A Companion to Kant's
Critique of Pure Reason

A Companion to Kant's
Critique of Pure Reason

Matthew C. Altman

Central Washington University

Westview
PRESS

A Member of the Perseus Books Group

Copyright © 2008 by Westview Press

Published by Westview Press,
A Member of the Perseus Books Group

Find us on the World Wide Web at www.westviewpress.com.

Westview Press books are available at special discounts for bulk purchases in the United States by corporations, institutions, and other organizations. For more information, please contact the Special Markets Department at the Perseus Books Group, 2300 Chestnut Street, Suite 200, Philadelphia, PA 19103, or call (800) 255–1514, or e-mail special.markets@perseusbooks.com.

Designed by Linda Mark

Library of Congress Cataloging-in-Publication Data
Altman, Matthew C.
  A companion to Kant's Critique of pure reason / Matthew C. Altman.
    p. cm.
  Includes bibliographical references and index.
   ISBN-13: 978-0-8133-4383-9
   ISBN-10: 0-8133-4383-6
  1. Kant, Immanuel, 1724-1804. Kritik der reinen Vernunft. 2. Knowledge, Theory of. 3. Causation. 4. Reason. I. Title.
  B2779.A39 2008
  121—dc22

                    2007029978

10 9 8 7 6 5 4 3 2 1

For Jorg Baumgartner

Contents

Preface

IT IS HARD to make sense of the *Critique of Pure Reason*. Its dense prose, complex arguments, and technical use of common terms are so difficult to decipher that those who are new to Kant have to reread each page many times, usually without understanding much, and trained philosophers often pass over particularly enigmatic passages in favor of more obvious claims. Indeed, the *Critique* provides a formidable challenge even to the most educated reader. It requires a familiarity with the history of ancient, medieval, and (especially) early modern philosophy; it struggles with issues in epistemology, metaphysics, logic, science, and the philosophy of mind; and its conclusions have implications for ethics, aesthetics, and religion. In short, it is hard to be a Kant specialist without specializing in just about everything—an impossible task.

This may excuse the vast majority of people from knowing much of anything about Kant's masterwork, but it is cold comfort for students who are charged with reading the *Critique* or for those who simply have an interest in modern intellectual history. *A Companion to Kant's "Critique of Pure Reason"* is designed to answer the questions that readers invariably have about the book: to explain its key concepts, to walk them through its most important arguments, and to give a sense of its place in the history of philosophy. In short, it makes the book accessible to the educated layperson.

The larger goal is to save students the expensive medical treatment they incur from Kant-induced anxiety attacks or from beating their heads against walls in frustration. As a student, my own first, second, and third readings of the *Critique* resulted in incomprehension, and those I teach are similarly confused. They need explanations of Kant's most basic claims in order even to begin a dialogue about the text in the classroom. The *Companion* is designed to get them to the point where they can approach Kant's writing critically, can appreciate more difficult secondary materials, and can engage one another as philosophical peers, with questions more interesting than "What the heck is going on?"

There are a number of available commentaries on the *Critique of Pure Reason*, but many of them are outdated, and most of the recent crop of books are beyond the grasp of those who are encountering Kant for the first time. They often deal with critical debates that distract from the *Critique* itself, and they largely neglect the epistemological approaches to which Kant was responding. The *Companion* illuminates the *Critique* by setting out the views of Kant's predecessors, focusing almost exclusively on the text itself, and presenting the material in a way that is accessible to those who are unfamiliar with Kant. I follow the order of the book as Kant himself organized it so that the reader can see how successive arguments build upon one another; I provide numerous examples to clarify the book's vocabulary, claims, and conclusions; and I repeatedly remind the reader of how the different pieces of the book fit into the ultimate goal of the critical project: to address metaphysical questions that philosophy had previously been unable to answer.

Of course, the *Companion* has a particular perspective on the material; it is primarily informed by recent Anglo-American approaches to Kant's theoretical philosophy. Accordingly, I conceive of the *Critique* as an investigation into the conditions for the possibility of making objective claims about the world rather than an inauguration of an absolute metaphysical distinction between appearances and things in themselves. I understand both Kant's response to his philosophical predecessors and his legacy for us in those terms. Although I employ an interpretive framework, the *Companion* does not try to dispel scholarly disagreements or to defend a revolutionary reading of the text. Instead, it attempts to chart common ground on which most Kant scholars agree. Those who want to pursue Kant in more depth will thus have a starting point from which to explore the vast secondary literature and to sort out in more detail his most crucial and opaque arguments.

This book is not intended to take the place of reading the *Critique* itself. I do not claim to do justice to the scope and complexity of Kant's original. It is called a "companion" because it is best used as a supplementary guide, when it is being studied next to an open copy of the *Critique*. However, I make extensive use of Kant's own writing in order to explain the arguments as Kant himself makes them, interpreting the jargon so that what is not quoted directly in the *Companion* can be understood when it is encountered in its original context.

One cannot fully appreciate the enormous impact that Kant has had on the history of philosophy, and indeed on the very ways that we understand ourselves and our experience, without at least struggling to make sense of the *Critique of Pure Reason*. What Kant says there cannot be made simple without being oversimplified, but it can be clarified to the point where such struggles are productive. With the *Companion*, I have attempted to illuminate Kant's writing without sacrificing depth or intellectual rigor. It has been said that every philosopher after Kant must take a position on the *Critique of Pure Reason*; it cannot be ignored. By making the book more accessible, the goal of the *Companion* is to help people participate in the most important conversations in modern and contemporary philosophy.

Acknowledgments

THE INSPIRATION for the *Companion* came from repeated attempts to illuminate the *Critique* for several confused groups of students. Many of the explanations and examples that made their way into the book emerged out of exchanges with those who pressed me to elaborate on difficult concepts. This book is a tribute to their eagerness and persistence.

My interpretation of the *Critique* has been deeply influenced by my time at the University of Chicago, where I studied Kant primarily under the direction of Robert Pippin. Undoubtedly, much of this book bears his stamp.

My wife and colleague, Cynthia Coe, has contributed to this work at every point in its development— suggesting interpretations of Kant's arguments, helping me to articulate my own thoughts, and repeatedly proofreading and offering comments for revision. She has made me a much better writer and teacher than I otherwise would be.

I also owe special thanks to Werner Pluhar, Phillip Downes, Sean Burns, Gary Bartlett, and Clinton Tolley for their various suggestions.

Finally, thanks to my parents, Doug and Sheryl, and to my sister, Lisa, for their unwavering encouragement.

M. C. A.
Ellensburg, Washington

Note on Sources and
Key to Abbreviations

FREQUENTLY CITED WORKS by Kant and others are referenced in the text parenthetically according to the abbreviations listed below. When available, I have referred to the standard English translation. Where there is no reference to an English version, the translation is my own. Works cited only in notes are given with their full publication information.

Works by Kant

As is standard in Kant scholarship, references to Kant's writings cite the pagination of the Royal Prussian Academy edition, which is included in the margins of the translations.

A/B   *Critique of Pure Reason*. Trans. Werner S. Pluhar. Indianapolis: Hackett, 1996.

CPrR   *Critique of Practical Reason*. Trans. Werner S. Pluhar. Indianapolis: Hackett, 2002.

Pro   *Prolegomena to Any Future Metaphysics That Will Be Able to Come Forward as Science*. 2d ed. Trans. Paul Carus. Rev. James W. Ellington. Indianapolis: Hackett, 2001.

Works by Others

DM   Descartes, René. *Discourse on the Method*. In *The Philosophical Writings of Descartes*, vol. 1, trans. John Cottingham, Robert Stoothoff, and Dugald Murdoch. Cambridge: Cambridge University Press, 1985.

E   Locke, John. *An Essay Concerning Human Understanding*. Ed. Peter H. Nidditch. Oxford: Clarendon, 1975.

EHU   Hume, David. *An Enquiry concerning Human Understanding*. In *Enquiries concerning Human Understanding and concerning the Principles of Morals*, ed. L. A. Selby-Bigge, rev. ed. P. H. Nidditch. 3d ed. Oxford: Clarendon, 1975.

M   Descartes, René. *Meditations on First Philosophy* and *Objections and Replies* [to the *Meditations*]. In *The Philosophical Writings of Descartes*, vol. 2, trans. John Cottingham, Robert Stoothoff, and Dugald Murdoch. Cambridge: Cambridge University Press, 1984.

PE   Leibniz, Gottfried Wilhelm. *Philosophical Essays*. Ed. and trans. Roger Ariew and Daniel Garber. Indianapolis: Hackett, 1989.

PHK   Berkeley, George. *A Treatise Concerning the Principles of Human Knowledge*. Ed. Jonathan Dancy. Oxford: Oxford University Press, 1998.

T   Hume, David. *A Treatise of Human Nature*. Ed. L. A. Selby-Bigge. Rev. ed. P. H. Nidditch. 2d ed. Oxford: Clarendon, 1978.

Introduction

THE *CRITIQUE OF PURE REASON* is one of the most important books in the history of philosophy, and also one of the most difficult. When it was first published in 1781, it was met with a general sense of bewilderment, but we now recognize it to be a formidable challenge not only to Kant's immediate predecessors but to a certain kind of epistemic arrogance. Indeed, with the *Critique*, Kant questioned a number of assumptions that had governed philosophy for hundreds of years, and he inaugurated a new way of looking at the world that continues to impact philosophy to the present day.

Among its many effects, the *Critique of Pure Reason* has spawned something of an industry, prompting generations of philosophers to write thousands of books and articles trying to make sense of it. But much of what has been written is still beyond the ken of nonspecialists and is largely incomprehensible to the educated layperson. This book is intended to fill this gap by providing both beginning and advanced students of Kant with understandable explanations of the *Critique*'s central arguments. Not only will this make possible a more productive reading of the text itself, but it will also prepare those with a deeper interest in Kant to navigate the complex claims of other secondary scholarship.

To accomplish these tasks, Chapter 1 of the *Companion* surveys the historical background of the *Critique* in order to place it in its philosophical context. Rationalism and empiricism were then the two most important schools of thought, with opposing methodologies but the same overarching goal: to discover mind-independent reality, either by means of reason or by means of the senses. Studying rationalism and empiricism in general, as well as some of the specific positions of their proponents, will allow us to see more clearly what Kant is responding to and to understand how innovative his epistemology was at the time.

Chapter 2 begins with Kant's pre-critical period as a prelude to an overview of Kant's critical turn. We will see how Kant conceives of the purpose of the *Critique*—to put metaphysics on a firm foundation—and how transcendental idealism, the thesis that we know only appearances and never things in themselves, helps us to resolve the metaphysical controversies that plague philosophy. This chapter covers the prefaces and the introduction, setting out some important technical terms and distinctions that Kant uses and outlining the structure of the book as a whole.

After this preliminary material, Chapters 3, 4, and 5 of the *Companion* examine the three main parts of the *Critique* in order: the Transcendental Aesthetic, where Kant argues that objects appear to us in space and time because of the way that sensations are given to us; the Transcendental Analytic, where he sets out the rules that we use to make sense of experience and attempts to prove that they are a necessary condition for objective representations; and the Transcendental Dialectic, where he explains why traditional metaphysical questions must be approached differently. We can know nothing about the soul, freedom, or God, even whether there are such things. Instead, they must be approached as matters of practical faith. I then discuss some of the arguments in the *Critique of Practical Reason*, so readers can get a sense of how Kant addresses these questions in his later work. I conclude the book with a brief consideration of Kant's importance: how the Copernican revolution in philosophy—the idea that the world must conform to our representation of it, rather than vice versa—has not only affected the history of the discipline but changed our conception of ourselves more generally.

At times, the density of Kant's writing can intimidate even the most experienced reader of philosophy. Among other things, he uses a technical vocabulary that must be clarified if his larger project is to be understood. Although I explain important concepts throughout the book, I have also included a glossary of key terms at the end of the *Companion* for quick reference when reading particularly difficult passages of the *Critique*.

Although it is a milestone in modern intellectual history, the *Critique of Pure Reason* is not a flawless piece of philosophy. In the body of the text and in notes, I have pointed out some of the major objections that subsequent philosophers have made to Kant's various assumptions and conclusions. The purpose of the book, however, is not to assess Kant's arguments. We can neither praise nor criticize a position until we have attempted a charitable understanding of it. A lot of time and effort is required before a productive debate can begin, and my intention here is to explain what Kant is saying as a prelude to evaluating it. The vast secondary literature has itself become an object of interpretation in which competing views, objections, and responses are taken up, challenged, and compared, but this is not my goal. For those who are interested in fully appraising the success or failure of the *Critique*, or those who would like to pursue some of Kant's claims in more depth, I have provided a selected bibliography of secondary works at the end of the *Companion*.

≈ CHAPTER ONE ≈

Kant's Philosophical Environment

THE HISTORY of early modern philosophy consists of a diversity of opinions, but it can be characterized initially by philosophers' self-conscious break with the Aristotelianism that dominated the Middle Ages. Although Aristotelianism had reigned for hundreds of years, philosophy had failed to achieve unanimity on any of the most important philosophical questions. Wild, dogmatic claims were advanced, each with its own complex and seemingly strong argument. But many of these claims contradicted one another. Metaphysical speculation about such things as how many angels can dance on the head of a pin led to unresolvable conflicts among inconsistent beliefs. What unites the early modern philosophers is a general feeling of disillusionment about the state of philosophy at the time. They attempted to right the ship by establishing a new method in order to pursue these questions more reliably. In this atmosphere of frustration and a desire for new beginnings, philosophy came to be dominated by two very different approaches, rationalism and empiricism. Both of these movements were part of what is called the Enlightenment, a period in intellectual history marked by the appeal to reason as a corrective to tradition and superstition.

Continental Rationalism: Thinking as the Way to the World

René Descartes is called the father of modern philosophy because he dramatically shifted the concern of philosophy from what is the case (ontology or metaphysics) to a consideration of how we know things (epistemology). Of course, Descartes and the other modern philosophers are ultimately concerned with the world and our place in it, just as medieval philosophers had been. But Descartes is one of the first to address what exists through an initial consideration of our own epistemic capacities. One of his most important works is the *Discourse on the Method of rightly conducting one's reason and seeking the truth in the sciences* (1637). In order to discover the truth, Descartes says, we must begin by finding out how we as finite beings ought to justify our claims.

Among people unfamiliar with it, philosophy seems to involve a lot of unfounded speculation about things that we can never know. But argument and evidence—in philosophy, this usually means giving reasons—are central to the discipline, and Descartes recognizes this. To see why it is important, contrast the following two scenarios. First, imagine that you wake up in a windowless room and flip a coin: "Heads, it's raining; tails, it's not raining." It comes up heads and you conclude that it must be raining. If it is in fact raining, your conclusion is correct. But now imagine that, instead of flipping a coin, you wake up, look out the window, and witness a deluge. The voice of the local meteorologist comes out of your clock radio: "We've already received an inch of rain today, and at this rate, we expect a lot more." Your roommate returns with a wet umbrella and tracks mud all over the room. She says, "It's really pouring outside." Trusting your eyes and your ears, you conclude that it is raining, and you put on your raincoat before heading out the door. In both of these cases, you have the same true belief: It is raining. However, in which case are you more likely to say that you *know* it is raining? Even though the beliefs are the same and the facts are the same, you have much better evidence in the second case. True belief is not the same thing as knowledge. To know something, what you believe must also be justified in the right way.

What distinguishes Descartes and the other rationalists—most notably Baruch Spinoza and Gottfried Wilhelm Leibniz—is the claim that even this kind of (sensory) evidence is not enough. Our senses sometimes deceive us. Descartes notes that we could be hallucinating or dreaming, and it is even possible that we are constantly being deceived by some malevolent being, what he calls a "malicious demon" or an "evil genius" (M 15). The senses are undoubtedly fallible, and thus we cannot know anything with certainty on the basis of the senses alone. If sensory evidence is to be trusted—and this is a big "if"—then it must first be validated by reason. Only by reasoning can we justify our beliefs about the world and achieve knowledge of the way things must be.

Descartes begins with this surprising revelation: *Everything* he has come to believe has been given to him either directly from the senses (things he has experienced himself) or through the senses (things he has been taught by others or has learned as a matter of custom) (M 12). If the senses can be doubted, and if our aim is to achieve certainty, we must begin anew. The firm foundation on which Descartes tries to erect a philosophical system with scientific certainty is, famously, his own existence as a thinking thing:

> But immediately I noticed that while I was trying thus to think everything false, it was necessary that I, who was thinking this, was something. And observing that this truth 'I am thinking, therefore I exist' was so firm and sure that all the most extravagant suppositions of the sceptics were incapable of shaking it, I decided that I could accept it without scruple as the first principle of the philosophy I was seeking. (DM 127)

Despite the 'therefore,' we should not be misled into thinking that Descartes is advancing some kind of typical argument, with premises and a conclusion. Rather, there is an intuitive inference from my thinking to my existing; my existence is "self-evident by a simple intuition of the mind" (M 100). If I doubt what I know, then even if I know nothing else, I at least know that I (who am doubting) exist. Of course, I do not know anything about *what* I am, but I know *that* I am.

Think of what Descartes is doing as an attempt to traverse a swamp. What had seemed like solid ground—what he thought he knew on the basis of the senses—is now a quagmire of doubt, and he is slowly testing whether there is some way to proceed. At this point, he has discovered one thing that cannot be doubted, one firm patch of ground: *Cogito, ergo sum.* Of course, as I think along with him, he has not proven his existence (to me). I know only that I exist. But the mere fact that I exist tells me nothing about the external world, or even if there is such a thing. At this point, I am left with only my existence and the ideas that I have in my head—if in fact I have a head. For example, I have the idea of a table. I can picture it: brown and rectangular, with four legs. On the basis of this idea, I usually make a judgment that there is an actual table out there, distinct from me, that corresponds to this idea. Although I cannot be mistaken in saying that I have the idea of a table, my claim that there actually is a table in front of me may be false. The question for Descartes then becomes: Do I have any ideas that necessarily, without a doubt, imply the existence of something besides me? This would expand my knowledge beyond the mere fact of my own existence.

I have all sorts of ideas: ideas of colors, tables, unicorns, people, historical events. Descartes thinks that all of these things could have come from me. But there is one idea that outstrips my power of imagination. The idea of God must be innate, produced in me at my creation by God himself:

> By the word 'God' I understand a substance that is infinite, <eternal, immutable> independent, supremely intelligent, supremely powerful, and which created both myself and everything else (if anything else there be) that exists. All these attributes are such that, the more carefully I concentrate on them, the less possible it seems that they could have originated from me alone. So from what has been said it must be concluded that God necessarily exists. (M 31)

From my own existence as a thinking thing, I could have derived any of the ideas I have except the idea of God. The idea of an actual perfection could not have been produced by a limited being such as myself; it could only have come from a perfect being. Therefore, God exists.

Because the idea of an infinite perfection must have come from a being who is without flaw, God cannot be a "malicious demon." Consequently, I know that an external world exists; a perfect being would not allow me to be constantly deceived about such a thing. Furthermore, because God is not a deceiver, I cannot err as long as I correctly use the powers that God gave me. I can make justifiable claims about the world based on the proper use of the senses. Thus Descartes validates the senses by an appeal to reason—that is, by deducing God's existence and what logically follows from it.

From this starting point, Descartes proceeds to establish a variety of metaphysical theses, including the immateriality of the soul. I clearly and distinctly perceive myself as a thinking thing, a thing whose essence is thinking, which is not extended in space. But I also perceive my body as something different, as extended stuff for which thinking is not essential. Because God is not a deceiver and therefore would not allow what I clearly and distinctly perceive to be false, the soul must really exist as a simple (without parts), immaterial substance distinct from the divisible, corporeal body.

From my thinking alone, I have deduced that I have an immaterial soul, but what is the material world like? The nature of objects and their relations are also discoverable through reason. Sensations are caused by bodies in space but are not adequate signs of the nature of things. The senses give us fleeting perceptions that shift with a person's perspective, vary among different observers, and change over time—color, smell, and taste are indistinct—but the fact that objects are substances is true independently of how they are perceived. Anything that is given to me in sensation is nothing but a confused form of what I already know (or can know) about the world through my thinking. We get at truth through the *a priori* investigation of what must be the case given the ways that we rationally conceive of the world. Thus the essence of material bodies is extension, taking up a certain space, and such pure shapes are governed by the laws of geometry. The universe consists of objects mechanically related by these immutable laws. This is the foundation of Cartesian physics.

Following Descartes's rational method, Spinoza and Leibniz attempt to correct the fallible senses by modeling philosophy on mathematics.

Like mathematics, philosophy should be an *a priori* investigation—
that is, it should not be based on experience—that proves its claims to
be necessarily true. A geometrician knows the sum of the interior
angles of any triangle by determining what it must be based on our
conception of a triangle, not based on the actual measurements of
particular triangles. More generally, the essence of things follows
logically from our rational conception of them; they are not derived
from given appearances. Just as it is certain at all times and in all places
that the interior angles of a triangle total 180 degrees, so too it is
absolutely necessary that God exists and the soul is an immaterial
thing (Descartes), that God is the one substance of which all other
things are attributes (Spinoza), or that each individual substance
expresses the whole universe (Leibniz).

Spinoza and Leibniz go beyond Descartes, however, in adapting
mathematical reasoning more methodically to a treatment of philosophical and metaphysical subject matter. They set out to establish their
claims by putting forward an initial set of definitions and axioms,
which they take to be indisputable, and deriving from them all other
truths (in the form of propositions). Spinoza's "geometrical method" is
modeled explicitly on the *Elements* of Euclid. Thus, in the *Ethics*
(1677), Spinoza cites at each new proposition the definitions and/or axioms from which the proposition logically follows. Leibniz spells out
his methodology in his essay "Primary Truths" (1689): "all remaining
truths are reduced to primary truths with the help of definitions, that is,
through the resolution of notions; in this consists *a priori proof*, proof
independent of experience" (PE 31). Because all truths are generated
by an appeal to axioms and definitions, neither of which depend on experience for their truth value, all truths are *a priori* and analytic—contained in the very concept of the thing about which the claim is being
made. Reasoning can tell us what is necessarily true of the world, or
even what is the case beyond all possible experience, which is more
than the senses ever could tell us.

Spinoza and Leibniz draw a number of specific conclusions from
this method, and they disagree on a number of points, but most of
them are not important for understanding the philosophy of Kant.
What is important is what makes their philosophies characteristic of

rationalism: Things as they are apart from our perceptions can be known only through reason. By thinking about the nature of our ideas, God, or objects, we can determine the way things must be, regardless of what our fallible senses tell us.

British Empiricism: Furnishing the Empty Cabinet

Like the rationalists, the empiricists were similarly discouraged by the fact that there was no established method for adjudicating among the great number of competing philosophies and claims that confronted them. John Locke, the first of the British empiricists, noted that this had led to a general sense of frustration concerning the very possibility of knowledge. Thus he also devised a method that would help to distinguish sense and nonsense and that would once and for all establish certainty in the sciences. While Descartes, Spinoza, and Leibniz attempted to erect a system of ideas on the basis of rationally necessary first principles, Locke attempted a similar foundationalism, but one based on what is immediately known through the senses.

In order to establish the tenability of empiricism as a whole, Locke begins the *Essay Concerning Human Understanding* (1690) with several arguments against the existence of innate ideas. Only if innate ideas are first ruled out can he claim that all human knowledge is discovered *a posteriori*—that is, from experience, on the basis of the senses. Although Locke formulates a number of complex arguments and sub-arguments, his overall strategy is simple enough: Innate ideas would have to be universally acknowledged or agreed upon by all people, yet no ideas (including the idea of God) are assented to by everyone. Even when there is general agreement among the subclass of people who have "come to the use of reason" (a vague and ambiguous phrase), the fact that they do not recognize the ideas before being introduced to them is more amenable to an empiricist explanation (E 51). They agree with these claims because they have similar experiences and a shared language based on those experiences. Any disagreement with empiricism concerning the origin of these ideas is merely apparent.

If the rationalist claims that an idea is innate because people assent to it when they hear it, then that implies that everything people believe is innate. Indeed, all truths are innate in this sense, even if people never hear about them, just because they *would* assent to them if asked. But this way of speaking is imprecise. Instead, the *capacity* to know is innate; *what* we know is acquired. Locke himself uses the following example: Everyone would agree that "white is not black," but how do we come to know what white and black are, and how do we learn to compare them (E 57)? We learn of these colors through the senses, and we learn to compare them by reflecting on their differences. The fact that there is universal assent to this proposition shows that those who have seen black and white can recognize that they are different. But this does not imply that the ideas were somehow implanted in us before we opened our eyes.

Of course, this is just a sketch of how Locke proceeds. But if he does in fact demonstrate that there are no innate ideas, then we must acquire them by means of the senses. Indeed, according to Locke, all ideas, even the most abstract, must ultimately be derived from perceptions:

> The Senses at first let in particular *Ideas*, and furnish the yet empty Cabinet: And the Mind by degrees growing familiar with some of them, they are lodged in the Memory, and Names got to them. Afterwards the Mind proceeding farther, abstracts them, and by Degrees learns the use of general Names. In this manner the Mind comes to be furnish'd with *Ideas* and Language, the Materials about which to exercise its discursive Faculty . . . . (E 55)

The mind is nothing but an "empty Cabinet"—Locke also calls it a *tabula rasa*, a blank slate—that must be filled up with information in order for us to know anything. It gets this information from sensations that are given to it from without and from reflection on its own ideas (E 105). This is the heart of empiricism. Although we may reflect on what we are given in experience—we can compare two experiences in our head to think about how they are alike—the building blocks of what we think are provided by the world as it affects our senses. I know a table is there because I see it, or because I feel my way around it in the dark. Even abstract concepts are merely extrapolations from particular perceptions, so that when we understand classes of things or we make general claims, we do so on the basis of what we have experienced. My idea of what tables are in general is derived from common features I have noticed among tables that I have seen.

In order to clarify what we know, then, we have to examine how we sense the world and what we can claim on the basis of our sensations. To do this, Locke makes a fundamental distinction between what he calls "original or primary Qualities"—characteristics of the object itself that do not depend on how it is perceived, such as its size, shape, motion, and texture—and sensible or "secondary Qualities"—characteristics that result from how our senses are affected by the object, such as its color and taste (E 135). The difference between primary and secondary qualities can be illustrated by looking at two examples in which people make contradictory claims about what they experience. Imagine that you and your roommate go outside, and she puts on her coat because she feels cold. But you feel fine, so you say, "It's not cold out." In this case, neither of you is right or wrong, because what she means to say is that the temperature is too cold *for her*; what you mean to say is that the temperature does not bother *you*. The feelings you have depend on not only the temperature of the air but how it affects you. Now think about a different scenario: You present your roommate with a birthday cake and tell her that there are twenty candles on top. Your roommate looks at the cake and responds, "There are only nineteen candles here." In this case, someone miscounted; at least one of you is wrong. Number does not depend on how things affect us. It depends entirely on the way the world is.

Of course, as we saw with the last example, our senses can deceive us. Someone saw the wrong number of candles. Descartes went beyond occasional mistakes and emphasized the possibility of constant hallucinations and dreams, saying that we could never achieve certainty by means of the senses. Locke responds by deriding Descartes's philosophical aspirations:

> if after all this, any one will be so sceptical, as to distrust his Senses, and to affirm, that all we see and hear, feel and taste, think and do, during our whole Being, is but the series and deluding appearances of a

long Dream, whereof there is no reality; and therefore will question
the Existence of all Things, or our Knowledge of any thing: I must de-
sire him to consider, . . . that *the certainty of* Things existing *in rerum
Naturâ* [in the nature of things], when we have *the testimony of our
Senses* for it, is not only *as great* as our frame can attain to, but *as our
Condition needs.* (E 634)

By clarifying what we in fact sense when we have experiences—by
distinguishing primary and secondary qualities, for example—we can
achieve a kind of understanding whose reliability attests to its veracity.
What we know empirically helps us to get along in the world. This is
good enough because it works.

George Berkeley and David Hume would later refine Locke's insights and formulate what they take to be more consistent empiricist
positions. Both Berkeley and Hume agree "that all our ideas are nothing but copies of our impressions, or, in other words, that it is impossible for us to *think* of any thing, which we have not antecedently
felt," but they disagree with Locke about *what* is known by the senses,
or what we can claim about the world based on our impressions
(EHU 135). According to Berkeley and Hume, so-called primary
qualities can never be directly apprehended. In addition, although
objects are typically postulated on the basis of sensory qualities in the
mind, such an inference—to the continued and distinct existence of
mind-independent material objects—cannot be warranted. Hume
makes this point in his *Treatise of Human Nature* (1739–40): The
senses give us only different, unconnected impressions at different
times, and they never allow us to perceive the object as it is in itself. To
assume that an object exists as the cause of our impressions, and thus
to infer its existence on the basis of what we sense, is to beg the
question (T 211–12).[1] We can never know whether the qualities of
substances themselves actually correspond to what we experience.
That would require a view from nowhere, a perception of the object as
it is unperceived. For Hume, this leads to skepticism about the very
existence of material objects. We cannot know whether there are such
things, even though we habitually act as if such things exist.

Berkeley goes beyond Hume's skepticism about materialism and advances a contrary position called "immaterialism" or "Berkeleyan idealism." Secondary qualities are relative to the perceiver. For example, the same lukewarm water will feel hot to someone who has recently been in cold water and cold to someone who has recently been in hot water, a solid color will appear different to different observers under different lighting conditions, and the same peach may taste sweet or sour depending on the person's eating habits. Given the dependence of secondary qualities on the perceiver's senses, Berkeley argues that primary qualities are similarly mind-dependent, because "original qualities are inseparably united with the other sensible qualities, and not, even in thought, capable of being abstracted from them" (PHK 106). For example, a body's extension must be marked out by its distinguishable color, and its motion and size are measured relative to the speed and position of the perceiver (PHK 106). Therefore, primary qualities are in the mind as much as secondary qualities are; because sight and touch are mind-dependent, so are motion, size, and extension. What we take to be objects are in fact groups of sensible qualities, or "ideas" that we relate to one another.

Hume and Berkeley both conclude that we cannot warrant a commitment to material things. This is consistent with the basic premise of empiricism, which restricts itself to what we directly perceive or what we can legitimately extrapolate from those perceptions. Nonsensical and baseless propositions—concerning, for example, freedom and the soul—arise when pure thought is taken to tell us something substantive about what exists. By considering only evidence based on the senses— the way that we access the world—we can avoid such metaphysical speculation, which is exactly what has led philosophy astray.

Humean Skepticism and the Problem of Induction

The split between empiricism and rationalism dominated the philosophical atmosphere in which Kant initially found himself, and, as we will see, these two approaches played important roles in the development of his own position. Kant was especially struck by a particular argument in Hume's *Enquiry concerning Human Understanding* (1748), the so-called "problem of induction." Kant's recognition of the challenge Hume posed for both rationalists and empiricists would inspire him to undertake a new direction in his work that would eventually give rise to the *Critique of Pure Reason*.

Hume begins his analysis by making an important distinction, known as "Hume's fork." He argues that every claim can be classified either as a relation of ideas or a matter of fact, depending on what warrants it and whether it is contingently true or necessarily true. The first kind, relations of ideas, are propositions that are known to be true without appealing to experience:

> Of the first kind [that is, relations of ideas] are the sciences of Geometry, Algebra, and Arithmetic; and in short, every affirmation which is either intuitively or demonstratively certain. *That the square of the hypotenuse is equal to the square of the two sides*, is a proposition which expresses a relation between these figures. *That three times five is equal to the half of thirty*, expresses a relation between these numbers. Propositions of this kind are discoverable by the mere operation of thought, without dependence on what is anywhere existent in the universe. Though there never were a circle or triangle in nature, the truths demonstrated by Euclid would for ever retain their certainty and evidence. (EHU 25)

Such claims cannot be false, because we cannot think of them in any other way; they have to do with how the concepts are related. Mathematical truths are a good example. It cannot be the case that two minus one is anything other than one. Whenever you have two of something and you take one away, one thing always remains—it does not matter when you do it (now or a thousand years from now) or where you do it (here or on Mars). Relations of ideas are also analytically true, or true by definition. 'All bachelors are unmarried males' is true because that is what we mean when we call someone a bachelor. If we analyze the meaning of 'bachelor,' we discover that it is synonymous with 'unmarried male'. Relations of ideas are also called analytic claims, because the predicate can be discovered simply by analyzing the concept of the subject. We do not have to go to bachelors and ask them one by one, "Are you married?" Of course, we cannot know prior to experience who is a bachelor or whether there even are any bachelors. But given the meaning of the terms, we can know independently of experience (*a priori*) that whoever is a bachelor must be an unmarried male. Because relations of ideas are *a priori* and analytic, they are true necessarily and universally.

By contrast, matters of fact depend on the way the world is set up and the way we experience it:

> Matters of fact, which are the second objects of human reason, are not ascertained in the same manner [as relations of ideas]; nor is our evidence of their truth, however great, of a like nature with the foregoing. The contrary of every matter of fact is still possible; because it can never imply a contradiction, and is conceived by the mind with the same facility and distinctness, as if ever so conformable to reality. *That the sun will not rise to-morrow* is no less intelligible a proposition, and implies no more contradiction, than the affirmation, *that it will rise*. We should in vain, therefore, attempt to demonstrate its falsehood. Were it demonstratively false, it would imply a contradiction, and could never be distinctly conceived by the mind. (EHU 25–26)

Relations of ideas are necessarily true simply because of what the terms mean and how they are related, but matters of fact are contingently true based on what happens to be the case. For example, we cannot discover the height of the tallest peak in Malaysia just by analyzing "tallest," "peak," and "Malaysia." Rather, it depends on what the world is like. Off the top of our heads, most of us do not know whether the tallest peak is 5,000 feet or 20,000 feet. And even if we do know how tall it is, it does not have to be that way. The mountain could have ended up shorter than it is now. By contrast, it can never and could never have been the case that two minus one totals something other than one.

Hume uses this distinction to address an epistemological problem: On what basis do we know things beyond what we are experiencing now and what we remember experiencing? I may have experienced a lot firsthand, but most of what I claim to know is based on inferences from what I have experienced directly. When I hear a knock at the door, I assume that there is someone on the other side, even before I see her with my own eyes. I expect a person there because every time I have heard a knock before, a person has been there. If a friend says that he is going to France, and I later receive a postcard bearing a French postmark and a handwritten note from him, I assume that he is in France, even though I do not have my arm around him under the Arc de Triomphe. If I knock a billiard ball into another billiard ball, I expect it to roll in a certain direction—even before I have seen it—because that has happened whenever I have played pool in the past.

According to Hume, every claim about what I am not experiencing, either because I am not there or because it has not happened yet, is an inductive inference that I make from cause to effect or from effect to cause. When I make such an inference, I am generalizing from particular experiences I have had to general principles that govern other events. We believe that the future will conform to the past because what has happened gives us evidence of causal laws. Scientists do this all the time. For example, when a pharmaceutical company undertakes clinical trials to discover the side effects of a new drug, its scientists take a sample of potential consumers, give them the drug, and compare their reactions to other potential consumers who are not taking it. If a number of people in the experimental group grow extra heads, the scientists discontinue its use. They make an inductive inference: The drug is causing the side effect, and this will happen if other people take it too. Similarly, our knowledge of anything we do not directly experience depends on inferences from what we know directly to what we think we know on the basis of those facts. I believe that the force of the billiard ball will push the other one along because I have seen it happen a lot. I believe that my friend is in France because, in prior experience, I have found that people tend to be in the place from which the postcard is sent.

Having answered the question as to how we know things beyond what we immediately experience, Hume proceeds to ask whether such inferences are warranted. He does this by investigating which of our capacities causes us to believe that the future will be like the past. Not coincidentally—because they correspond to relations of ideas and matters of fact, as well as rationalism and empiricism—the two main candidates are reason and the senses.

Hume gives several arguments as to why causal inferences are not warranted by reasoning alone. First, he says, we cannot merely look at an object and determine what its effect will be or what caused it:

> Let an object be presented to a man of ever so strong natural reason and abilities; if that object be entirely new to him, he will not be able, by the most accurate examination of its sensible qualities, to discover any of its causes or effects. Adam, though his rational faculties be supposed, at the very first, entirely perfect, could not have inferred from the fluidity and transparency of water, that it would suffocate him, or from the light and warmth of fire that it would consume him. No object ever discovers, by the qualities which appear to the senses, either the causes which produced it, or the effects which will arise from it; nor can our reason, unassisted by experience, ever draw any inference concerning real existence and matter of fact. (EHU 27)

It is important that Hume refers to Adam here: the first person, newly discovering the world, with no help from others' experiences. Try to put yourself in Adam's position. You see a clear pool, very still. How will it behave? What effect will it have if you jump in (or on) it? From just looking at it, you cannot tell what it will do. In fact, you do not even know what water is. Air is fluid and transparent, and that does not hurt you. This stuff is just a little thicker. Maybe you should test it: put your hand in, or dunk your head under the surface. It is not solid. It conforms to your shape, just like air. But if you try to breathe it in, you choke. In that case, you are *experiencing* how it affects you. You will not try to breathe it in again, because you do not want to drown. But you did not deduce this; you experienced it.

Of course, it is hard to imagine yourself as Adam, without any experience. Imagine instead that I place an object in front of you that you have never seen before. What is it going to do? What effect will it have? You cannot tell simply by looking at it. You may think that it looks like the sort of thing that would bounce around the room. But it may not. If we look at an unfamiliar object, we realize that there are all sorts of things it could do. If we expect a particular effect without actually seeing what it does, we will be deciding arbitrarily that it will act that way. This is Hume's second point. Our thinking *a priori* gives us no reason to expect one thing rather than another, to expect it to bounce around rather than shoot flames out of its sides while playing the tuba. You do not expect it to do this because you have not seen anything do this before. Perhaps you are comparing it to something you have seen before, and you are inferring on that basis that it too will bounce around. But it will not necessarily do the same thing. And even if it does, you will have extrapolated on the basis of past experience. How it will behave (the effect) cannot be discovered in the object itself (the cause) through reasoning alone. If we want to know what something does, we have to see what it does. If we have certain expectations about its behavior, either we have arbitrarily decided upon it, or we have based our expectations on experience.

When you see a pool of water, you tend to assume that you know how it is going to behave simply by thinking about it, but actually you are making an inference based on what others have told you, or because of your experience of how water has behaved in the past. Hume thinks that such reactions become second nature and that we often forget their origins in our past experience.

It seems that reason alone cannot warrant inductive inferences because we always need the assistance of experience to get us there. If we have not experienced something, we cannot make a causal claim about it. Of course, you probably do not find this particularly troublesome. We tend to think that induction comes through the senses anyway. Scientists cannot know how a drug will behave until they do clinical trials. Only when they see its effects on hundreds or thousands of people can they know what it is going to do. But this leads us to a different problem, a question that only a philosopher would ask: How do the senses give us the belief in cause and effect, or how do they justify inductive inferences from past experiences? What is it about past experiences that warrants a general claim about future experiences?

To approach this part of Hume's argument, we must pause for a moment and consider what we actually experience when we see one event cause another event. For example, one billiard ball rolls toward another, they come into contact, you hear a noise, and then the other ball starts rolling. You see one thing happen, then another, and you assume that the first thing causes the second because they are "constantly conjoined" (EHU 42). You always see the one thing followed by the other. However, at no time do you actually see the first ball *cause* the second ball to move. It is not as though we see the first billiard ball roll toward the second, and then see some force pass between them that indicates causation. Instead, we see one ball move, and then another. The physicist would measure the mass and velocity of each ball before and after the collision and (taking into account friction) would conclude that the first ball has transferred momentum to the second one. But even in this case, we see two balls, each with a certain amount of kinetic energy, and then a change in each ball's kinetic energy upon contact. To say that the change was caused by the contact goes beyond what is given to us in experience—simply a series of events, one after another. Because the second action always follows the first, we assume that there is some "secret power" that makes the same object have the same kind of effect over and over again, but we never experience any such power (EHU 33).

We must concede this to Hume. However, because the events always happen one right after the other, we believe that we are still on solid ground when we infer that there is such a causal relationship. We *conclude* that one thing causes another *on the basis of* their constant conjunction. And this is where Hume's fork again becomes important. If such inferences are to be justified, either they must be based on our perceptions (matters of fact) or they must be rationally necessary in the way that mathematical claims are (relations of ideas). How should we categorize inductive inferences, as relations of ideas or matters of fact?

First Hume considers whether causal inferences are relations of ideas. Perhaps our knowledge of causality is achieved through reasoning. Perhaps a particular effect must follow from a particular cause because that is the only way I can conceive of the events. When the first ball hits the second one, it must move in a particular way, just in the way that two minus one must equal one. But, Hume says, this cannot be so, because any two events could have been otherwise; they are not related necessarily, as, for example, mathematical concepts are. Given the meanings of 'one', 'two', and 'minus', it would be contradictory to say that two minus one equals anything but one. However, it is not contradictory for the same cause to bring about a different effect on successive occasions. It is conceivable that the sun may not rise tomorrow, or that a billiard ball running into another billiard ball will cause them both to do an Irish jig.

Here again, one may agree with Hume without any worries. Any of these things *may* happen, but they are very unlikely, because we have seen the sun rise every day and billiard balls have never danced. Our experience has led us not to expect a change. So, while reasoning cannot get us to necessity, experience can get us to probability. What Hume asks, then, is whether the claim that these effects are unlikely is actually warranted by experience. He concludes that experience cannot justify such inferences without circularity:

> We have said that all arguments concerning existence are founded on the relation of cause and effect; that our knowledge of that relation is derived entirely from experience; and that all our experimental conclusions proceed upon the supposition that the future will be conformable to the past. To endeavor, therefore, the proof of this last supposition by probable arguments, or arguments regarding existence, must be evidently going in a circle, and taking that for granted, which is the very point in question. (EHU 35–36)

Circular or question-begging arguments assume what they claim to prove, and thus they prove nothing at all. How do we know what the future will be like? Because of what has happened in the past. How do we know that the past will be a good guide to the future? Because it always has been (in the past). This is using induction to prove induction: Using induction to predict the future has always worked, so we inductively infer that induction will continue to work. Hume is asking why we believe in induction, why we assume that the next instance will happen like all of the previous instances. To say that we are sure because we have seen this happen many times, because induction has always worked, does not answer the question. *Why* is this a good reason for making such an inference? There is no answer, except to say that it has always been like this. This assumes the truth of induction rather than proving it.

Hume has demonstrated that, although we see things conjoined in regular ways, neither reason nor the senses support any causal claim or inductive inference about the world. Nonetheless, we do anticipate what will happen based on what has happened before. I expect the sun to rise tomorrow, and I expect the first billiard ball to push the second one along. Hume claims that we believe in induction regardless of its lack of justification because of what he calls "custom" or "habit." The conjunction of two events again and again, over the course of time, produces in us the belief that they are related by a causal connection: "For wherever the repetition of any particular act or operation produces a propensity to renew the same act or operation, without being impelled by any reasoning or process of the understanding; we always say, that this propensity is the effect of *Custom*" (EHU 43). We believe that the future will be like the past because we are used to its being this way. We expect it because we are creatures of habit, even though this is not a warranted expectation. Every Cubs game that my friend has watched on television has ended with a Cubs loss. There is a constant or repeated conjunction between his watching the game and the losses. So, the next time he watches a game (if I cannot stop him), I expect the Cubs to lose. His viewing patterns obviously do not affect the players, but I expect it nonetheless. Our normal judgments concerning causality may feel more certain, but they are just as baseless, grounded in nothing but habit.

Because causality is warranted neither by experience nor by reason, it is not and cannot be justified. Indeed, Hume says, claims that cannot be verified by being traced back to sensation or reflection are meaningless. They are nonsense, like talk of angels on the head of a pin:

> One event follows another; but we never can observe any tie between
> them. They seem *conjoined*, but never *connected*. And as we can have
> no idea of any thing which never appeared to our outward sense or
> inward sentiment, the necessary conclusion *seems* to be that we have

no idea of connexion or power at all, and that these words are absolutely without any meaning, when employed either in philosophical
reasonings or common life. (EHU 74)

Hume has explained why we make such inductive inferences, but he
has also shown that such inferences are completely unjustified and
meaningless when considered in objective terms—that is, as properties of the world. The connection between the two is a connection in
my thought, what I habitually expect. When I talk about causality, I
am not making any claims about the objects themselves. I am merely
voicing an unjustified bias that I have. Causality is not a necessary
relation among objects but is contingent on my habitual association
of two things. This is why Hume calls his explanation a "sceptical
solution" (EHU 40). When we make causal inferences, we are describing not objective relations in the world but our own subjective,
psychological associations. These cannot in principle be right or
wrong. How are we to make judgments about someone's association
given that every causal inference is without justification? You relate
the knock with a person at the door; I relate my friend's viewing patterns with the Cubs' record. Neither claim is justified by reasoning
or any amount of experimentation.

It follows from this that natural science consists of merely descriptive
claims—how we *do* associate things—rather than normative claims—
what we *ought to* believe about the world. Science does not reveal objective, causal laws. Rather, it clarifies and reports on the customary
associations that we tend to make. Berkeley similarly criticizes the
scientists of his day for their grand claims, which transgress the
boundaries of what they can investigate: sensible qualities or ideas,
rather than material objects governed by natural forces (PHK 139ff.).

The problem of induction has profound implications not only for
natural science but for the ambitious claims of the rationalists and empiricists. Neither reason nor the senses can warrant inductive inferences,
and induction is the only way to know anything beyond what we immediately experience. Therefore, what we know is severely limited. What
seem to be objective claims about the world are merely subjective claims
about my own psychology. Given that Descartes had shifted the focus

of philosophy from ontology to epistemology, Hume's skepticism essentially confines philosophy to a marginal or secondary role: clarifying the proper domain of the sciences, identifying which philosophical questions are meaningful, and making our language more precise.[2]

Like many others, Kant was convinced by much of Hume's argument, which impelled him to try to explain how to justify objective claims, including knowledge beyond immediate experience. Kant believes that we must make sense of the world in terms of causal relations rather than merely subjective associations. The question then becomes: How can the problem of induction be resolved while avoiding Hume's "sceptical solution"?

CHAPTER TWO

The Copernican Revolution
in Philosophy

LIBERATING PHILOSOPHY from the thrall of scholasticism began with Descartes's turn inward, but the divisions between rationalism and empiricism clearly indicated that the scientific aspirations of the Enlightenment had not been achieved. Different epistemic approaches had failed to explain definitively how we are related to the world and had also failed to resolve questions concerning, among other things, whether we are free, whether we have souls, and whether God exists. Philosophy was still in disarray, despite numerous attempts to set it right.

With the publication of the *Critique of Pure Reason* in 1781, Immanuel Kant would recast the philosophical debate in ways that reverberate to the present day. Empiricists are right to insist on the givenness of sensations, because knowledge must answer to something external to me if it is to be meaningful or have content. However, if sensations are merely given to me, then they can never amount to knowledge, because getting something right or wrong is possible only if I make judgments about my experience, as the rationalists emphasize. Any adequate account of the nature of cognition must respect the truths of empiricism and rationalism while avoiding their shortcomings. But how do we keep activity and passivity together in a unified treatment of the subject? What is the relationship between sensibility (the faculty that receives sense data) and understanding (the faculty of judgment)?

If our thinking requires given sensations in order to have content, we can know things only as they are given to us. And if we must make judgments about those sensations in order to have knowledge, then none of our cognitions can ever get us beyond how we take things to be. This conclusion, which Kant calls "transcendental idealism," rules out the traditional ontology that had dominated the scholastic period and that many of Kant's contemporaries continued to practice. If we can know things only as they appear to us, then questions about freedom, the soul, and God are beyond our epistemic capacities. Rationalist philosophers who make theoretical claims about these things wrongly insist that our thinking gives us knowledge beyond appearances and thus engage in what Kant calls dogmatic metaphysics.

Responding to Kant's discovery of the limits of human knowledge, the German poet Heinrich Heine called the *Critique of Pure Reason* an "executioner's sword," a "destructive, world-crushing thought."[1] Indeed, Kant's critical philosophy did destroy a world of metaphysical speculation, even as it created another, in which epistemology, the philosophy of language, and the philosophy of mind set about understanding our place in the world.

Kant's Pre-Critical Period

Early in Kant's philosophical career, he adhered to a form of Leibnizian rationalism carried on by Christian Wolff, who attempted to derive the principle of sufficient reason[2] from the law of identity ('A is A')[3] and to use the former principle as the basis of a systematic metaphysics. Leibniz had strictly distinguished the study of the world as it appears to us, which is the subject matter of science, from the world as it really is—as it is perceived by God—which is the subject matter of metaphysics. We can understand the ultimate nature of reality not by doing experiments but by speculating about how things must be, given how we must conceive of them. We can approach a godlike understanding of the world through reason.

Continuing this Leibnizian/Wolffian project, the young Kant sought to provide an absolute foundation for a metaphysics of nature that would fulfill the Leibnizian program: to discover "the general principles of corporeal nature and even of mechanics [which] . . . belong rather to certain indivisible forms or natures as the causes of the appearances, than to the corporeal mass or to extension" (PE 51–52). Philosophers should not distract themselves with mere appearances but should turn their attention to things as they are apart from how they appear to finite beings—that is, things as they are in themselves. Although such things are beyond the reach of the senses, we can rationally deduce the laws that stand behind and govern the material world. Particularly in such works as *Thoughts on the True Estimation of Living Forces* (1746–47) and the *Physical Monadology* (1756), Kant tries to discern the "something more real" that underlies causal change (PE 51), to give a "certain and decisive" account of the *a priori* foundation of a Leibnizian science.[4]

By his own account, Kant was awakened from his "dogmatic slumber" by confronting the philosophy of David Hume (Pro 260). As we saw in Chapter 1, Hume demonstrates that there is no purely rational basis for causal claims: Because the effect is distinct from the cause, the effect cannot be discovered in the very concept of the cause. As intelligent as Adam is, he cannot determine the causal powers of things in the world based on reasoning alone (EHU 27). If real relations cannot be determined through the logical connections among concepts, then *a priori* analytic truths (like the principle of sufficient reason) can never add anything to our knowledge of objects. They merely explicate the definitions of terms. Rationalists like Leibniz, Wolff, and the early Kant dogmatically assume that pure rational concepts correspond to the way the world is, but Hume shows that this is unjustified. Rationalist metaphysics is bound to fail.

By demonstrating the failure of rationalism, however, Hume seems to preclude the very possibility of objective knowledge, for as Kant would later claim, we require "necessity and strict universality" (B4), which is achievable only *a priori*, in order "to give coherence to our presentations of the senses" (A2). As we understand it, the natural world is governed by causal laws, according to which "we say that everything in a sequence of events is subject to rules to the point that nothing ever happens without being preceded by something that it always follows" (A112–13). For us to have a coherent experience of events, we must locate them in a temporal series in which they are necessitated by prior events. For example, to say that a bridge collapsed for no reason—that it "just happened"—makes no sense to us. There must have been some structural defect, or its load limit was surpassed, or there was an earthquake. Only then can we explain why the event happened or was bound to happen. Every event has a cause, or a sufficient reason for its occurrence.

The problem is that, according to Hume, empiricism also cannot make sense of this. Based solely on what we know empirically, we cannot say that the earthquake caused the bridge to collapse. The best we can say is that we associate the two. However, I could just as easily associate the bridge collapse with the black cat I saw, the movement of the stars, or the burrito I had for lunch. When we try to explain something, we are after more than this. We usually think that there are right and wrong associations to make. I may associate the bridge and the burrito, but *in fact* the earthquake caused the structure to crumble. By making objective claims—that is, claims about objects that can be right or wrong—we attempt to describe the way things are, as opposed to our own psychological tendencies. The world does not make sense as a series of events that we just happen to relate to one another. We have to relate things with law-like connections, but such relations among objects are not given to us empirically.

Experience gets us merely to constant conjunction and habitual association, not to causal necessity; and by reasoning we know only about how we think, not about the world as it is apart from our thinking. But if, as Kant contends, we need law-like relations between events for us to make sense of the world—a coherent world, with necessary causal connections—and if Hume has shown that we cannot get them by appealing either to reason or the senses, how are we supposed to know anything?

Kant realized that his rationalism had been fatally undermined, but he was not willing to accept Hume's "sceptical solution" as a viable alternative. Hume claims that objective causal necessity is a fiction, because it is neither a relation of ideas nor a matter of fact. But Kant says that we use it all the time, and that it is necessary to make coherent judgments about the world. So, where does this idea come from? This is the question Kant thinks Hume posed for us: "It was a question concerning the *origin* of the concept, not concerning its indispensability in use" (Pro 259). In other words, Hume knew that we needed causality, but he did not know how to validate it. He was giving us a problem to solve. How, then, can philosophy make sense of the world while avoiding the pitfall of skepticism?

Kant often describes the problem in broader terms. We have certain ways of conceiving of reality—for example, we think that there must be a cause of every event—but what reason do we have to think that these concepts actually characterize the world? Why is the world amenable to human understanding? Sensations are given to us from mind-independent things, yet concepts are products of our own thinking. It would be easy to explain their relation if the mind simply created the world through its thinking, or if we had only empirical concepts derived from experience. However, Kant realizes that "our understanding, through its representations, is neither the cause of the object . . . , nor is the object the cause of the intellectual representations in the real sense."[5] In other words, the mind does not give itself sensations through thinking alone, but what experience gives us does not exhaust our way of conceiving of objects. Causal necessity, for example, is not arrived at empirically, but we do use that concept in our thinking about the world. If objects are not derived from our concepts and our concepts are not derived from objects, how is our thinking applicable to experience? Specifically, how is the concept of causality reflected in actual objective relations among objects?

These questions struck Kant with such force that, during his so-called "silent decade" from 1771 to 1780, he published virtually nothing. Instead, he thought about and eventually devised his own solution to the problem. The result was his major theoretical work, the *Critique of Pure Reason*, whose innovative approach to how we know things would profoundly influence the history of modern philosophy.

Overview of Kant's Solution

The *Critique of Pure Reason* is notoriously difficult to understand, but Kant's general strategy sounds simple enough: Rationalism and empiricism are incomplete, so they must be synthesized. Any experience is necessarily related to what is given in sensation—we cannot know about specific relations in the world without observation—but the world only makes sense to us because we organize our experience in certain ways. Thus our experience involves not only what Kant calls sensible intuition but also the discrimination of our perceptions according to pure concepts. Empiricism was right to stress the need for experience, and rationalism was right to stress the role of judgment in understanding the world. However, neither is sufficient on its own. We cannot know things about the world if we just think about it, and we cannot relate to the world in a coherent way if we just passively receive it. We have to get something from the world *and* make judgments about it.[6]

This may sound unusual, because it seems like experience is entirely passive. We see things just as they are given to us. But you can understand the plausibility of Kant's project if you concentrate for a moment on your own experience. Look at your surroundings. What do you see right now? If you are in a typical classroom, you probably see a table or a series of desks, chairs, walls surrounding you. You may respond, "There's a table in front of me," or "There's a chair in the corner of the room." Of course, you can be wrong about these things. You can think you are seeing a chair when there is not one there. The fact that you can be right or wrong tells you that you are making a judgment.

When I asked about what you saw, you did not just yell, "Brown!" Although it is true that you had the sensation of brown, that would tell me merely what you were sensing. Instead, you may have said, "The table is brown." When you experience objects in the world, you are making objective *claims*—that is, claims about objects rather than mere reports of your (subjective) sensations—and you can be right or wrong in a way that you could not be if you were entirely passive. There is a normative element to your experience. You see patches of color, but what distinguishes the patches of brown (the chairs) from the patches of white (the walls), or from other patches of brown (the table)? You not only see them as different colors, but represent them as adjacent and distinct things. And you see that they are different things because you are cutting up your sensations in certain ways. Experience is not simply given to you, but is the result of your making judgments about what is given to you. Kant thinks that such judgments are possible only when we organize our sensations according to certain *a priori* rules that govern the operation of our understanding. Of course, at this point, we may not understand or agree with this conclusion. One of the primary purposes of the *Critique of Pure Reason* is to establish its veracity.

The State of Metaphysics

Although one of the *Critique*'s aims is to solve the problem of induction, Kant's ultimate purpose is to address some of the unanswered questions that continue to plague humankind—for example, whether God exists, whether we are free, and whether we have immortal souls. As rational beings, we are drawn to these kinds of questions, even though their answers always escape us: "Human reason has a peculiar fate in one kind of its cognitions: it is troubled by questions that it cannot dismiss, because they are posed to it by the nature of reason itself, but that it also cannot answer, because they surpass human reason's every ability" (Avii). Because of the very nature of reason, we inquire into the ultimate basis of what we know empirically. Kant calls this our need to know the "unconditioned." For example, every event in the world has some cause; everything is conditioned by some prior thing. But when we realize that, questions naturally arise: How did it all get started? Is there such a thing as an absolutely free, uncaused/unconditioned act that begins the chain of (conditioned) effects? We want to know this. We cannot just set metaphysics aside.

And so, philosophers have advanced a number of different but convincing arguments in defense of opposing hypotheses. Some have argued that there must be some first cause of all things, because an unending series of causes and effects does not explain why this particular causal chain exists rather than some other. An explanation entirely in terms of causal laws thus cannot account for why things are as they are; it fails as an explanation. Other philosophers have argued for the contrary position, claiming that it makes no sense for something to happen that itself is uncaused. For it to come about, it must be caused by a prior event. Otherwise, no explanation could be given for why it occurs. If there are reasonable arguments for both claims, however, we arrive at the following contradiction: There must be a first cause *and* the idea of a first cause is nonsensical. Kant calls this an "antinomy" of reason (in particular, the Third Antinomy [A444/B472ff.], which we will examine in Chapter 5). If we try to give a complete explanation of natural events, reason leads to equally valid but (seemingly) incompatible conclusions, and thus it is in conflict with itself.

The fact that metaphysical speculation has led to such equally valid contradictory opinions shows that we have gone about answering these questions in the wrong way. In the *Critique*, Kant attempts to show how we ought to approach metaphysics in order to eliminate the contradiction in which reason finds itself. In other words, he wants to put metaphysics on a firm foundation: to establish metaphysics as a science, or at least to establish once and for all that it cannot be a science. We may realize that metaphysical questions simply cannot be answered or that there is a different way of addressing them that previous philosophers have neglected. Either way, we will have made some progress.

The Method: Critique

In an effort to establish metaphysics as a science, Kant scrutinizes reason and the extent of its powers so that we can see what we can and cannot know, and we can understand the basis of our objective claims. As Kant says, the *Critique of Pure Reason* is not an exercise in metaphysics; it does not make conclusions about what exists beyond the senses. Rather, it investigates how it is that we know, so that the questions—regarding God, freedom, and immortality—can be addressed properly: "The critique is a treatise on the method [of the science of metaphysics], not a system of the science itself. Yet it does set down the entire outline of metaphysics, including the bounds of this science as well as its entire internal structure" (Bxxii). By looking at the nature of human cognition and the limits of what we can know, Kant clarifies whether and how we can progress in metaphysics.

Like Descartes, Kant is trying to establish metaphysics as a systematic whole, grounded in certain foundations and (like other sciences) capable of progress in figuring things out. But in order to answer questions regarding metaphysical entities, we must first understand how we know things. Thus the *Critique of Pure Reason* is what Kant calls a *"propaedeutic* (preparation)" to a systematic metaphysics (A841/B869). This is also in the Cartesian tradition—an emphasis on epistemology as a prerequisite to metaphysics—but in this case it is even more radical. Kant believes that in order to defend empirical cognition from the consequences of Humean skepticism, and in order to make possible the epistemic meaningfulness of universal and necessary judgments (such as 'Every event has a cause'), he must first demonstrate that the *a priori* concepts governing how we think are applicable to the way the world works. This is something Descartes failed to do.

Kant sets himself a difficult task, to say the least. He proposes to answer Humean skepticism, to warrant the application of pure concepts to experience, and to correct the errors that plague the work of his philosophical predecessors. In doing so, he will overcome the general sense of disillusionment with philosophy (because of its lack of progress) and will make possible a well-founded inquiry into the existence (or nonexistence) of God, the soul, and human freedom, among other things.

For metaphysics to get on track and make real progress, Kant says that we must first look at how we make and justify our claims. All of these ambitious plans can be accomplished through a critique of the faculty of reason itself:

> [This indifference to philosophy] is evidently the effect not of the heedlessness but of the matured *judgment* of our age, which is no longer willing to be put off with seeming knowledge. And it is a call to reason to take on once again the most difficult of all its tasks—viz.,

that of self-cognition—and to set up a tribunal that will make reason
secure in its rightful claims and will dismiss all baseless pretensions,
not by fiat but in accordance with reason's eternal and immutable laws.
This tribunal is none other than the critique of reason itself: the *critique
of pure reason*. (Axi–xii)

Here Kant is referring to the very indifference that Locke talked
about, a frustration as to the possibility of achieving any knowledge
through philosophical speculation (E 44). Just as Locke claimed that
philosophy had exceeded the boundaries of what it can address, so too
Kant concludes that rationalism has extended our reasoning beyond
that to which it meaningfully applies. To understand what we are able
to know on the basis of reason alone, we must examine reason itself.
In this sense, the *Critique* is an exercise in self-cognition.

To explain what this means, Kant uses a judicial metaphor: The
person who engages in dogmatic metaphysical speculation exceeds his
rightful claim. It is as if he owns a piece of property and he is building
beyond the property line. He does not have the right to go beyond
what he owns, just as pure logical concepts are not rightfully applicable beyond our ways of thinking. The only way to establish what one
is entitled to is to appeal to a court of law to determine where the
property line is located; in this case, a tribunal is needed to determine
the proper use of pure concepts. This is discovered through an investigation of the power by which such claims are made, so that we can
understand what is rationally warranted. The cognizing subject must
first take account of the faculty of cognition. By "critique," then, Kant
does not mean that reason must be criticized. This is not an evaluation
of its worth, which is not really in dispute. Rather, a critique of pure
reason looks at how and what we know about the world by examining
how we conceive of the world.

Unfortunately, Hume has already shown that *a priori* investigations
into how we conceive of the world cannot tell us what the world is
actually like. Adam cannot deduce that water will drown him, and we
can tell nothing about the weather by sitting in a windowless room and
thinking about it. If a critique of pure reason is to help us understand

the world, Kant must confront this problem. How can such an inquiry help us? How can we know anything about objects *a priori*?

Although it is too early to understand the reasons for this, Kant will conclude that a critique of pure reason can help us to understand the world because we (in part) actively constitute the world that we experience. The world that we know is the result of not only what is given to us from without but also how we make judgments about what we are given, according to pure concepts.

Other Sciences: Logic, Mathematics, Natural Science

When trying to figure out how to erect metaphysics on a firm foundation, Kant looks to other inquiries that have been more successful in establishing themselves as sciences: logic, mathematics, and natural science. Beginning with logic, Kant says that Aristotelian logic is complete and has achieved stability. We can see by its systematic unity that Aristotle has given us an exhaustive list of logical rules—"the formal rules of all thought"—and that any further advances we could make within logic would merely simplify what is already there (Bix).

The problem is that logic is empty of content. For example, we know that the following (modus ponens) form is truth-preserving . . .

If A, then B.

A⎯⎯⎯⎯⎯⎯⎯

Therefore, B.

. . . but we do not know what A and B *are*. The form of the argument cannot tell us what is true. This is why Wolff and the other rationalists could not warrant their metaphysical claims. They assumed (wrongly) that logical rules could tell us about the way the world is in itself. But the law of identity, for example, is merely a formal restriction on how we think.

Mathematics provides Kant with a much more useful model for understanding human cognition. Mathematics has also achieved the status of a science, and as we saw in Chapter 1, the rationalists looked to mathematics for guidance in overhauling philosophy. But Kant uses its insights differently. Mathematical relations are reflected in the world because we experience the world in terms of our own mathematical concepts:

> When the *isosceles triangle* was first demonstrated, something dawned on the man who did so. . . . He found that what he needed to do was not to investigate what he saw in the figure, nor—for that matter—to investigate the mere concept of that figure, and to let that inform him, as it were, of the figure's properties. He found, rather, that he must bring out (by constructing the figure) the properties that the figure had by virtue of what he himself was, according to concepts, thinking into it a priori and exhibiting. And he found that in order for him to know anything a priori and with certainty about the figure, he must attribute to this thing nothing but what follows necessarily from what he has himself put into it in accordance with his concept. (Bxi–xii)

The mathematical properties of an isosceles triangle cannot be determined merely by measuring a particular figure. That could tell us the characteristics that *one* triangle *has*, but it would not tell us the characteristics that *all* isosceles triangles *must have*. Thus we do not derive our conception of an isosceles triangle from experience. Merely thinking about the definition of a triangle, however, does not provide us with any content. An isosceles triangle is not a conjunction of predicates—a plane figure with three sides, two of which are of equal length—but a series of lines that actually exhibit these characteristics. To understand what an isosceles triangle is, we must produce a figure by our thinking *through* the concept. We understand an isosceles triangle not by memorizing its definition but by imagining an actual shape that exhibits those characteristics. We know the characteristics such a triangle must have not because we have experienced it, nor because we have the bare concept of an isosceles triangle. Rather, the properties of an actual triangle in experience must correspond to our *a priori* concept because we construct such an object in accordance with the concept— that is, we form an object that exhibits the predicates.

Natural science took much longer to hit on a systematic method. In the beginning, science merely catalogued what people witnessed, or it appealed to variable, supernatural causes to explain events. To predict things, science must discover necessary causal laws that govern the natural world in general. For example, medical science would not be worth much if the future effects of a drug could not be determined based on clinical trials. Hume seems to have demonstrated that such objective relations cannot be justified; we are left only with subjective associations. However, according to Kant, the world only makes sense to us in terms of natural laws. Under Hume's "sceptical solution," nature has no rational coherence. Scientists can only recognize such coherence in nature if they reject Hume's empiricism and acknowledge the role of thinking activity in our experience. Kant credits Francis Bacon, Galileo, and others with realizing this relatively recently, in the seventeenth century.

> What all these investigators of nature comprehended was that reason has insight only into what it itself produces according to its own plan; that reason must not allow nature by itself to keep it in leading strings, as it were, but reason must—using principles that underlie its judgments—proceed according to constant laws and compel nature to answer reason's own questions. For otherwise our observations, made without following any plan outlined in advance, are contingent, i.e., they have no coherence at all in terms of a necessary law—even though such a law is what reason seeks and requires. When approaching nature, reason must hold in one hand its principles, in terms of which alone concordant appearances can count as laws, and in the other hand the experiment that it has devised in terms of those principles. Thus reason must indeed approach nature in order to be instructed by it; yet it must do so not in the capacity of a pupil who lets the teacher tell him whatever the teacher wants, but in the capacity of an appointed judge who compels the witnesses to answer the questions that he puts to them. (Bxiii)

Scientists formulate hypotheses about how nature behaves and subsequently test them against observational evidence. Kant gives the example of Galileo's famous experiment in which he rolled balls of different weights down an inclined plane (Bxii). In doing so, he falsi-fied the theory that the rate of acceleration depends on an object's mass. Instead, the data was consistent with his theory that the distance covered would be proportional to the square of the time. Galileo did not concoct this claim on the basis of rolling balls. Rather, the experi-ment supported what he already thought.

Science brings to light our own understanding of how things are. Any experiment is done to show which principle of ours is in fact reflected in nature. It is not merely a matter of recording what we perceive: "There is heat. The copper is expanding." That is not sci-ence. Scientists make different kinds of claims: "Heat makes copper expand." As Hume rightly demonstrated, we cannot arrive at that conclusion based solely on observation. Our claims to know and recognize these necessary relationships are possible only if we as-sume that the world conforms to our manner of conceiving of it in accordance with certain principles. If Kant wants these judgments to elucidate the way the world is, then, he must warrant their applica-bility to objects in a way that rationalism failed to do.

The Copernican Turn

Ordinarily, we think that our knowledge of the world derives wholly from our observation of what happens, rather than anything we contribute to it. When a bridge collapses after an earthquake, we assume that what we actually saw was an effect of the tremors on the structure of the bridge. The act of observing is simply the reception of sense data that does nothing to change the unfolding of events. If we perceive the same table on repeated occasions, we think that the table is the same because it really *is* the same. What do we have to do with it?

In part, Kant agrees with this ordinary understanding. He does not deny that there is an actual table apart from the image in our heads, or that the earthquake shook the bridge. We know all of these things because we experience them. However, he wants to explain how it is possible for us to know that these things are "really" the case. How does our way of understanding the world—in terms of spatiotemporal objects and causal relations—relate to the way things actually are?

To understand how such concepts are applicable to the world, we must assume that nature corresponds to how we think of it. This sounds pretty familiar so far. Descartes used a methodological skepticism concerning the external world, but he concluded that the world beyond the senses exhibits our rational conception of it—namely, that it is a world of geometrical objects governed by mechanical laws. However, Hume also demonstrated that we cannot get "out there" by an appeal to reason alone. Mechanical laws cannot be derived *a priori*. So, Kant asks, if Hume is correct that we cannot make judgments about objects based on our *a priori* concepts (including the concept of causal necessity), how can we claim that the propositions of mathematics and natural science describe the world?

In order to explain how *a priori*, subjective concepts could be applicable to objects, Kant proposes an experiment:

> Thus far it has been assumed that all our cognition must conform to objects. On that presupposition, however, all our attempts to establish something about them a priori, by means of concepts through which our cognition would be expanded, have come to nothing. Let us, therefore, try to find out by experiment whether we shall not make better progress in the problems of metaphysics if we assume that objects must conform to our cognition. (Bxvi)

If we are trying to catch up with the world as it exists independently of us, we can never know anything just by looking at how we think about it. In addition, although we normally believe that we learn about the world simply because it affects our senses, Hume has shown that this only yields habitual associations. Kant hopes to show that in order to make objective judgments about the world, the world must conform to the *a priori* rules that we use to understand it. The world as we experience it is governed by how we organize our perceptions.

In an effort to explain how the world is an object of cognition for us, then, Kant is going to explore the subjective conditions for the possibility of objective experience. What about us as subjects makes our experience of the world have the characteristics it has? He likens this to what Copernicus did:

> The situation here is the same as was that of *Copernicus* when he first thought of explaining the motions of celestial bodies. Having found it difficult to make progress there when he assumed that the entire host of stars revolved around the spectator, he tried to find out by experiment whether he might not be more successful if he had the spectator revolve and the stars remain at rest. Now, we can try a similar experiment in metaphysics, with regard to our *intuition* of objects. If our intuition had to conform to the character of its objects, then I do not see how we could know anything a priori about that character. But I can quite readily conceive of this possibility if the object (as object of the senses) conforms to the character of our power of intuition. (Bxvi–xvii)

The retrograde motions of the planets (when other planets seem to move backward in relation to the fixed stars) cannot be explained given an immobile earth at the center of a Ptolemaic model of the universe, so Copernicus theorized a heliocentric system instead. If the earth orbits around the sun, we can understand why it is that the other planets seem to undergo retrograde motions: Their movements are witnessed from a revolving and rotating observational point (the earth) that makes the simple motions of the planets seem less than regular. Similarly, the fact that *a priori* concepts such as causality apply to actual objects is inexplicable if the world that we experience is taken to be a fixed point, absolutely distinct from the understanding. Like Copernicus, Kant reconceives how we experience things by claiming that they too depend on the activity of the observer. We will discover what the world is like by looking at how we understand it.

This overcomes the gap between thinking and the world that the rationalists simply ignored, as well as the gap that Lockean empiricists thought could be bridged by immediate experience. They assumed that reason would be reflected in mind-independent reality. Kant's approach is very different. He is not saying that we will look at reason to figure out what the world is like in itself but asserting that the world appears to us only as we judge it to be a certain way. Just as the measurements of the planets result in part from the movement of the observer, so too does experience result in part from the judgment of the perceiver. The objects that we experience are mere appearances, the result of how we represent them by means of pure concepts. We can never know things as they are in themselves—that is, apart from such concepts. Discovering the sources and limits of human cognition will, Kant hopes, eventually resolve the antinomy of pure reason and give us a strategy for answering metaphysical questions.

Kant's Distinctions

Kant begins this task in earnest in the introduction to the *Critique*, where he makes some important distinctions. Kant seems to be adopting Hume's fork, but he introduces a crucial difference. Rather than a two-pronged fork—analytic *a priori* and synthetic *a posteriori*—Kant describes a third kind of judgment: synthetic *a priori*. Hume had not recognized the latter as a possible kind of judgment, but establishing its possibility is essential for the Kantian project.

	analytic	synthetic
a priori	• (first prong of Hume's fork)	• (Kant's addition, not recognized by Hume)
a posteriori	None (Hume and Kant agree)	• (second prong of Hume's fork)

According to Kant, an analytic *a priori* judgment is a judgment in which the predicate is "contained in" the concept of the subject (A6/B10). It is *a priori* because we do not need to investigate what is going on in the world to know whether it is true, and it is analytic because all we have to do is analyze the meaning of the terms.[7] As an example, Kant presents the claim "All bodies are extended" (A7/B11). This is analytic because by 'body' we mean a thing that is extended in space, and it is *a priori* because we do not need to experience particular bodies to know that this proposition is true. 'All bachelors are unmarried males' is another example. A bachelor is an unmarried male by definition. We may also think of analytic truths as logical truths that cannot be denied without self-contradiction. To say that bodies are nonextended is self-contradictory, because anything that is a body must be extended in space.

Because the truth of an analytic proposition is established simply by the meaning of the terms themselves, there is no such thing as an analytic *a posteriori* judgment: "to base an analytic judgment on experience would be absurd, because in its case I can formulate my judgment without going outside my concept, and hence do not need for it any testimony of experience" (B11). The fact that a judgment is analytic means that the concept of the predicate is contained in the concept of the subject. We need not appeal to experience in order to warrant the claim. We do not have to poll bachelors as to their marital status. If they are in fact bachelors, then we know that they are unmarried males. That is what it means to be a bachelor. We simply need to analyze the concept.

A synthetic *a posteriori* judgment is any judgment in which the predicate is not contained in the subject (not analytic) and whose truth is warranted by experience (not *a priori*). Most of the claims we make are synthetic *a posteriori*: "Class begins at eleven o'clock," "It's sunny outside," "The *Critique* is heavy," "I have a daughter named Lucy," and so on. "The door is open" is a synthetic *a posteriori* judgment, because simply analyzing the meaning of the word 'door' cannot get us to its being open. We have to look at it. Kant notes that such synthetic judgments are "*expansive*" because they add something to the concept of the subject in a way that analytic judgments do not (A7/B11). Claiming that all bachelors are unmarried males does not help us to learn anything new about bachelors. But if I tell you that Sam is a bachelor, you now know something about Sam that you could not know *a priori*. It is not contained in the concept of Sam that he is a bachelor. Otherwise, it would be a contradiction in terms for him to be married.

Note that, because analytic judgments are *a priori*, they hold necessarily and universally, whereas *a posteriori* judgments do not. Any bachelor we encounter *must be* an unmarried male. If he were married, then he would not be a bachelor. But empirical claims are not strictly necessary or universal. The door may be open now, but it may have been otherwise, and it may be closed tomorrow. It is always possible that any generalization we make on the basis of experience may be contradicted by further experience. For example, if someone claims that bachelors get a lot of Chinese take-out, it is possible that there are some bachelors who do not. Even if this rule holds generally, it does not hold necessarily and universally. This is because we can never experience every possible instance of the thing about which we are making a judgment (not universal), and because, if we have to experience something to make a judgment about it, that means that it could possibly have been otherwise (not necessary).

The best observation can do is to provide us with what Kant calls "empirical universality," something that happens to hold in all cases, but whose opposite is not inconceivable (B4). Repeated observations have shown us that the sun rises in the east, and this may in fact be true for the remainder of the earth's existence. But only *a priori* judgments can tell us what things of a certain kind must be like with necessity and strict universality—for example, 'All bodies are extended'. It is impossible for there to be a body that does not occupy space, but it is logically possible that the sun could have risen in the west, or that it may not rise at all tomorrow, just as it is possible that the tallest peak in Malaysia could have ended up taller or shorter than it actually is.

A posteriori judgments can do something that it seems *a priori* judgments cannot, however: They can tell us about the world. We know that all bachelors are unmarried males, but we cannot know *a priori* whether any bachelors exist. We know that all bodies are extended, but without experience, we do not know the shape of any particular bodies. Looking at the door can tell us whether it is open, and this tells us something about the world that we did not know before we looked at it.[8]

The importance of these distinctions has yet to be seen. So far, Kant has said nothing that distinguishes his position from Hume's fork. There are analytic *a priori* claims having to do with the meaning of concepts, and there are synthetic *a posteriori* claims having to do with what we experience. If these exhaust the kinds of claims we make, then, as Hume rightly noted, we can make no necessary judgments about the world. Any empirical judgments are contingent and could have been otherwise, including claims about causal necessity. Copper does not have to expand in the presence of heat, even though the two have been conjoined (and subjectively associated by us) in the past. The very same cause could bring about a very different effect tomorrow; there is no necessity. If all of our experiential claims are synthetic *a posteriori*, then we cannot justifiably commit ourselves to objective natural laws. But if, as Kant insists, events must be causally related in order for them to make sense to us, then we again face the threat of Humean skepticism.

Synthetic *A Priori* Judgments

As we saw earlier, Kant is interested in how mathematics and natural science achieved the status of sciences, and he comes back to these two fields in the introduction. Both can say things about the world—that is, their claims are expansive—but they also hold necessarily. Descartes rightly thought that the world is governed by mathematical relations (the laws of physics), but he failed to explain why our thinking is reflected in our experience of objects. Mathematical relations that characterize our experiences cannot be derived simply by inspecting our own mathematical concepts, yet we understand what happens with regard to mathematical relations among things by (so to speak) understanding them in terms of our own *a priori* rules. For example, we know that the base angles of an isosceles triangle are equal, but this is not an analytic proposition. An isosceles triangle is a three-sided figure with two congruent sides, but there is nothing in the meaning of these terms that says anything about the base angles. Nonetheless, this judgment holds necessarily, so it cannot be *a posteriori*. In the introduction to the *Critique*, Kant uses an example from arithmetic: $7 + 5 = 12$ (B15–16). In thinking the union of seven and five, we are not already thinking the concept of twelve; the union of seven and five does not somehow "contain" twelve. Hence, it is not analytic. However, it does hold necessarily, in all possible worlds, that $7 + 5 = 12$.

Because the necessity of this relation cannot be established by repeated trials, it must be *a priori*.

Similarly, the claims of pure natural science are necessarily true of the world, but they are not derived from observation. What Kant calls pure natural science is composed of the most basic claims that any science assumes in doing its investigations. For example, that Coke causes tooth decay is a specific claim about what causes what. It is based on experiments and evidence. But the fact that every event has a cause is a matter of pure natural science. In addition, the existence of particular objects is determined empirically, but it is a physical law that matter is neither created nor destroyed, "that in all changes in the corporeal world the quantity of matter remains unchanged" (B17). Matter is defined simply as the substance that constitutes physical objects, so the concept of matter itself does not contain the idea of indestructibility. This is not an analytic proposition. However, this holds necessarily with regard to any matter in the universe, and the necessity of this law could not be achieved simply by generalizing from experience. It must be *a priori*. The practice of science is a matter of applying such rules to what we experience, as when we understand the bridge collapse through the concept of causality. By allowing us to make necessary and universal propositions about objects, synthetic *a priori* judgments give both mathematics and natural science firm foundations as sciences.

Unlike analytic propositions, synthetic judgments are expansive. The predicate adds to our understanding of the subject rather than merely clarifying what the concept means. A metaphysics that relies on analytic propositions can only look at how we think about the world. It does not warrant "the valid use of such concepts in regard to the objects of all cognition generally" (B23–24). This is why rationalism can never get to an understanding of the world: Descartes, Spinoza, and Leibniz tried to move from definitions—of God, or of substance—to what exists, but this move is unjustified. Only synthetic claims enlarge our knowledge.

An *a priori* judgment, however, does not rely on experience. We do not need to verify it in particular cases; it holds necessarily and universally. Combining these characteristics (of synthetic judgments and *a priori* judgments), we can conclude that a synthetic *a priori* judgment is a proposition whose predicate tells us something more about a subject than what is already contained in it (synthetic), but which is not justified by an appeal to experience (*a priori*). In short, it tells us something about the way the world must be, necessarily and universally.

	analytic	synthetic
a priori	•	•
a posteriori	None	•

To gain an understanding of synthetic *a priori* propositions, let us look at a familiar example: 'Every event has a cause.' Note that this is not the same thing as 'Every effect has a cause.' The latter proposition is analytic, because the notion of an effect already contains within it the notion of its being caused. But 'Every event has a cause' is synthetic. An event is just something that happens. The concept of an event does not "contain" the concept of its being caused. In addition, this is a universal claim: *Every* event is caused by some prior event. Because experience can never provide us with strict necessity or universality, 'Every event has a cause' must be *a priori*, not *a posteriori*.

Even though mathematical relations and natural laws are taken to hold necessarily, it is unclear how we can make such judgments. It is obvious how looking at the door expands our knowledge—we now know that it is open, which we did not know before we looked at it—but how could something that is not based on experience expand our knowledge about objects—for example, that every event has a cause, or that matter can neither be created nor destroyed? Furthermore, how can nonanalytic judgments pertain universally to every possible experience? If synthetic *a priori* principles are necessary for mathematics and natural science to be sciences, how does Kant warrant our commitment to such principles? In short, "*how are synthetic judgments possible a priori?*" (B19).

Transcendental Idealism

These are important questions, because only by answering them can Kant provide an alternative to Humean skepticism. Kant's solution involves the experiment that we discussed earlier, the Copernican turn in philosophy. The passage bears repeating:

> If our intuition had to conform to the character of its objects, then I do not see how we could know anything a priori about that character. But I can quite readily conceive of this possibility if the object (as object of the senses) conforms to the character of our power of intuition. (Bxvi–xvii)

We can know about the world by looking at the understanding only if we suppose that the world as it appears to us must conform to our faculty of judgment, rather than the understanding's having to conform to (or find out about) the world in itself.

Synthetic *a priori* judgments about the world are not possible if the empiricists or the rationalists are right. Both of them assume that a world that exists independently of our thinking is the ultimate object of cognition. We are trying to get at what is true either by perceiving the world through the senses or by conceiving of the world through reason. But, Kant says, if the world is not separate from my thinking, if the objects I perceive are in part created by me because of how I conceive of them, then it makes sense that the world would conform to my understanding of it, because the world that I experience is structured by that very understanding. We normally conceive of ourselves as learning about the world by passively receiving sense data. It is certainly true that we can understand particulars—for example, which events have which causes—only through sensation, but to relate these particulars in a causal relationship, we have to be making a judgment based on what we require of the world conceptually.

At the beginning of the *Critique*, Kant says that he will try this as an experiment. The task of most of the *Critique* will be to show that this hypothesis is true, that our formal constraints on what is given to the senses are conditions for the possibility of our experiencing objects. Kant calls what he is doing transcendental philosophy: "I call *transcendental* all cognition that deals not so much with objects as rather with our way of cognizing objects in general insofar as that way of cognizing is to be possible a priori. A *system* of such concepts would be called *transcendental philosophy*" (A11–12/B25). In short, a transcendental inquiry is an inquiry into the *a priori* conditions for the possibility of experience rather than the content of experience, how we cognize things rather than the objects of cognition. As we will see later in the book, we can know the formal features of any possible experience because sensations are represented by us according to what Kant calls the forms of sensible intuition and the pure concepts of the understanding.

Because the experience we have results not only from the sensations that are given to us but also from our making certain discriminations that are not given through sensation, the world as we know it is distinguishable from the world as it is apart from our subjective conditions of knowing. The world considered in abstraction from the knowing subject is necessarily inaccessible to us. Kant calls this position 'transcendental idealism,' according to which we can know only appearances ("phenomena") and never things in themselves ("noumena").[9]

Is Metaphysics Possible as a Science?

It is easy to lose track of why Kant is interested in all of this, given the ultimate purpose of the book: to put metaphysics on a firm foundation. Kant clarifies this in the *Prolegomena to Any Future Metaphysics*, which was published in 1783 (two years after the first edition of the *Critique*) to explain his revolutionary work to a confused public.

As we saw, pure mathematics and pure natural science are composed of synthetic *a priori* claims, such as '7 + 5 = 12,' and 'Every event has a cause.' But metaphysical claims are also synthetic *a priori*. By definition, *meta*physical (as opposed to physical) claims transcend experience (Pro 265). We do not come around the corner and notice God, like we would notice an open door. And we cannot introspect in order to discover whether we have souls. We have self-consciousness, but we do not directly intuit a thing that makes consciousness possible. So, Kant says, metaphysical claims must be *a priori*.

They are also synthetic. When one says that the soul is an immortal substance, the concepts of immortality or substantiality are not contained in the concept of the soul. Aristotle, for example, could consistently maintain that animals and plants have souls, and that the soul is merely the essence (or form) of a living thing, such that it is not a substance and cannot exist without a body.[10] If we claim that the soul is a substance and that it is immortal, we are adding something to the concept. Similarly, claims about God's existence make assertions. If it is not a contradiction in terms to say that God does not exist, then 'God exists' is not analytically true, or true by definition.[11]

The soul, God, and freedom are not discoverable through experience or by merely reflecting on the meaning of terms. The problem is: How could we know anything about what exists—including God, the soul, and freedom—without experience? This leads to one of the guiding questions of the *Prolegomena*, "'whether such a thing as metaphysics be at all possible?'" (Pro 255).

Kant investigates pure mathematics and pure natural science to figure out how synthetic *a priori* judgments are possible. How can we know that the interior angles of every triangle total 180 degrees? How can we know that every event has a cause? Ultimately, the point of asking these questions is to illuminate the basis of metaphysical claims, which are also synthetic *a priori*. If we can find out how mathematical and scientific claims are possible, we can also understand how (or whether) metaphysics is possible as a science. Talking about these other fields of inquiry is only a means to an end. And what Kant discovers is that synthetic *a priori* judgments are possible because the world conforms to our way of understanding it (according to pure concepts) and our way of receiving it (in space and time). If this is so, we can only know the world as it appears to us, because we cannot know the world as it is apart from our subjective conditions.

That means if we do apply *a priori* concepts beyond the boundaries of experience, we would be using them the wrong way. If they are based on such concepts, any claims made about things in themselves are unjustified: "as soon as we leave this sphere, these concepts retain no meaning whatever" (Pro 315). The problem is that when we engage in metaphysical speculation, that is exactly what we do. Instead of explaining how metaphysics is possible, then, Kant will explain why metaphysics is impossible: Metaphysical claims are the result of misapplying *a priori* concepts to things in themselves. The bulk of the *Critique of Pure Reason* is an attempt to prove that our knowledge is in fact limited in this way and that the traditional way of approaching metaphysics is misguided.

Contents of the *Critique*

Before we consider which *a priori* conditions make coherent experience possible and why we should believe that they do, let us take a step back and ask a few more basic questions. Why should we focus on experience if we are interested in finding out what we can know about the world? In other words, why is experience so important in epistemology? These sound like trick questions, but answering them will put us on the right track. We must begin with experience because our capacity to know about objects—and as Kant will show, our capacity to know ourselves—is limited by what we are able to perceive. We become familiar with the world when we first open our eyes and ears, and we come to know ourselves by reflecting on our thoughts and feelings.

But this is just part of the story. We are passive, but we are also active in our cognitions. We are discursive thinkers; that is, we arrive at our experience through the process of thought. We are given sensible intuitions upon which our cognition is based, but we also interpret our perceptions as representations of objects:

> There can be no doubt that all our cognition begins with experience. For what else might rouse our cognitive power to its operation if objects stirring our senses did not do so? In part these objects by themselves bring about presentations. In part they set in motion our understanding's activity, by which it compares these presentations, connects or separates them, and thus processes the raw material of sense impressions into a cognition of objects that is called experience. . . . But even though all our cognition starts *with* experience, that does not mean that all of it arises *from* experience. For it might well be that even our experiential cognition is composite, consisting of what we

receive through impressions and what our own cognitive power sup-
plies from itself (sense impressions merely prompting it to do so). (B1)

Because we are in a passive relationship to what is given through the
senses *and* we must actively organize the information we receive in order to have objective experience, Kant divides his analysis into one
part that examines the conditions of our receptivity and another part
that examines the activity of the understanding—the Transcendental
Aesthetic and the Transcendental Analytic, respectively. The Transcendental Aesthetic explores the forms under which we receive sensations, or the conditions of receptivity. At this point, we have not
gotten to concepts, only to the way that our senses are affected.[12] The
activity of judgment is discussed only in the Transcendental Analytic,
where Kant enumerates the pure concepts of the understanding and
warrants their applicability to experience.

   The way that Kant divides up the *Critique of Pure Reason* says a lot
about how his position is related to rationalism and empiricism. (See
Figure 2.1.) The Transcendental Aesthetic investigates how we sense
things—what Kant calls the forms of sensibility—apart from a consideration of the understanding. There can be a distinct philosophical
critique of how things are given to us, logically prior to how we conceive of them. For rationalists like Descartes, Spinoza, and Leibniz,

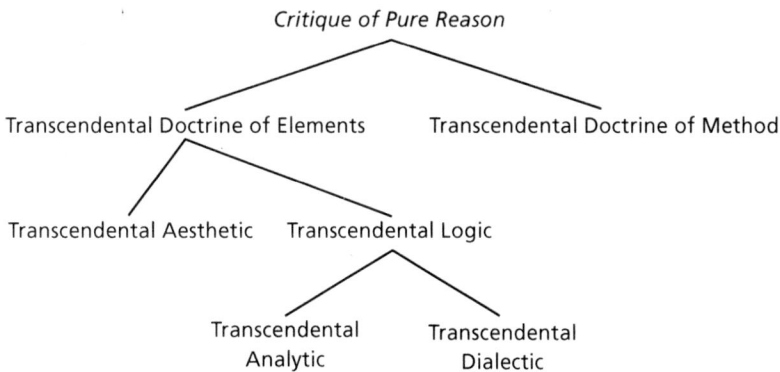

FIGURE 2.1 The parts of the *Critique*

getting at what we know by looking at sensation would be misguided. Sensibility ought to be corrected by clarifying what rationally must be the case *a priori*. Kant rejects this and, incorporating an element of empiricism, argues that the understanding can give us warranted claims about the world only if it is applied to the material of sensation.

The Transcendental Analytic is devoted to how we must intellectually discriminate our sensations, according to the pure concepts of the understanding. For empiricists like Locke, Berkeley, and Hume, investigating our way of thinking could never get us to knowledge about the world. The understanding merely abstracts from what is given to the senses. Kant rejects this and, incorporating an element of rationalism, argues that we must discriminate among our perceptions in certain ways in order to arrive at objective claims. Experience is the result of making judgments according to *a priori* rules.

Kant establishes his epistemology in the first two sections of the *Critique*. In the third part, the Transcendental Dialectic, he spells out the implications of transcendental idealism for metaphysics. There he applies his earlier claims about the conditions for the possibility of experience both to refute specific metaphysical positions (such as Descartes on the substantiality of the soul) and, by limiting our knowledge to appearances rather than things in themselves, to establish the possibility for a new metaphysics based on practical considerations. Among other things, this is where Kant solves the antinomy of pure reason, showing that the conflict of reason with itself is merely an apparent conflict, as a result of our applying *a priori* concepts beyond their proper use.

The book's concluding section reflects on the place of the *Critique* in a projected system of pure reason. In addition to going into more detail about Kant's views on mathematics, the Transcendental Doctrine of Method primarily sets out a complex taxonomy of the functions that reason can perform, as well as how the different areas of philosophy are related. As Kant explains it, the Doctrine of Elements has "assessed the building equipment available to us," or has given us an inventory of what we can know, and the Doctrine of Method provides us with "the plan" by which we can "erect a firm residence" for metaphysics (A707/B735). As we will see, Kant severely limits the materials that we have for this project, so the scope of speculative philosophy is correspondingly narrow, and the last part of the *Critique* is appropriately slight in comparison to the preceding parts. The first three parts of the *Critique*—the Aesthetic, Analytic, and Dialectic—are most important for understanding Kant's philosophical and historical importance, so we will concentrate our efforts there.

~ CHAPTER THREE ~

The Transcendental Aesthetic

BECAUSE THE WORLD is accessible to us only through the senses, Kant first inquires into the conditions for the possibility of receptivity. In examining these conditions, Kant encounters what he considers to be an epistemological problem that must be solved. The objects we receive information about (or "intuit") are in space and time, but space and time are neither concepts nor sensations:

> if from the presentation of a body I separate what the understanding thinks in it, such as substance, force, divisibility, etc., and if I similarly separate from it what belongs to sensation in it, such as impenetrability, hardness, color, etc., I am still left with something from this empirical intuition, namely, extension and shape. These belong to pure intuition, which, even if there is no actual object of the senses or of sensation, has its place in the mind a priori, as a mere form of sensibility. (A20–21/B35)

Objects are extended things that have certain shapes, which means that they take up space and are bounded by it in particular ways. However, their being situated in space is not attributable to what we sense of the object. We do not perceive space like we perceive colors. We see an object's color, but we see its shape *in* space. An object's extension and shape are also not the result of our bringing it under concepts. We intuit the object *directly* in space. Even if we simply reported our immediate sensations without making judgments about them, what we perceive would still be spatially located—a patch of color, for example, has certain dimensions. The same is true of time. Things appear to us at certain times without our making any kind of conceptual judgment about when they exist, and time is not a sensation but a way that sensations are received (in time).

If space and time are not sensations and they are not a result of our making a judgment, what are they? Space and time are intuitions, because sensibility is the faculty whereby the mind directly relates to objects as they are given to us. And they are *a priori* because our perception of the world must be in space and time, necessarily and universally. Therefore, space and time are what Kant calls "pure forms of sensible intuition." Space and time are not things that exist outside of the mind but rather modes of apprehension. In other words, they have to do with how we receive sensory data. It is the task of the Transcendental Aesthetic to demonstrate this.

The Metaphysical Exposition of the Concept of Space

By "metaphysical exposition," Kant means that he is defining space in terms of its characteristics and thereby explaining what it is (or must be). The Metaphysical Exposition of the Concept of Space[1] begins easily enough: Kant observes that it is only by means of the senses that we know anything about objects, and that such sensations are always of objects locatable in space. Indeed, to have an experience, something must be given to me: I see the open door, or I bump into a table in the dark. That is how I have access to the world—through the senses. And anything that is part of the world around me must be spatially oriented. Objects are close to or far from one another, and they have particular shapes: The table is rectangular, and it is closer to me than the round clock. How such spatial relations and dimensions are possible, however, is the very thing at issue.

During Kant's time, there were two dominant explanations for why we experience the world this way: Either space and time are "actual beings," or they are "only determinations of things, or . . . relations among them," positions defended by Newton and Leibniz, respectively (A23/B37). Isaac Newton claimed that all things exist and are related to one another within an infinite space, and that all motion is not only in relation to other objects (relative motion) but also set against this all-encompassing space (absolute motion). All particular relations among objects are merely parts of the infinite space in which all things (including all particular spaces) exist. Thus space is a kind of independently existing container.[2] Unlike Newton, who argued for an absolutist account, Leibniz advanced a relational or reductionist view: Our conception of space arises from our perception of the relations among objects. Space is not an independently existing thing but an imaginative invention derived from things that we perceive together. In other words, space is merely the coexistence of events ("an order of coexistences"), so there is no such thing as empty space (PE 324).[3] We just see objects as separate and posit empty space between them. Newton's and Leibniz's differing accounts of time follow a similar pattern: We perceive all things within an "absolute, true, and mathematical time,"[4] or time is discovered by relating two things that occur one after another ("an order of successions") (PE 324).

What follows in the Metaphysical and Transcendental Expositions is a series of arguments that rule out both of these possible explanations of space, exclude a third possibility (space as a concept), and advance Kant's position as the only coherent alternative. Our representation of space cannot be accounted for as a result of the application of any universal spatial concept, as derivative from experience, or as part of an absolute space. Therefore, space must be an *a priori* intuition.

The overall argument structure of the Metaphysical Exposition is composed of two disjunctive syllogisms. First, space is either derived from relations among representations (*a posteriori*) or *a priori*; it is not *a posteriori*, so it must be *a priori*. Second, space is either a universal concept or an intuition; it is not a concept, so it must be an intuition. From these arguments, Kant concludes that our representation of spatially located objects is a matter of how we perceive things rather than something that we discover through our perceptions or a concept that we use to discriminate among particular spaces.

Refuting Leibniz: Space Is Not *A Posteriori*

In the first and second arguments (labeled #1 and #2), Kant rules out the Leibnizian hypothesis: "Space is not an empirical concept that has been abstracted from outer experiences" (A23/B38). In the First Metaphysical Exposition, Kant reaches this conclusion based on the following argument:

> For the presentation of space must already lie at the basis [or be presupposed] in order for certain sensations to be referred to something outside me (i.e., referred to something in a location of space other than the location in which I am). And it must similarly already lie at the basis in order for me to be able to present [the objects of] these sensations as outside and *alongside* one another, and hence to present them not only as different but as being in different locations. (A23/B38)

I would not be able to relate any objects to one another unless they were already spatially distinguishable from me ("outside me") as I occupy a particular location in space. Space is a prerequisite for my having external objects to compare in the first place. In addition, space could not be derived from two distinct objects unless I confronted those objects already as distinguishable from one another ("*alongside* one another") in space. Two objects must originally occupy different regions of space in order to be numerically distinct, two things rather than one. To say that space depends on the existence of particular objects or spatial relations presupposes space that is not derived empirically: Our representation of space depends on our relating distinct representations, and the existence of distinct representations depends on an *a priori* representation of space. Thus Leibniz's theory cannot explain space unless it is supplemented by a contradictory theory. This is nonsensical. We can conclude that our orientation in space is not achieved *a posteriori*, as a result of comparing different objects: "Accordingly, the presentation of space cannot be one that we take from the relations of outer appearance by means of experience; rather, only through the presentation of space is that outer experience possible in the first place" (A23/B38). Space is not given to us by the things themselves. Rather, we intuit things in space because of our particular kind of sensibility.

Kant makes a similar kind of argument in the *Prolegomena,* where he uses the example of incongruent counterparts to demonstrate that spatial relations cannot be derived from objects and their relations. Incongruent counterparts are things that are distinguishable by us in space ("incongruent") but are not qualitatively different ("counterparts"). For example, your left hand and your right hand are mirror images of one another. They are different—one is a right hand and the other is a left hand—even though they are qualitatively identical— they take up the same amount of space, and every quality had by one hand is reflected in the other. Kant claims that if Leibniz were correct, we could not distinguish incongruent counterparts as different things; one would have to be substitutable for the other. However, your right hand cannot be replaced (without difference) by your left hand; your left hand does not fit properly into your right glove. The two hands are qualitatively identical, but they are not substitutable for one another because, "notwithstanding their complete equality and similarity, the left hand cannot be enclosed in the same bounds as the right one (they are not congruent)" (Pro 286). For Leibniz, two such objects with identical properties would have to *be* identical because there is no difference in the relations of the parts of the hands; the index and middle fingers on the left hand are the same distance apart as the corresponding fingers on the right hand, the thumbs bend the same way, and so on. They have identical properties—"no internal differences"—and therefore, according to Leibniz, they are indistinguishable (Pro 286). Because we can differentiate two such qualitatively identical things, we must be judging them each in relation to a universal space that is independent of the objects themselves and their relational properties.

The fact that we must represent individual spaces as parts of a universal space forms the basis of the Second Metaphysical Exposition. If space were derived from the relations among objects, particular spaces and things would not be apprehended in relation to a universal space. Yet this is necessary for any representation, because any representation must occur *in* space:

> Space is a necessary a priori presentation that underlies all outer intu-
> itions. We can never have a presentation of there being no space, even
> though we are quite able to think of there being no objects encountered
> in it. Hence space must be regarded as the condition for the possibility
> of appearances, and not as a determination dependent on them. Space is
> an a priori presentation that necessarily underlies outer appearances.
> (A24/B38–39)

Some commentators have interpreted this as a kind of contingent psychological thesis about what we can and cannot imagine, but this
misses Kant's point. Any representations, including representations of
particular spaces, always presuppose a universal space in which they
occur; but this universal space does not presuppose particular representations, because it is possible to have an empty space without any
objects or relations among objects. We cannot do away with space, but
we can do away with objects in space. If universal space were derived
from particular representations, however, it would not make sense to
have an empty space.

Space Is Not a Concept

To this point, Kant has rejected Leibniz's claim that we represent space
as a relational feature among objects. Space is not derived (*a posteriori*)
from the relations of things in space but must be an *a priori* representation underlying objective experience. In the Third and Fourth Metaphysical Expositions (labeled #3 and #4), Kant moves on to the
second disjunction and rules out the possibility that space is a concept
by which we classify our representations: "Space is not a discursive or,
as we say, universal concept of things as such; rather, it is a pure intuition" (A24–25/B39). Here Kant denies that space is the result of a
judgment that we make through the understanding. By showing that
space must be an intuition, Kant hopes to explain why we represent
things spatially by appealing to how we receive things sensibly.

Before we delve into the second half of the Metaphysical Exposition, however, we need to clarify what Kant means when he talks
about intuitions and concepts. Unfortunately, Kant provides little
guidance in this part of the *Critique*. He does say repeatedly that there

are two elements involved in our experience: a receptive element by which we sense things and an active element by which we make judgments about sensations. These correspond to intuition and concepts, respectively. Having shown that our representation of space cannot be abstracted from the relations among things but is rather *a priori*, Kant asserts that space must either be a matter of how we take things in or how we think about them through the understanding. In either case, because our representation of space is *a priori*, it must be something that we bring to experience. But what is the difference between an intuition and a concept?

Kant distinguishes them in the Transcendental Dialectic: "Cognition is either *intuition* or *concept* (*intuitus vel conceptus*). An intuition refers directly to the object and is singular; a concept refers to the object indirectly, by means of a characteristic that may be common to several things" (A320/B376–77). Intuitions refer to particular representations that can be brought under general concepts. I see something walking down the sidewalk (intuition) and call it a dog (concept), or I hear someone speaking (intuition) and identify the language as Italian (concept). Because intuitions are always singular, they are immediately related to the object, while concepts are only mediately related to what is being represented: By identifying the thing I see as a dog, I am understanding it in terms of a general class of things. By means of a concept, the understanding picks out certain marks or distinguishing features (*Merkmale*) given through sensation, so the concept is "a universal representation, or a representation of what is common to several objects."[5] The animal has a certain head shape and size, paws, and a tail. The words have Latinate roots and the person speaks them with an identifiable intonation and rhythm.

Initially, this taxonomy may seem to share a lot with Lockean empiricism: Some ideas are given directly through the senses, and others result from reflection upon those sensations. For Kant, intuitions are particular sensations that are conceptually distinguished by the thinking subject. For example, if someone shows you a new paint color, you intuit that particular color, but you understand the kind of color it is by relating it to previous, similar colors: "It's a shade of blue." In fact, like Locke, Kant also describes this as a process of reflection.[6]

The difference for Kant is that space must be *a priori* and thus cannot be merely received in sensation or abstracted from particular sensations; it is not an *empirical* intuition or an *empirical* concept. We learn to call different things blue by relating different color experiences to one another. 'Blue' is an empirical concept. But space is something that the subject brings to experience. It is not derived from experience. The question then becomes: Does space have the immediacy and singularity of an *a priori* intuition, or is it an *a priori* concept by which we classify different experiences? In other words, are things represented in space because of how we receive sensations, or does this result from our making a judgment about those sensations?

The Third and Fourth Metaphysical Expositions set out to answer these questions. In both arguments, Kant trades on the characteristics that distinguish intuitions and concepts. He rules out the possibility that space is a concept first by showing that space is singular (in #3), underlying all particular conceptual judgments, then by showing that we are directly related to space through sensation (in #4). He begins with the singularity criterion:

> first, we can present only one space; and when we speak of many spaces, we mean by that only parts of one and the same unique space. Nor, second, can these parts precede the one all-encompassing space, as its constituents, as it were (from which it can be assembled); rather, they can be thought only as *in it*. Space is essentially one; the manifold is in it, and hence also the universal concept of spaces as such, rests solely on [our bringing in] limitations. It follows from this that, as far as space is concerned, an a priori intuition of it (i.e., one that is not empirical) underlies all concepts of space. (A24–25/B39)

There is just one space within which other spaces are represented. Because space is singular, it must be an intuition. Our concepts of particular spaces—the dimensions of a classroom, the size of Central Park, the shape of the Taj Mahal—are not instances of a universal concept but parts of a singular space. Concepts are applied to particular sensations, but all conceptual discriminations occur within an all-encompassing space. These particular spaces could never be added onto one another to achieve the universal space, any more than repeatedly adding one plus one could get us to infinity. When we specify a particular space according to concepts, then, it is merely an instance of universal space, a part of our general representation of a singular space.

The Fourth Metaphysical Exposition plays upon the idea that we *apply* concepts to different particulars, but that space *contains* all particulars within it. Space must be an intuition because things are directly apprehended in space:

> We present space as an infinite *given* magnitude. Now it is true that every concept must be thought as a presentation that is contained in an infinite magnitude of different possible presentations (as their common characteristic) and hence the concept contains these presentations *under itself*. But no concept, as such, can be thought as containing an infinite multitude of presentations *within itself*. Yet that is how we think space (for all parts of space, *ad infinitum*, are simultaneous). Therefore, the original presentation of space is an a priori *intuition*, not a *concept*. (B39–40)

Concepts may be applied to an infinite variety of sensible intuitions, but things to which we apply concepts are in space. In other words, using concepts to make sense of perceptions is different from having perceptions that are spatially oriented. To clarify the contrast, think about what it looks like to bring representations together under the concept of causality: Heat makes copper expand, Coke rots your teeth, Sam placed the personal ad. We conceive of these effects as similarly necessitated by their causes because they share certain features: their constant conjunction in an experimental setting, or evidence we have that only the proposed cause explains the subsequent event. Even though all of these things are related as instances of causality, however, space contains things (objects and particular spaces) in a different way. Particular spaces are *parts of* an actual, given infinity, and particular objects are located *in* space. By contrast, particular instances of a given concept are *members of* a class. The size of Central Park is a limited part of an all-encompassing space, but Sam's placing the personal ad is not a part of causality; it is a particular case of causally related things.

Refuting Newton: Space Is a Form of Sensible Intuition

Collectively, the arguments of the Metaphysical Exposition amount to a refutation of Newton's view that space is a mind-independent thing. If Kant has succeeded, then he has demonstrated that space is an *a priori* intuition. Because space is an intuition rather than a concept, we know that space is not the result of a judgment we make but a matter of how we take things in. Because space is *a priori*, our spatial orientation is not something that we learn about in experiencing the world. Instead, space is a necessary condition of any possible experience we could have.

As a pure intuition, space is a matter of how we receive what we are given through the senses. Objects appear to us in space not because that is how they are in themselves, but because space is contributed by us (*a priori*) to experience. Space is a formal condition by which the content of experience is organized, a pure form of sensible intuition. Consequently, space is not a Newtonian thing but a subjective condition governing our experience of things. There is no absolute space.[7]

The Transcendental Exposition of the Concept of Space: The Argument from Geometry

Expositors of Kant disagree as to whether the Transcendental Exposition is a further argument for the claim that space is a form of sensibility or whether it is intended merely to demonstrate the applicability of space to actual experience. Were it meant to serve the former purpose, it would be largely redundant. The four arguments of the Metaphysical Exposition have the combined result of proving that space is not a concept but an intuition, and that space is not derived from experience but *a priori*. As a result (and contrary to the claims of Leibniz and Newton), we know that space is a pure form of sensible intuition. For our purposes, then, we will treat what follows in the Transcendental Exposition as a kind of test case for Kant's position in which he exhibits the explanatory advantages it has over Newton's position in particular.

Despite critical disagreement concerning the purpose of this section, Kant's strategy is clear: Only if we assume that space is a pure form of sensible intuition can we account for a common phenomenon that we all accept. As we saw earlier, when Kant talks about a transcendental inquiry, he is investigating conditions for the possibility of experience. In the Transcendental Exposition, Kant investigates the conditions for "the possibility of other synthetic a priori cognitions"—in particular, the claims of geometry (B40).

The argument from geometry relies on an epistemic consideration: If space were not a pure form of sensible intuition, we could know nothing about the truths of geometry that characterize all existing spatial relations. We could not know what we do about space if space were a thing in itself, or if it were derived from relations among representations. Rather, the truth of geometrical propositions can be explained only if space is *a priori* and an intuition:

> Geometry is a science that determines the properties of space syntheti-
> cally and yet a priori. What, then, must the presentation of space be in
> order for such cognition of space to be possible? Space must originally
> be intuition. For from a mere concept one cannot obtain propositions
> that go beyond the concept; but we do obtain such propositions in
> geometry. . . . This intuition must, however, be encountered in us a
> priori, i.e., prior to any perception of an object; hence this intuition
> must be pure rather than empirical. For geometric propositions are one
> and all apodeictic, i.e., linked with the consciousness of their neces-
> sity—e.g., the proposition that space has only three dimensions. But
> propositions of that sort cannot be empirical judgments or judgments
> of experience; nor can they be inferred from such judgments. (B40–41)

Geometrical propositions about space cannot be derived from concepts, because such propositions go beyond what is contained in the concepts. The concept of a triangle, for example, is nothing but the concept of a three-sided plane figure, but we can build a geometric proof to show that its interior angles must total 180 degrees. If this is not discoverable in the very concept of a triangle, how do we know this? We proceed by "constructing" the geometric concept of a triangle in pure intuition—that is, by means of a representation not based on experience—then undertaking a series of other constructions whereby we deduce the sum of the interior angles (A713/B741).[8] The resulting proposition, that the interior angles total 180 degrees, holds of all triangles. Kant actually gives this proof (at A716/B744–A717/B745) in order to demonstrate that the synthetic *a priori* propositions of geometry are possible because the space we use to construct those propositions is an *a priori* intuition. *A posteriori* generalizations are not universal or necessary, so the geometrical proposition must be derivable *a priori*.

We can understand Kant's argument by trying a little experiment. Look at the following triangles:

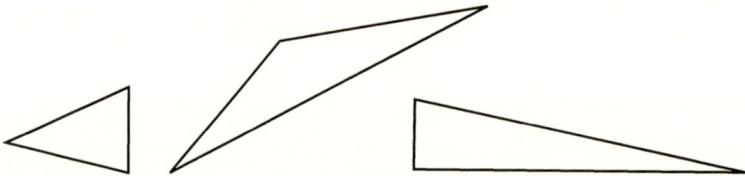

The total of the interior angles of each of these triangles is 180 degrees. But these are only three examples. At the end of this chapter, there is another triangle. What is the total of the interior angles of *that* triangle? If you think that the total is 180 degrees, you are right. But how do you know that? Did you look at the triangle, measure the angles, and then add the numbers? Probably not. Are you generalizing based on your measurements of the interior angles of a lot of previous triangles, including these three? That could not get you to what the next one will be like *necessarily*. All you could get is some degree of probability, as if, for example, you saw a lot of white swans and determined that, probably, all swans are white. But the next one could be black. By contrast, the interior angles of the triangle at the end of this chapter *must* total 180 degrees. It is not like looking at another swan.

We know that geometrical propositions are *a priori* for two reasons. First, given the meaning of *a priori* as knowable independent of experience, the fact that we have knowledge of actual geometrical relations before we experience them—the interior angles of the next triangle we see, even though we have not seen it yet, will total 180 degrees—demonstrates that they are *a priori*. Second, given necessity and strict universality as criteria of *a priority*, the fact that objects necessarily adhere to geometrical rules—the interior angles of *every* triangle *must* total 180 degrees—also shows that they are *a priori*.

But geometrical propositions are also synthetic. 'Having interior angles totaling 180 degrees' is not contained in the meaning of the word 'triangle'. If they were analytic, geometrical propositions would tell us nothing about the world. However, they do expand our knowledge; the truths of geometry are reflected in the characteristics of existing objects. We know that the interior angles of the next triangle we see will total 180 degrees. How is this possible? How can we know anything about the world *a priori*? Specifically, why must actual triangles conform to our conception of triangles?

As long as it is assumed that space is mind-independent, there is no way to dispel this puzzlement. We could know nothing about what space must be like necessarily if we merely learned about it through experience. Were there an absolute Newtonian space, our knowledge of space would be extremely limited, because we would have experienced very little of it. Yet we can discover geometrical propositions that hold necessarily and universally for actual spatial relations. The only way to explain this is to assume that objects must conform to our spatial understanding, rather than vice versa. In other words, space is a way that we have of apprehending the world rather than something that affects us from without:

> How, then, can the mind have an outer intuition which precedes the objects themselves, and in which the concept of these objects can be determined a priori? Obviously, this can be so only insofar as this intuition resides merely in the subject, as the subject's formal character of being affected by objects and of thereby acquiring from them *direct presentation*, i.e., *intuition*, and hence only as form of outer *sense* in general. (B41)

Space, including the spatial relations that characterize geometrical propositions, does not exist apart from how we perceive things. Only if space is a pure form of sensible intuition can we understand why objects must conform to the *a priori* synthetic judgments of geometry.

If we assume that the geometer's space—the way that we think about spatial relations—is the very same thing as the space actually "out there," we can solve the mystery as to the empirical applicability of *a priori* mathematical concepts: We can anticipate characteristics of the next triangle because the space that defines it is something that we contribute to our representation of the world. The space in the phenomenal world is the same as the space that is a formal condition of our sensibility. Kant's position thus has an explanatory advantage over Newton's hypothesis:

> Now suppose that there did not lie within you a power to intuit a priori; that this subjective condition were not, as regards its form, at the same time the universal a priori condition under which alone the object of this (outer) intuition is itself possible; and that the object (the triangle) were something in itself, even apart from any relation to yourselves as subject. (A48/B65)

Here Kant has us imagine that his hypothesis is wrong. If we perceive things as they are in themselves rather than as they appear to us relative to our subjective conditions, what would that imply? What follows is a *reductio ad impossibile* of this realist position: If this were the case, then no strictly necessary judgments could be made regarding possible experience. Geometrical propositions concerning triangles, for example, would not necessarily apply to actual triangles.

> If that were so, how could you say that what necessarily lies in [or belongs to] your subjective conditions for constructing a triangle must also belong necessarily to the triangle itself? For, after all, you could not add to your concepts (of three lines) anything new (the figure) that would therefore have to be met with necessarily in the object, since this object would be given prior to your cognition

rather than through it. Hence you could not synthetically a priori establish anything whatsoever about external objects if space (and similarly time) were not a mere form of your intuition, an intuition that a priori contains conditions under which alone things can be external objects for you—these objects being nothing in themselves, apart from these subjective conditions. (A48/B65–66)

Geometry makes sense only if objects must conform to our way of sensing those objects. We know that the interior angles of the next triangle we see must total 180 degrees, but we could not know this synthetic claim to be true if we always had to adjust our geometrical claims based on our limited experience of some absolute space.

Therefore the following is not merely possible—or probable, for that matter—but indubitably certain: Space and time, as the necessary conditions of all (outer and inner) experience, are merely subjective conditions of all our intuition. Hence in relation to these conditions all objects are mere appearances, and are not given to us in this way on their own. And that is why much can be said a priori about these objects as regards their form, but not the least can ever be said about the thing in itself that may underlie these appearances. (A48–49/B66)

We can make synthetic judgments *a priori* only if we do not experience the world as it is in itself, but as it is subject to our conditions of knowing it. Because space is a subjective form of sensible intuition, mathematical relations function as constraints on what could be apprehended by us empirically. The transcendental ideality of space—or the idea that space is applicable only to things as they appear to us—is therefore proven ("indubitably certain") because it makes sense of geometry. By demonstrating that space is an *a priori* intuition, Kant has shown how synthetic judgments are possible *a priori*. They are not possible under Newton's account of space.

Here Kant also corrects a mistake made by Descartes (and rationalism generally). As we saw in Chapter 1, Descartes deduced the objects of the world as geometrical objects made real. They were conceived to be objects in themselves, as they are apart from how we (confusedly) experience them. However, Descartes failed to warrant the application of *a priori* principles to objects. Indeed, he could not do so as long as these objects are considered apart from our conditions of knowing them. The application of synthetic *a priori* principles to objects makes sense only if they must conform to our epistemic constraints. And objects considered according to these subjective conditions are distinct from objects as they are in themselves. Therefore, geometrical laws apply only to the world as it appears to us—obviously a dramatic change from the rationalists' insistence that such laws can help us transcend empirical reality.

Before moving on to Kant's treatment of time, it should be noted that the argument from geometry has been criticized by a number of philosophers primarily because of its underlying assumptions that actual space corresponds to Euclidean geometry, and that Euclidean geometry consists of a series of synthetic *a priori* propositions. We now recognize a number of non-Euclidean geometries, and theoretical physics is committed to a view of space that is decidedly non-Euclidean.[9] In addition, some people now contend that pure geometry is a closed explanatory system that follows from analytic truths, and that the propositions of applied geometry, with relevance for actual physical space, are nothing more than empirical hypotheses.[10] Because of these objections, the question of whether the argument from geometry is needed to establish the transcendental ideality of space is quite important.

Kant's argument should not be abandoned too quickly. A defender of Kant could say that space seems to be structured by Euclidean geometry given our (and Kant's) prior Euclidean assumptions, but that actual spatial relations among objects are governed by a non-Euclidean system. In ordinary life, we interpret spatial relations in Euclidean terms, but this may be the wrong interpretation of what we are perceiving; judgments about our perceptions are not always reliable. We may actually perceive things according to a non-Euclidean framework, something Kant simply failed to recognize. This would mean only that Kant mischaracterizes the actual structure of physical space as it appears to us, not that we have reason to doubt that space is a pure form of sensible intuition.

The Metaphysical and Transcendental Expositions of the Concept of Time

Commentators usually focus on section one of the Transcendental Aesthetic, which deals with space, because there Kant initiates a pattern of argument that basically recurs (with less clarity) in the second section, where he deals with time. But his arguments for time as an *a priori* intuition are also of interest because, like space, time is typically considered to be something that we discover *a posteriori*, by witnessing change in our perceptions. The second section dispels this misconception and demonstrates that time is also a pure form of sensible intuition, or a subjective mode of apprehension.

Just as in the first section on space, Kant's first two arguments here are meant to prove that time is not *a posteriori*, that it cannot be merely abstracted from the changes that we experience. The first argument had shown that space cannot be abstracted from the appearance of objects because a condition of our relating objects in the first place is their locatability in space. Similarly, in the First Metaphysical Exposition of the Concept of Time (labeled #1), Kant claims that time cannot be abstracted from experience, for in order to be presented with objects related in time (through motion or change) in the first place, they must appear to us in time—either simultaneously or successively. The argument that space is necessary for any experience in outer sense appears in a parallel form here as well (labeled #2): All things necessarily occur in time; even though we can remove all appearances in time, time itself remains as their condition. Time therefore cannot be arrived at on the basis of experience but is rather an *a priori* condition of any possible experience.

At this point, the Metaphysical Exposition of time diverges from the pattern of section one. Kant's Third Metaphysical Exposition (labeled #3) parallels the argument from geometry, and it is meant to demonstrate that time is not a thing in itself but rather the form in which we receive sensations.[11] Just as there are geometrical propositions that hold necessarily of every possible experience, there are also axioms concerning time that are absolutely necessary (or "apodeictic"), and such necessity could not be achieved if we learned about time through our experience of an absolute time. Kant gives the following proposition as an example: "Time has only one dimension; different times are not simultaneous but sequential" (A31/B47). For this to be true of all possible times, it cannot be something that we learn based on what we have witnessed. Otherwise, it may be generally true (like 'all swans are white'), but it would not hold with strict necessity. If we can make such a claim about any possible set of different times, then time must also be a form of sensible intuition.

We can illustrate this with the same kind of thought experiment that we did with the triangles. Here is a randomly chosen time: 9:47 A.M. on Thursday, May 11, 1972. At the end of this chapter, I have listed a *different* time. Is that time simultaneous with this time, or is it sequential—that is, coming either before or after 9:47 A.M. on Thursday, May 11, 1972? Obviously, if it is a different time, then it must have come either before or after the time listed. Otherwise, it would be the same time. It must be sequential. Yet how can we know this with absolute certainty even without looking at the end of the chapter? We know that this *must* be so because the way that we experience time is reflected in actual events. Our experience of the world corresponds to our subjective conditions of knowing—in this case, time as a form of sensible intuition. If we were after some absolute time, as Newton thinks we are, then necessary synthetic propositions about time would be impossible. We could make only empirical generalizations, such as "In my experience, different times have been sequential. But I've experienced only a small part of absolute time. Perhaps tomorrow I'll be more familiar with absolute time and discover that different times are sometimes simultaneous." Such generalizations are incapable of achieving the level of necessity. If there are some necessary propositions concerning time (just as there are some necessary [geometrical] propositions concerning space), this makes sense only if objects must conform to our way of perceiving them, rather than vice versa.

Following the third argument, Kant continues to parallel the arguments of the Metaphysical Exposition of the Concept of Space. In #4 and #5, he argues that time is not a pure concept that we use to discriminate among sensible intuitions. Different times are parts of one and the same (singular) time; they are not brought under a general category. The latter characterizes the use of concepts; the former characterizes intuition. Kant also returns to the point made in the previous section: The axioms of time are not discovered by analyzing concepts, since axioms like 'Different times are not simultaneous but sequential' are synthetic. We cannot derive the fact that different times are sequential simply by analyzing the words 'different' and 'time' any more than we could determine the interior angles of a triangle just by analyzing what it means to be a three-sided figure. In addition, time itself is unlimited, and determinate times are contained in a universal time. Concepts apply to determinate things in experience, but time forms a condition of experience as a whole. Our representation of time is singular and immediate, so it must be an intuition.

Based on these arguments, Kant concludes that time is not derived from experience (*a posteriori*), nor is it a concept that is applied to experience by the understanding. Rather, time is an *a priori* intuition. Like space, time is a subjective way of perceiving the world that necessarily constrains our sensory data. All sensations—of objects in the world and ideas in our heads—occur in time.

Empirical Realism and Transcendental Idealism

Given the arguments in the Transcendental Aesthetic, we can now see that space and time are pure forms of sensible intuition. Objects appear to us in space and time as a result of how we perceive what is given to us, but we cannot know what things are like apart from these subjective conditions—that is, we must apprehend the world in space and time. This amounts to transcendental idealism, or the theory that we can know only phenomena and never things in themselves:

cross to previous chapter.

If we take objects as they may be in themselves—i.e., if we abstract from the way in which we intuit ourselves inwardly, and in which by means of this intuition we also take into our power of presentation all outer intuitions—then time is nothing. Time has objective validity only with regard to appearances, because these are already things considered as *objects of our senses*. But time is no longer objective if we abstract from the sensibility of our intuition, and hence from the way of presenting peculiar to us, and speak of *things as such*. Hence time is merely a subjective condition of our (human) intuition (an intuition that is always sensible—i.e., inasmuch as we are affected by objects); in itself, i.e., apart from the subject, time is nothing. Nevertheless, time is necessarily objective in regard to all appearances, and hence also in regard to all things that we can encounter in experience. We cannot say that all things [as such] are in time; for in the concept of things as such we abstract from all ways of intuiting them, while yet this intuition is the very condition under which time belongs in the presentation of objects. If now we add the condition to the concept, and say that all things as appearances (objects of sensible intuition) are in time, then this principle has all its objective correctness and a priori universality. (A34/B51–A35/B52)

We receive sensory information successively and from particular vantage points. We thus perceive objects in space and time because we apprehend the world empirically. They are necessary conditions of any objective experience, forms of sensible intuition rather than independently existing things. Although they are not characteristics of the world as it is in itself (considered apart from how we perceive it), space and time do characterize any possible experience of the world that we could have. These claims have been well established in sections one and two of the Transcendental Aesthetic.

To this point, we have followed Kant's arguments rather quietly, but we have arrived at a startling conclusion. If space and time are not things in themselves, does that mean that what we see in space and time is a product of our own imagination? If space and time are subjective modes of apprehension, are things not really "out there" in space? Is the external world merely a fiction based on our inner perceptions? Against Berkeleyan phenomenalism, Kant makes what initially seems like a puzzling claim. Time and space are not only transcendentally ideal but empirically real:

Hence the doctrine we are asserting is that time is *empirically real*, i.e., objectively valid in regard to all objects that might ever be given to our senses. And since our intuition is always sensible, no object that is not subject to the condition of time can ever be given to us in experience.

On the other hand, we dispute that time has any claim to absolute reality; i.e., we dispute any claim whereby time would, quite without taking into account the form of our sensible intuition, attach to things absolutely, as a condition or property. Nor indeed can such properties, properties belonging to things in themselves, ever be given to us through the senses. In this, then, consists the *transcendental ideality* of time. According to this view, if we abstract from the subjective conditions of sensible intuition, then time is nothing, and cannot be included among objects in themselves (apart from their relation to our intuition) either as subsisting [as such an object] or as inhering [in one]. (A35–36/B52)[12]

This claim may seem contradictory, but when we examine it, we realize that Kant is merely summarizing the conclusions of the metaphysical and transcendental expositions of space and time. Because human experience is limited to objects as they are constituted (in part) by the formal conditions of sensible intuition, space and time cannot be applied to things as they are in themselves. If we distinguish appearances from things in themselves—as we must, given the applicability of space and time only to appearances—we must conclude that space and time are "nothing" with regard to things considered apart from our way of perceiving them. Space and time are transcendentally ideal, in that they are not independently existing things but subjective conditions for the possibility of experience.

But this does not mean that space and time are inapplicable to objects. Objects are given to us directly in space and time, insofar as objects are external and real for us only as they are subject to these conditions. We see the door in front of us, then we see the table in the middle of the room. Our representations of the door and the table occupy space and time—one is farther from us than the other, and they appear to us in succession. All empirical judgments involve determinations of spatially arranged phenomena that appear to us at different times.

In addition, spatiotemporality makes such objects possible outside of us, as constituting objects distinct from our subjective sensation of objects. We distinguish the subjective ideas of objects from objects themselves, and such objects—as objects of outer sense—are real, in that they affect us directly through the senses and they occur to us as subsisting things that, for example, exclude other substances from their spaces. The table that I bump into is a real object in space, distinct from the image of a table in my head. I do not have to walk around my idea of a table. Space and time are empirically real in this sense.

Kant's distinction here is not identical to the empiricist's distinction between primary and secondary qualities, but the two do overlap. As we saw in Chapter 1, Locke distinguishes an object's secondary qualities, such as its color, which belong to the object only because I am affected by it in a certain way, from its primary qualities, such as extension, which belong to the object itself (E 132–43). The object as a bearer of primary qualities is empirically real in Kant's sense—it is distinct from the subject and is intuited immediately through the senses—but Locke dogmatically presumes that this object is also the thing in itself. For Locke, once we exclude or get beyond the variable qualities of objects as they appear to different observers, we have the object as it really is. This is true for Kant in the sense that objective claims can be made only about spatiotemporally located perceptions, with (primary) qualities like extension (in space). Color, for example, is not a property of the object.

But transcendental idealism also distinguishes the object that has certain primary qualities from the thing as it is in itself, apart from the conditions under which we perceive it. Space is a subjective condition of something's being an object for us, so the extension that characterizes the object does not characterize the thing in itself. The object as a spatiotemporally located substance is the result of our perceiving the object under the pure forms of sensible intuition. The object is in part determined by the formal conditions that we require of it.

This is certainly confusing, and Kant recognizes that Locke's two-place distinction is much more familiar to us:

> It is true that we commonly make this distinction about appearances: we distinguish what attaches to their intuition essentially and holds for the sense of every human being in general, from what belongs to that intuition only contingently by being valid only for a special position of

this or that sense, or for the spacial organization of that sense, but not valid for the relation of [the intuition to] sensibility in general. We then speak of the first kind of cognition as presenting the object in itself, and of the second as presenting only its appearance. (A45/B62)

Empiricism distinguishes the object "in itself" (with its primary qualities) from the mere appearance of the object (its secondary qualities). The color of an object can look different to different people, but the shape of the object is a fact that does not depend on how we perceive it. Locke's position amounts to what Kant calls transcendental realism: Our perception (or "idea") of an object corresponds to some real object that stands behind it. Although we can be mistaken—our idea may correspond to no actual object—generally our perceptions resemble the world as it is in itself.

But Kant's arguments for space and time as formal conditions of experience complicate Locke's picture. We not only have the variable appearances of objects and the objects themselves. Under transcendental idealism, spatiotemporal objects are mere appearances that can be distinguished from things in themselves, which can never be known:

This distinction [between the object and its variable appearance], however, is only empirical. If (as is commonly done) we fail to go beyond it and do not (as we ought to do) regard that empirical intuition in turn as mere appearance, in which nothing whatever belonging to some thing in itself is to be found, then our transcendental distinction is lost. We then believe after all that we cognize things in themselves, even though in the world of sense, however deeply we explore its objects, we deal with nothing whatever but appearances. (A45/B62–63)

Locke was right to distinguish primary qualities from secondary qualities. The table may look brown or red in different light, but it occupies the same space under any environmental condition. Kant agrees. However, this is merely an empirical distinction, or how we separate two kinds of things in our experience. Given the claims supported by the Transcendental Aesthetic, we must make not only the empirical distinction between appearances and objects but also the transcendental distinction between the object (which possesses primary qualities) and the thing in itself (whose qualities cannot be known). Kant illustrates this complicated taxonomy with the example of a rainbow:

> Thus it is true, e.g., that when during a rain accompanied by sunshine we see a rainbow, we will call it a mere appearance, while calling the rain the thing in itself. And this is indeed correct, provided that we here take the concept of a thing in itself as meaning only something physical. We then mean by it something that in general experience, and in all its different positions in relation to the senses, is yet determined thus, and not otherwise, in intuition. But suppose that we take this empirical something as such, and that—without being concerned about its being the same for the sense of every human being—we ask whether it presents also an object in itself (not whether it presents the rain drops, for these, as appearances, will already be empirical objects). In that case our question about the presentation's relation to the object is transcendental, and the answer is: Not only are these drops mere appearances; rather, even their round shape, and indeed even the space in which they fall, are nothing in themselves. They are, rather, mere modifications, or foundations, of our sensible intuition. The transcendental object, however, remains unknown to us. (A45–46/B63)

We can speak of objects as they are, apart from how they appear to different people. Even though my senses are struck by the colors of a rainbow, I know that I am merely seeing the effect of light refracted through small droplets of water. The colors will vary depending on light conditions and my shifting perspective, but there is some objective truth about the number and shape of the water droplets. The drops occupy certain spaces, and that does not vary among different observers.

This is how Kant guards against Humean skepticism. We share a common world (albeit a phenomenal one), and we make judgments about objects that we all experience through the senses. Because of this, we can make knowledge claims rather than merely associating things subjectively. We can disagree about things and eventually discover which judgment reflects the truth of the matter. It was once believed that smoking cigarettes provided health benefits, and we now believe that it causes cancer. The earlier causal claim was mistaken, and we know this because the latter hypothesis more accurately explains the experimental evidence. Science is never perfect; some of our current hypotheses will eventually be falsified. But there is some truth we are after. The earth is either at the center of the universe, or it is not. Judgments about the world are not subjective in the sense that they are relative to whatever each individual happens to believe. If I claim that Coke provides the body with nine essential vitamins and minerals, I am wrong, even if I sincerely believe it. The formal conditions of experience are subjective because they are necessary forms of sensibility for us, but this does not make experience purely individual or personal.

Kant says that his position is a form of empirical realism, in the sense that we do perceive an external world that exists independently of our representation of it and that is given to us through the senses. Kant is not denying that there are objects out there. He is not saying that the world is unreal or that everything we experience is an illusion with no truth to it, as if they were figments of our imagination. In fact, Kant claims, we would not have any experience unless there were things out there to affect the senses: "otherwise an absurd proposition would follow, viz., that there is appearance without anything that appears" (Bxxvi). This is where he agrees with the empiricists. Sensations are given to us by an external world that is independent of our thoughts.

Kant is not making any claims about the existence of things. He is interested in how we experience those things and what it means for something to be an object of experience. Objective claims are about the world rather than merely associated states of consciousness, but our experience of objects depends on certain subjective conditions. The drops of water have certain shapes and the sun has a particular location because our sensations come to us under space as a pure form of sensible intuition. In other words, an object's spatial characteristics—

its shape, size, texture, location, all of the object's primary qualities—as well as its position in time are the result of how we as subjects receive sensations. Although spatial and temporal qualities apply to the sun or the rain as objects of experience, we cannot know what they are like apart from our subjective conditions of knowing. The thing in itself is in neither space nor time, so although it is not a possible object of experience, it is in principle distinguishable from the physical objects that we apprehend every day. The objects that we experience are "mere appearances" because we know them (and can only know them) as they appear *to us* in space and time (A46/B63).[13]

Because of this complicated conception of objectivity, Kant can say that space and time are both empirically real and transcendentally ideal, depending on whether we are talking about objects as they exist for us or objects considered apart from our conditions of knowing them—that is, as things in themselves. From an empirical perspective, the water droplets do occupy space, and there are a specific number of drops out there that I experience directly through the senses. Sensations are given to me, the objects exist independently of my perception of them, and (if I am right) any person similarly positioned will come to the same conclusion. From a transcendental perspective, however, the space that the water inhabits is a subjective mode of apprehension. As they are in themselves, the drops are not in space and time. And even though I can conceive of them in this way, knowing what they are like is necessarily beyond my grasp, because they can only be objects of cognition for me subject to the pure forms of sensible intuition. I can never know them as they are apart from how I must experience them.

Objectivity and Subjectivity

One risk in talking this way is that we start to feel as if we are not as capable of objective certainty as we once were. Calling the objects that we experience *mere* appearances gives the impression of something that is lacking in substance or that is a pale copy of the truth. Such a conclusion is unwarranted. Kant has not demonstrated that knowledge is impossible. We never did grasp the object as it is in itself. The certainty we now have is the certainty that we have always had. To think that we can no longer know what is true and false, or that the very idea of objective truth is being overthrown, is to misunderstand how Kant conceives of the object. Experience is not subjective in the sense that it is entirely up to me. I have to be responsive to intuitions that are given to me. I cannot will my invisible friend into existence just by sincerely believing in him. Physical objects exist or do not exist, and they may or may not correspond to what we perceive.

What has changed is that the objects we are talking about are not the same things that we thought we experienced when we previously claimed to know something. We should not respond to Kant with skepticism, because he is in fact warranting our claim to know in a way that neither the empiricists nor the rationalists could. His is a well-founded knowledge. Taking it as an occasion to doubt whether we in fact know objects is to misconstrue the nature of objectivity:

> I am saying, then, that the intuition of external objects and the self-intuition of the mind both present these objects and the mind, in space and in time, as they affect our senses, i.e., as they appear.[14] But I do not mean by this that these objects are a mere *illusion*. For when we deal with appearance, the objects, and indeed even the properties that we ascribe to them, are always regarded as something actually given—except that insofar as the object's character depends only on the subject's way of intuiting this given object in its relation to him, we do also distinguish this object as *appearance* from the same object as object *in itself*. (B69)

The objects of our experience are real in that they are given from without, directly to the senses. They are not figments of our imagination. This is the truth of empiricism. We are in contact with the world through sensible intuition. But they are appearances in that they are objects for us only subject to the formal conditions of cognition. The sphere of Locke's empiricism is restricted to objects considered empirically, and we must be careful not to confuse these objects with things in themselves. Indeed, it is just such confusion that has plagued the history of philosophy prior to Kant and has led to the errors of metaphysics that he diagnoses in the Transcendental Dialectic.

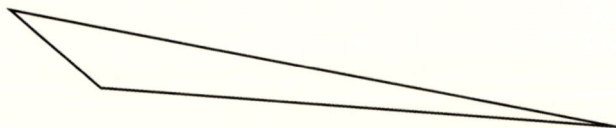

6:44 A.M. on Tuesday, July 13, 2004

CHAPTER FOUR

The Transcendental Analytic

THE SECOND MAJOR SECTION of the *Critique*, the Transcendental Logic, turns from an investigation of the formal requirements for how we receive sensations to an inquiry into how we make judgments about sensible intuitions: Aesthetic is "the science of the rules of sensibility as such," while logic is "the science of the rules of the understanding as such" (A52/B76). In the first part of the Logic, the Transcendental Analytic, Kant sets out to discover the *a priori* rules ("categories" or "pure concepts") that the understanding employs and to establish them as conditions for the possibility of experience.¹ Without them, he claims, we could never distinguish our subjective sensations and associations from objective and causally related representations that we perceive in space and time.

Kant divides this complex argument into roughly three parts. First, he uses pure general logic as a clue to determine how the understanding functions. Kant distinguishes pure general logic from other forms of logic by the fact that it abstracts completely from all content ("general") and it is not derived from our particular psychology ("pure") (A54/B78). Although pure general logic cannot provide us with objective knowledge, Kant claims that an analogous list of rules governs the operation of the understanding with regard to empirical cognitions. In the second part of the Analytic, Kant sets out to prove the validity of the categories for us. In other words, he argues that experience is only possible subject to these particular rules, and he explains how they are necessary in particular for our kind of sensible intuition (in space and time). The Transcendental Deduction of the Categories is the most important part of the *Critique*, because it not only demonstrates why an investigation of the understanding can tell us anything about experience in general but also firmly establishes the truth of transcendental idealism and provides the tools for Kant's analysis of metaphysical speculation. In the last part of the Transcendental Analytic, Kant outlines the more specific principles that we use to organize and relate our representations. Among other things, we must posit a permanent substance that underlies all apparent change, and we must conceive of events as causally related. Here Kant responds to Humean skepticism and Berkeleyan idealism and clarifies his critical reevaluation of rationalism.

The Distinction Between Sensibility and the Understanding

Rationalism fails on many counts: The formal conditions that we require of the world can tell us what the world is like in general, but they cannot tell us about particular events in the world; we can only know *a priori* how we must understand the world, not how it is in itself; and the understanding, not reason, is the faculty of cognition by which our perceptions of the world are organized. This is more than an academic distinction. Although reason and the understanding are related, they serve different functions: The understanding unifies appearances according to rules that apply to "the objects of all cognition generally," but reason attempts to unify the rules of the understanding under absolutely general principles (B24). Reason tries to make sense of the unconditioned basis of the whole of experience, but the understanding helps us to make sense of particular perceptions by bringing them under concepts.[2] The applicability of the understanding to the world thus depends on and is related to sense data in a way that reason is not. How we think of things rationally does not necessarily characterize how things are. The truth of empiricism is that we can know about the world only through sensible intuition.

Although Kant rejects rationalism in part, he accepts the idea that looking at our way of thinking can tell us the formal conditions that any object must meet in order to be perceived by us; for example, every event has a cause. Our experience of the world is not simply a matter of the sensations that are given to us. What we perceive is the result of how we discriminate our perceptions according to *a priori* concepts. This is the truth of rationalism, and it is where empiricism fails on its own.

To surmount these shortcomings, Kant synthesizes the two positions. Any theoretical cognition must involve both (the pure concepts of) the understanding and what is given to us in sensibility:

> Our cognition arises from two basic sources of the mind. The first is [our ability] to receive presentations (and is our receptivity for impressions); the second is our ability to cognize an object through these presentations (and is the spontaneity of concepts). Through receptivity an object is *given* to us; through spontaneity an object is *thought* in relation to that [given] presentation (which [otherwise] is a mere determination of the mind). Intuition and concepts, therefore, constitute the elements of all our cognition. Hence neither concepts without an intuition corresponding to them in some way or other, nor intuition without concepts can yield cognition. (A50/B74)

We comprehend the world in objective terms, as a set of material things that exist apart from our perceptions of them and that are related according to causal laws. However, these concepts are merely formal ways of considering experience. Without sensing the world, we do not know which objects exist or which causes bring about which events. In addition, receptivity alone is inadequate, because as Hume shows, spatiotemporal objects that persist apart from our perceptions cannot be justified solely on the basis of (subjective) sensations, and only habitual associations follow from the constant conjunction of perceptions. Without relating given perceptions to one another according to our concepts, we would not have objective experience.

If objective experience is to be possible, the necessary claims that we make on the basis of *a priori* concepts must be strictly distinguished from empirical generalizations:

> Both intuition and concepts are either pure or empirical. They are *empirical* if they contain sensation (sensation presupposes the actual presence of the object); they are *pure* if no sensation is mixed in with the presentation. Sensation may be called the matter of sensible cognition. Hence pure intuition contains only the form under which something is intuited, and a pure concept contains solely the form of the thought of an object as such. Only pure intuitions or concepts are possible a priori; empirical ones are possible only a posteriori. (A50/B74–A51/B75)

The specific and relatively general propositions that are made on the basis of empirical evidence function differently than the necessary claims that are warranted on the basis of pure concepts and the pure forms of sensible intuition. Pure intuitions give us *a priori* synthetic judgments concerning spatiotemporal objects, but empirical intuitions give us particular facts. We know that the interior angles of any triangle must total 180 degrees, but we need to look at a particular triangle to know the specific measure of each of its angles. Similarly, pure concepts characterize things universally and necessarily, but empirical concepts are merely useful generalizations. Empirically I have found that most dogs have coats of fur that cover their bodies, but I do not need to see any dogs to know that every dog—as a substantial thing—must occupy space.

Like the empiricists, Kant recognizes that we develop concepts based on experience. Such empirical concepts are the result of reflecting on and comparing our various encounters with the world. Kant's thinking on how these concepts are formed mirrors Locke's own description in the *Essay Concerning Human Understanding*. In the *Jäsche Logic*, Kant says that "an empirical concept arises from the senses through comparison of objects of experience."[3] To illustrate this process, he explains how we come to know what a tree is. We compare different kinds of trees and note their differences, then we reflect on their common traits and abstract from the unique features (quality, figure, etc.) of the particular trees we have experienced to arrive at the concept of a tree in general.

Kant distinguishes such empirical concepts from the pure (*a priori*) concepts of the understanding that he calls the categories; the former are derived (*a posteriori*) from experience, but experience itself is possible only by means of the categories. The categories are the rules by which the understanding makes sense of what is given to us perceptually and are thus conditions for something's being a representation of an object in the first place. The activity by which I arrive at experience is different from my attempt to make general claims about the world on the basis of that experience.[4]

For rationalists, especially Spinoza, Leibniz, and Wolff, the domain of human thought forms a continuum between sensibility and the understanding, in that being fully conscious of our innate ideas reflects the whole of human knowledge, including empirical knowledge. Sensibility is only a confused form of the understanding. We get at what is true of the world through an *a priori* investigation into what reason logically requires of it. For empiricists such as Locke and Hume, there is a similar continuum, but sensibility is the way to know the world. The understanding merely reflects *in abstracto* the raw data given to the senses and less clearly indicates what exists. What we know is the result of how the mind is affected by objects and how we conceive of the world on the basis of our perceptions.

In contrast to both of these positions, Kant opposes sensible intuition, which passively receives given sensations, and the understanding, which actively judges what is given according to concepts. The content of experience apprehended in time and space can be distinguished from the subject's judging about the content, yet in order for there to be experience at all, the formal conditions of experience and what is given in sensation must be conjoined. Kant's insight is that we can make claims about objects only if they are given to us empirically *and* if we organize our sensations in certain ways:

> Let us give the name *sensibility* to our mind's *receptivity*, [i.e., to its ability] to receive presentations insofar as it is affected in some manner.

> *Understanding*, on the other hand, is our ability to produce presentations ourselves, i.e., our *spontaneity* of cognition. Our *intuition*, by our very nature, can never be other than *sensible* intuition; i.e., it contains only the way in which we are affected by objects. *Understanding*, on the other hand, is our ability to *think* the object of sensible intuition. Neither of these properties is to be preferred to the other. Without sensibility no object would be given to us; and without understanding no object would be thought. Thoughts without content are empty; intuitions without concepts are blind. Hence it is just as necessary that we make our concepts sensible (i.e., that we add the object to them in intuition) as it is necessary that we make our intuitions understandable (i.e., that we bring them under concepts). (A51/B75)

In order for the categories to be about something other than merely formal relations among possible intuitions, material must be provided by sensations received according to the pure forms of sensible intuition (space and time). The resulting "manifold" of sensible intuition (sensations received spatiotemporally) forms the content of our experience. But in order for this content to be meaningful to us, as objects of cognition, the material must be actively selected, organized, discriminated, and compared. We must *do* something to it. And the rules that govern this activity are the categories.

In many ways, then, Kant's philosophy is simultaneously a rejection and a synthesis of empiricism and rationalism. Neither position is adequate in itself, but each contains an important element of the truth. The understanding can tell us only about the formal conditions that any possible experience must meet. We know *a priori* that every event has a cause, but we cannot know prior to experience which causal claims to make about the world—for example, what happens when copper is heated. For this, we must look to sensibility. However, to cognize objects (as opposed to merely relating perceptions), we have to make judgments about sensible intuitions according to the pure concepts of the understanding—for example, not just that I feel heat and associate it with copper's expanding, but that heat causes copper to expand. Such judgments can be right or wrong depending on whether they correspond to the way the world is, but applying the categories to our perceptions allows us to make such objective (and falsifiable) claims in the first place.

Concepts and the Claim to Objectivity

As we discussed at the end of Chapter 3, Kant's position does not amount to a form of subjectivism in which anything goes. My world is not entirely up to me. If it were, a shared objective world would be impossible. My world and your world would be merely two different sets of subjective associations, with no way to compare them and no way for us to get it wrong. This kind of relativism leads to absurd results. If I see a large rabbit named Harvey in the corner of the room and you see nothing, then we are both right because we each believe what we say: There is a rabbit there (for me) and there is not a rabbit there (for you). And if I think I see a rabbit, but I later come to my senses, I was right in both cases: There was a rabbit (for me), and now there is no rabbit (for me).

We do not just talk about what things look like to us or what we associate. Usually we make claims about what *exists* or *is there*. When we make objective claims about the way the world is (as opposed to what our sensations are), we can get it wrong. Either a rabbit is there or it is not. We are applying certain rules to our sensations, and we may be applying those rules correctly or incorrectly. In the case of Harvey, I am improperly applying the concept of existence to a hallucination.

We can use a rule when we should not, but we can also fail to apply a rule when it is applicable. For example, one should not think of events in the world as uncaused. If one billiard ball hits another one, and the second one is propelled forward, the motion of the second is attributed to the transfer of momentum from the first. It would be wrong to say that the first ball simply stopped for no reason and that the second ball started without any impetus. Even if the balls were controlled by magnets under the table, that would mean not that their motions were uncaused but that their motions had different causes than we originally thought. For any change in the world, we cannot say that it "just happened" without any possible explanation for why it happened. We must understand every event in the world as caused, according to the *a priori* concept of causality.

We can see, then, that there are rules for the possible discrimination of the sensory manifold. Furthermore, we know that these rules must be *a priori*, because they apply universally—*every* thing (such as Harvey) must either exist or not exist—and necessarily—every event (such as the movement of the billiard balls) *must* have a cause. Yet Hume had called into question causal necessity by, among other things, questioning the applicability of *a priori* concepts to experience. Kant appreciates this objection but rejects Hume's "sceptical solution":

> I tried first whether Hume's objection could not be put into a general form, and soon found that the concept of the connection of cause and effect was by no means the only concept by which the understanding thinks the connection of things *a priori*, but rather that metaphysics consists altogether of such concepts. I sought to ascertain their number; and when I had satisfactorily succeeded in this by starting from a single principle, I proceeded to the deduction of these concepts, which I was now certain were not derived from experience, as Hume had tried, but sprang from the pure understanding. This deduction (which seemed impossible to my acute predecessor and had never even occurred to anyone else, though no one had hesitated to use the concepts without investigating the basis of their objective validity) was the most difficult task ever undertaken in the service of metaphysics; and the worst was that metaphysics, such as it then existed, could not assist me in the least because this deduction alone can render metaphysics possible. (Pro 260)

We use concepts in our experience of the world, but we also do so when we make metaphysical claims—for example, when we assert that God *exists* or that the will is an uncaused *cause* of our actions. In order to determine whether we are justified in using such concepts, Kant has to investigate how the understanding functions. One of the main tasks of the Transcendental Analytic is to discern the *a priori* rules by which we discriminate the content of experience (the Metaphysical Deduction) and to warrant their applicability to the manifold of sensible intuition (the Transcendental Deduction). Only then will Kant discover the limits of our knowledge and set metaphysics on a firm foundation.

The Metaphysical Deduction: Pure General Logic as the *Leitfaden*

In the Metaphysical Deduction, the first part of the Transcendental Analytic, Kant enumerates the pure concepts of the understanding and tries to demonstrate that the table he gives is an exhaustive list of such concepts. He does this by relating pure general logic—the rules of thought systematized by Aristotle—to transcendental logic—the rules that the understanding uses in its interpretation of experience.

As we saw in Chapter 2, pure general logic consists of the principles that govern how we must relate ideas in our thinking; it describes the minimal structure of claim-making. But its rules are merely formal (without content) and are not directly related to any particular representation. For example, 'If A, then B' means that A logically entails B. However, we do not know what A and B are. In fact, this relationship remains even if A and B are replaced with nonsense:

'Twas brillig.
<u>If 'twas brillig, then the borogoves were mimsy.</u>
Therefore, the borogoves were mimsy.

The above claims (taken from Lewis Carroll) are logically comprehensible—indeed, the argument form (modus ponens) is valid, because the truth of the premises entails the truth of the conclusion—but they are without meaning. The formal requirements of pure general logic cannot generate objective claims about the world. Kant emphasizes this in an open letter to one of his supposed followers, Johann Gottlieb Fichte. Fichte begins his philosophy with the law of identity, but Kant insists that this strategy is fruitless: "the principles of logic cannot lead to any material knowledge, since logic, that is to say, *pure logic*, abstracts from the content of knowledge; the attempt to cull a real object out of logic is a vain effort and therefore a thing that no one has ever achieved."[5] Rationalism had improperly applied the rules of pure general logic to the world beyond our thinking, but the law of identity, for example, says nothing about what exists. It amounts to the claim that whatever exists is identical to itself, but such a claim is without content. As we saw earlier, Kant credits Hume with showing that *a priori* logical principles have no necessary import for external events. How we must think of things—in terms of the law of identity or the principle of sufficient reason—cannot get us to what is true.

Pure general logic does have some function with regard to actual cognitions, but its function is limited. Specifically, logic can prune out flawed thoughts that are necessarily (because analytically) false. For example, we know that a particular object cannot both exist and not exist. This is contradictory ('A and not-A'), so we know that such an object is logically impossible. However, for a thought to be in accordance with logical rules does not make it true. It only makes it a candidate for truth. For something to be logically possible—that is, not self-contradictory—the understanding must be in agreement with itself, but for a claim to be true, the thought must agree with its object. Both 'unicorns exist' and 'no unicorns exist' are logically possible. We know which proposition is true only by verifying one of the claims in experience, by examining the world and finding out whether unicorns do in fact exist. That cannot be determined *a priori*.

Although pure general logic cannot give us knowledge about the world, it can give us insight into the understanding. The conceptual discriminations made in pure general logic come from the understanding, so the understanding must discriminate objects according to analogous rules. Therefore, pure general logic is important for Kant's purposes because it provides the "clue" or "guide" (*Leitfaden*) to the systematic discovery of the categories. In the first part of the Transcendental Analytic, Kant shows the status of concepts and their nature by relating them to the general forms of (logical) judgment. In deriving transcendental logic from pure general logic, the *a priori* origin of the categories is proven, and the table of categories is shown to be an exhaustive list of the pure conceptual constraints on experience.

The Table of Logical Functions

Kant begins by enumerating the "formal rules of all thought" that constitute Aristotelian logic, which he takes to have definitively characterized the kinds of claims we are able to make (Bviii–ix). In the Metaphysical Deduction, Kant then derives the table of categories (A80/B106) from these twelve forms of judgment (A70/B95). (See Figure 4.1.)

Although the table may seem complicated, Kant is merely classifying the kinds of claims we make every day. Everything we say that can be true or false—that is, every proposition—can be characterized by one element from each of the four main headings. As an example, imagine that I state, "The door is open."

1. Quantity: The claim is *singular*, because I am talking about *one* door.

   If I were talking about *some* doors ("Some doors are open"), it would be a *particular* judgment. If I were talking about *all* doors ("All doors are open"), it would be a *universal* judgment.

1
Quantity of Judgments
Universal
Particular
Singular

2
Quality
Affirmative
Negative
Infinite

3
Relation
Categorical
Hypothetical
Disjunctive

4
Modality
Problematic
Assertoric
Apodeictic

FIGURE 4.1 The table of logical functions (A70/B95)

2. Quality: The claim is *affirmative*, because I am affirming that the door *is* something.

   If I said, "It is *not* the case that the door is open" or "The door is *not* open," it would be a *negative* judgment. If I said, "The door is *non*-open," it would be an *infinite* judgment. These two kinds of judgment (negative and infinite) may have the same truth conditions—they are called "obverses" of one another—but they have different logical forms.

3. Relation: The claim is *categorical*, because I am saying that it is true about the door.

   If I were to say that the door is open *if* certain conditions hold ("If class is in session, then the door is open"), it would be a *hypothetical* judgment. If I said that the door is *either* open *or* closed, it would be a *disjunctive* judgment.

4. Modality: The claim is *assertoric*, because I am asserting that something *is* true, or *happens to be* true, even though it is possible that it could have been false.

   If I said that it is *necessarily* the case that the door is open, it would be an *apodeictic* judgment. Only *a priori* claims are apodeictic; for example, "All bachelors are unmarried males" is universal, affirmative, categorical, and apodeictic. If I made a claim that something *may* be the case ("The door *could be* open"), it would be a *problematic* judgment.

According to Kant, every proposition makes sense only in terms of the functions listed in the table of judgments. However, this is merely a way of understanding the kinds of claims we can make. 'The borogoves were mimsy' and 'A is B' have the same formal structure as 'the door is open,' yet neither of the first claims is related to the world, or our experience of the world. By drawing on the table of logical functions, we are merely cataloguing the formal characteristics of a kind of claim, or how the subjects ('borogoves,' 'A,' 'door') and predicates ('mimsy,' 'B,' 'open') are related. These logical functions are not directly related to experience but are the only ways that we (by means of the understanding) can reflect on it and conceptualize it in language. For claims about our experience to make sense to us, we must articulate what we perceive—literally, recognizing the distinct parts and how they are connected—using these forms of judgment.[6]

The Table of Categories

Although such judgments are limited to how we think, each form of judgment listed in the above table has a corresponding judgment in the table of categories. It is by means of these categories that the understanding organizes sensations into a coherent experience. (See Figure 4.2.) The twelve forms of empirical judgment correspond to the twelve kinds of judgment in pure general logic. Indeed, Kant claims not only that the two kinds of formal conditions—forms of judgment and categories—are related, but that "the *categories* . . . are indeed nothing but precisely these functions of judging insofar as the manifold of a given intuition is determined in regard to them" (B143). Speaking somewhat loosely, pure general logic and transcendental logic look at the same

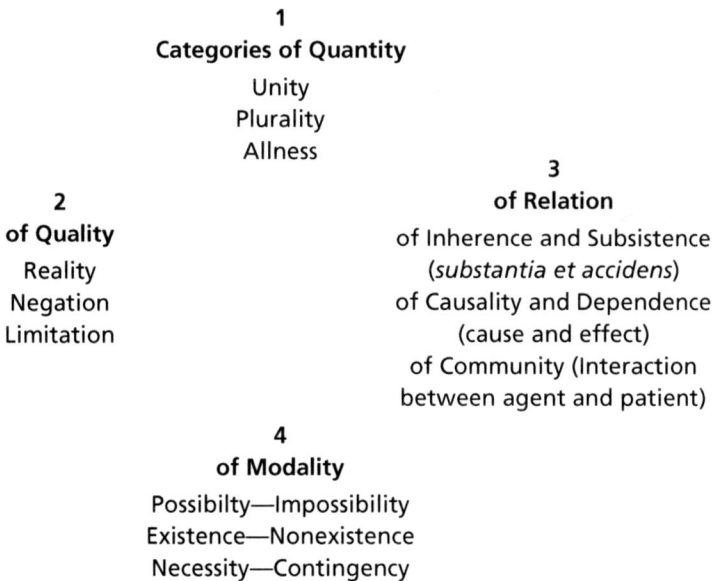

1
Categories of Quantity
Unity
Plurality
Allness

3
of Relation
of Inherence and Subsistence
(*substantia et accidens*)
of Causality and Dependence
(cause and effect)
of Community (Interaction
between agent and patient)

2
of Quality
Reality
Negation
Limitation

4
of Modality
Possibilty—Impossibility
Existence—Nonexistence
Necessity—Contingency

FIGURE 4.2 The table of categories (A80/B106)

judgments from different points of view. General logic is concerned with the purely formal features of a judgment, no matter what it is about. By contrast, transcendental logic is concerned with the features of the judgment that would allow it to be about (or represent) an object. In other words, general logic constrains our thinking about anything, but transcendental logic constrains our judgments about perceptions that purport to be objective experiences.

Pure general logic is relevant to Kant's transcendental investigation (into the conditions for the possibility of experience) because the unity of judgment is the same kind of unity given to representations in sensible intuition. The forms of judgment operative in pure general logic apply only to how we think, but their corresponding categories can tell us about how the world must appear because they are necessary constraints on how we make sense of experience.

Empirical judgments are possible only by means of these categories, because they are the most general principles by which we understand any sensible intuitions that are given to us. Unfortunately, Kant claims that no real definition can be provided for the categories, because what a definition does is pick out the characteristics of a possible object of cognition, to distinguish it from other cognitions (A241–42n). If we attempt to consider the categories apart from their empirical conditions—that is, as they would be used to make judgments about what appears to us in space and time—then nothing is left but "the logical function that they have in judgments" (A242). In other words, they are not objects but the rules by which we make judgments about objects. Thus they themselves could never be objects of cognition and could never be defined.

As we will see later in the chapter, the categories are given content only in their "schematized" form, in relation to space and time. To explain what the various categories mean, we must anticipate what he demonstrates later in the Transcendental Analytic: that the pure concepts can be related to our form of sensible intuition. We can then define the categories, because this gives them content in terms of which the different concepts, "as concepts of things as such," can be represented (A242).

With this caveat in mind, think about the kind of discriminations I am making when I perceive an open door in front of me. I am organizing the sense data that is given to me empirically according to the categories.

1. Quantity: The experience involves *unity*, because I am organizing successive impressions of the door over time into an experience of *one* door.

   If I interpreted successive impressions as the experience of *several* doors, then it would involve the category of *plurality*. If I were experiencing an entire class of objects, such as all the doors in the hallway, it would involve *allness*.[7] It is, Kant says, merely "plurality considered as a unity" (B111).

2. Quality: I am taking the door to be *real*, as an object that exists in time. In other words, it has the quality of *being* from moment to moment. Even when I am not sensing the door, it continues to exist.

   If I did not see an open door there, my experience would involve *negation*. *Limitation* measures the "degree or magnitude" of a sensation as it stands between reality and negation—in other words, the "transition" between a sensation's being judged to be nothing and its being judged to be something, or vice versa (A143/B182–83). Someone uses this category, for example, when she gradually recognizes a hallucination for what it is, or she comes to see something that she did not realize was there.

3. Relation: The quality of being open is a characteristic of the door, and thus I am making a judgment involving *inherence and subsistence*. In technical terms, I am experiencing the door as a substance (a bearer of properties) and openness as a property of that substance.

   If I saw a professor open the door, I would be relating them *causally*. Kant says that this is "the manifold's succession insofar as this is subject to a rule" (A144/B183). In other words, we experience different events as necessarily related by means of this category—in this case, the door is open because the professor opened it. We make judgments about a substance and its qualities (inherence and subsistence) or an event as a cause or effect of another event (causality and dependence), but we also experience the whole of things as reciprocally related. This is the category of *community*. If one thing causes another (and not vice versa), the first object is temporally prior to the second. Yet some objects coexist in time, such that my representations of them are reversible—I could represent either one first (A211/B258). The judgment I am making, then, is that the objects themselves are *"coordinated"* in time even though I am representing them in succession (B112). Entering a room and claiming, for example, that it contains both an open door and a table would involve the category of community. I can experience them as existing simultaneously because I can go from one to the other in a continuous series of perceptions that are related to one another, and this means that they are not separated by empty space and that they therefore affect one another (A212/B259).

4. Modality: I experience the open door as something that *exists* outside of me at a particular time. In other words, I am given sensible intuitions (experienced as an open door) at a particular time. The door may not have been open, but its openness—indeed, the existence of the door itself—is a contingent fact about the world.

Modality involves how actual or possible sensations are related to the pure forms of sensible intuition. In other words, it has to do with our own thinking of the object rather than the object itself. A *possible* object is one that is consistent with "the conditions of time as such" (A144/B184). Thus it could conceivably be an object of experience—for example, the door could be open, or there could be an open door in one of the rooms. The category of *necessity* is the concept of something that must always be true, because it follows from the

very conditions of experience. Such things are physically necessary—that is, necessary given the way we must conceive of
nature. As we will see, that matter can be neither created nor
destroyed is, according to Kant, one example of a necessary
fact about the world.

Note that the pure concepts of the understanding are relevant for
experience. The understanding interprets the manifold of sensibility
according to the categories, such that it is represented objectively—
that is, as objects in the world distinct from the sensations that I have.
Everyone before Kant recognized that 'The door is open' is a claim
that may be true or false, depending on whether I am hallucinating or
simply mistaken. But Kant sees the very experience of the door as an
exercise in claim-making. The experience I have is the basis of my articulation of the judgment ('The door is open'), but Kant argues that
judgment functions in the very having of the experience (seeing that
the door is open), prior to my conceptualization of the experience in
language.

This is one of Kant's most important advances over the empiricists. For someone like Locke, the raw data of experience is passively
received by the mind, which then reflects on and relates various
experiences to arrive at general concepts. The mind becomes active
only *after* the experience is given to it. At that point, claims are made
that are either true or false and that have forms in accordance with
the table of logical functions. But in the Transcendental Analytic,
Kant argues that it is the activity of understanding that makes
experience even possible. Using what is given empirically to the
senses, the mind in part constitutes the experience that the mind uses
to formulate its claims. This is why the world as we know it can only
be the world as it appears to us and never as it is in itself—because
we actively transform what we intuit of the world. We can never
have an experience that is prior to or otherwise independent of the
categories, one that passively reflects what exists independently of
the mind's conceptualization.

By formulating the table of categories and distinguishing it from
the table of logical functions, Kant also corrects an error made by the

rationalists concerning the relationship between thought and reality. According to philosophers like Descartes, the rules of pure general logic can tell us how the world itself must be. However, such an inference is unwarranted. There is a gap between the world and our thinking about the world, and rationalists have no explanation for why the one is applicable to the other. For Kant, the central logical term is judgment, the mental activity by which we combine our perceptions in certain ways, according to certain *a priori* concepts. The rules that constrain appearances are not the formal rules of thinking but functions of the understanding that make objective experience possible in the first place. Thus the content of our experience consists of things as they appear to us in accordance with these subjective conditions.

The relationship between pure general logic and transcendental logic may be difficult to understand, especially since the understanding is operative with regard to both. However, they function in distinct ways: Pure general logic deals with the formal relationship between a *subject* and its *predicates,* whereas the pure categories of the understanding structure the relationship between a *substance* and its *properties.* It is wrong to conflate these different kinds of judgment, but dogmatic metaphysics did not realize this. By distinguishing transcendental logic from pure general logic, Kant is rejecting the rationalists' attempt to relate our forms of thinking (our concepts of things) directly to forms of being (things as they are). Pure general logic and transcendental logic are certainly related—one provides a clue for the discovery of the other—but they are not the same thing. Pure general logic concerns our linguistic concepts, whereas the categories relate to representations: whether we are seeing one object or many, whether our sensations indicate a real thing or not, how those things are related to one another, and whether the object is necessary, is possible, or exists. Therefore, only transcendental logic, not pure general logic, makes possible "material knowledge."[8]

It may be easier to understand how the forms of our thinking in pure general logic are related to the forms of our judgment in transcendental logic if we look at another example. One logical form of our judgments is the hypothetical, 'If A, then B.' A and B are related such that if we accept A, we must accept B. This is a formal relationship between terms. For example, 'If 'twas brillig, then the borogoves were mimsy' is a hypothetical claim. Note that this is not a causal claim about the world. In fact, we do not even know what these terms mean. But we do know that the truth of the antecedent (''twas brillig') implies the truth of the consequent ('the borogoves were mimsy'), whatever they happen to mean.

The corresponding category that applies to experience is the concept of causality, 'If A happens, then it makes B happen.' This is a different sort of thing. It is a claim about A as the cause of B. This is an objective claim, and it is either true or false based on what the world is like. It says something different from the hypothetical statement. For example, 'heat makes copper expand' is true only if heat *does* make copper expand, only if there is in fact such a causal relationship.

In short, the hypothetical claim involves a relation between judgments, which may or may not be about objects, whereas causal relations necessarily concern relations between objects. The truth conditions of the corresponding claims are different. The antecedent and consequent in a hypothetical claim are not related in the same way as are the cause and effect in a causal claim. The conditional statement commits one only to the concurrence of two things: When you accept A, you also must accept B. But asserting that A *causes* B goes beyond their constant conjunction to the idea that an event in the world (A) gives rise to another event (B) necessarily. By itself, the mere concurrence of A and B would satisfy the conditional claim, but the causal claim requires an objective relationship between two states of affairs; that is, one event must be effected by the other.

As noted earlier, a statement in pure general logic is logically false only if it is self-contradictory; for example, 'A and not-A' must be false. But objective claims must accord with reality, which is only a subset of what is logically possible: "For even if a cognition accorded completely with logical form, i.e., even if it did not contradict itself, it could still contradict its object" (A59/B84). In other words, a claim that is logically coherent may nonetheless be materially false: 'If the second billiard ball moves, then it was pushed by a tiny monkey' is not self-contradictory, but given the absence of tiny monkeys in the pool hall, it is probably not the case. A formal judgment is logically false only if it is self-contradictory, but an objective claim—a causal claim, for example—is false if it does not correspond to the way the world is.

Possible Problems with the Metaphysical Deduction

Before continuing with the Transcendental Analytic, we need to pause momentarily and note some objections that have been raised about the Metaphysical Deduction. Although the derivation of the table of categories from the table of logical functions seems intuitively right, the Metaphysical Deduction is one of the most criticized parts of the *Critique*. If Kant does provide a complete table of judgments based on Aristotelian logic, then the table of categories is also complete, assuming that the two are connected in the way that Kant says they are. But a lot of this is questionable.

First, Kant offers no argument in support of his claim that the table of judgments is complete. Although he credits Aristotle with developing logic as a science, Kant adds to and subtracts from Aristotelian logic, purportedly in order to systematize what Aristotle had discovered piecemeal (Pro 323). For Aristotle, the categories are kinds of judgments about being, and he devised a list of ten such categories: substance ("what a thing is"), quantity, quality, relation, place, time, position, state, activity, and passivity.[9] Like a number of other philosophers, Kant revises the list significantly. He eliminates place, time, and position (which result from the pure forms of sensible intuition rather than the understanding) and adds several others. However, he gives no explanation of the decisions he makes in composing the first table and fails to justify the claim that these are the only logical functions. Famously, G. W. F. Hegel accused Kant of cobbling it together "empirically," as Aristotle had, merely giving it the appearance of systematicity.[10] Some critics even claim that Kant composed the table not based on a consideration of formal logic but vice versa, based on the list of categories he had devised. Thus his claim that "the table [of categories] lists completely all the elementary concepts of understanding" is undermined, because its systematicity depends on the presupposed systematicity of the table of logical functions, which is in doubt (B109).

A second, related objection is that we cannot know, in principle, that the forms of judgment constitute an entire system and that there are not others. Even if these two tables were complete in their own way, it is not inconceivable that there would be additional tables that similarly corresponded to one another. It would be analogous to someone who knows only the numbers one through twenty and divides them into odd and even numbers. The fact that it seems systematic does not mean that the list exhausts all possible numbers, any more than Kant's tidy-looking schema necessarily exhausts all possible forms of judgment. To justify the completeness of the table of logical functions, he refers to its historical stability—"thus far it . . . has not been able to advance a single step, and hence is to all appearances closed and completed"—but this is hardly convincing (Bviii). Even if it has been relatively consistent over time, that is not enough to prove the systematicity and completeness of the two tables.

Third, the idea that the two tables correspond to one another does little to justify the claim that all possible experience must conform to these specific categories. Kant's assertion that the categories are nothing but the functions of thought applied to the manifold of sensible intuition stretches the imagination in several instances. For example, the form of categorical judgment is supposed to correspond to the concept of substance. But on the face of it, there is no clear connection between 'A is B,' a merely formal relation between two terms, and the concept of a permanent substratum that underlies all physical changes. In short, Kant's main argument for the various categories is its relation to the table of logical functions, but his derivation of the specific categories is sometimes suspect.

Finally, if Aristotle's term logic is itself inadequate, then using that system to derive what is supposed to be the basic structure of human understanding is bound to fail. Beginning with the work of Gottlob Frege in the late nineteenth century, logicians began to adopt a truth-functional logic in which the truth value of a claim is a function of the truth value of its constituent parts, and a predicate calculus in which one can demonstrate inferences among predications—that is, statements in which properties are attributed to objects. Aristotle's syllogistic logic cannot handle everything that modern formal logic can.

In addition, Frege argues that Aristotelian logic depends too much on how we happen to think of things rather than on how thoughts themselves are related. Kant absorbs this bias when he says that logic shows us how the understanding works: "in logic the understanding deals with nothing more than itself and its form" (Bix). Kant conceives of the basic feature of a judgment to be the (internal) predicative relation it expresses rather than its (external) relation to a truth-value. But according to Frege, logical implication is a relation among claims—how the truth-value of premises and their components impacts the truth-value of a conclusion—rather than a description of how we relate those claims in thinking. Therefore, not only the formal structure of Aristotelian logic but Kant's entire inspiration is misguided. Logic gives us no insight into the understanding.

These are just a few of the challenges to the Metaphysical Deduction. Whether Kant is susceptible to these criticisms, or whether they undermine his broader claim that experience is the result of a rule-governed synthesis on our part, is a matter of debate.

Normativity

Even if Kant has successfully criticized rationalism by showing that logical functions are not directly related to objects, he has yet to show that empiricism is not a viable alternative. To determine whether our judgments are true, we have to experience the world. I know that horses exist because I have seen them. Because no one has seen a unicorn, unicorns probably do not exist. This is consistent with what Locke has to say. So, why should we believe that *a priori* concepts are conditions for the possibility of objective claims? Why is a critique of pure reason necessary, as opposed to an essay on sensibility?

The animating question behind Kant's epistemology is: What is an object of experience, as opposed to mere flashes of sensation? Hume and Berkeley were right to claim that independent objects cannot be warranted on the basis of perception alone. But we do distinguish the object from how it happens to appear to us, and this distinction is possible only if empiricism is wrong, or at least incomplete.[11]

Objective experience ("cognition") involves claims about the manifold of sensible intuition that have normative force beyond merely how we associate our perceptions. If I say that chocolate ice cream is the best and you say that strawberry is better, there is no problem here that needs to be solved. Neither one of us is wrong; we are just reporting our different preferences. Similarly, if I say that I associate the expanding of copper with heat and you say that you associate the expanding of copper with fuzzy bunnies, you still have not gotten anything wrong. You and I simply associate things differently. However, in making an objective claim—that is, a claim about objects—we are going beyond conventional rules (what everyone believes) or associated regularities (things that happen to be connected in a person's mind). Instead, we are making a judgment whose truth depends on whether it corresponds to the way the world is. If I say that heat makes copper expand and you deny it, I am right and you are wrong. Such a claim has normative import.

The pure categories of the understanding are rules for the discrimination of objects that make our experience capable of being right or wrong. They allow us to make judgments about the world. Indeed, the categories are applicable to experience because any experience we have is an act of claim-making. The world does not wholly determine our perception of it. Sensations are merely causal modifications of the sense organs, but this does not amount to knowledge. By organizing intuitions into objective representations, we relate to the object through sensation; such representations are not reducible to sensations. To have cognition, we must see the object *as* being in front of us, or *as* affecting another object. We must conceive of it in a certain way. The organization of our sensations is always the result of a rule-governed synthesis on our part: "the spontaneity of our thought requires that this manifold, in order to be turned into a cognition, must first be gone through, taken up, and combined in a certain manner. This act I call synthesis" (A77/B102). The categories are synthetic functions of human thought, the most general constraints on how we organize our perceptions in order to make experience possible.

The pure concepts of the understanding give us the ability to discriminate objective unities in the world, instead of saying "it just appears that way to me." When we make judgments about objects rather than merely reporting our subjective states, our experience has a normative dimension. We are capable of objective cognition. But such judgments are possible only given the operation of the categories—at least, that is what Kant attempts to show in the Transcendental Analytic.

How do we know that our representations of the world are necessarily structured by the pure concepts of the understanding that Kant lists in the table of categories? We know this because any experience we have involves an act of judgment or discrimination on our part, and the understanding is the faculty with which we make such judgments:

> Hence the cognition of any understanding, or at least of the human understanding, is a cognition through concepts; it is not intuitive, but discursive. All our intuitions, as sensible, rest on our being affected; concepts, on the other hand, rest on functions. By *function* I mean the unity of the act of arranging various presentations under one common presentation. Hence concepts are based on the spontaneity of thought, whereas sensible intuitions are based on the receptivity for impressions. Now the only use that the understanding can make of these concepts is to judge by means of them. But in such judging, a concept is never referred directly to an object, because the only kind of representation that deals with its object immediately is intuition. Instead the concept is referred directly to some other presentation of the object (whether that presentation be an intuition or itself already a concept). Judgment, therefore, is the indirect cognition of an object, viz., the presentation of a presentation of it. (A68/B93)

Our experience is not simply given to us ("intuitive") but is the result of our making judgments about sensible intuitions ("discursive"). We can therefore anticipate reality in our thinking because having an experience is a matter of putting sensations together according to certain *a priori* rules. It is possible because our understanding does not conform to the object, but the object conforms to our understanding. We look in the room and see a chair or a table, but all that we are given is a bunch of sensory impressions that we perceive in space and time. We make judgments about these impressions based on certain features (or marks) that they have in common. We only know the world as we organize it, subject to the *a priori* concepts by which we make judgments about what we are given. We do not know things as they are in themselves. Transcendental idealism follows from the Copernican turn.

The object affects the sensibility directly, but only according to the pure forms of sensible intuition, and it is this spatiotemporal representation that is organized by the understanding according to the categories, forming our objective experience. We thus have a spatiotemporal manifold (a presentation) that we also discriminate conceptually (a representation of a presentation).[12] As we saw earlier, intuition is immediately given, and conceptual discrimination is only mediately related to sensations. We can now understand how the different elements of experience are related:

Sensations (matter of experience) + Received under the forms of sensibility (space and time) = Sensible intuitions

Sensible intuitions + Pure concepts of the understanding = Experience

The rules of thinking are applicable to objects because thinking plays a role in their being objects (for us), rather than mere sensible intuitions.

At this point, however, Kant still must demonstrate that the use of pure concepts is a condition for the possibility of experience. And just as he does in the Transcendental Aesthetic, this is done through a deduction—in this case, a transcendental deduction of the categories.

The *Quid Iuris*

In the second-edition preface, Kant says that he will try *as an experiment* to assume that the object must conform to our manner of representing the object, rather than vice versa (Bxvi). The Metaphysical Deduction relates the table of categories (in transcendental logic) to the table of judgments (in pure general logic) and thus supports the idea that these are the pure concepts we would use. However, Kant has yet to justify that such principles are applicable to our experience of the world. This is what the rationalists failed to do. Of course, the categories cannot be derived *a posteriori* from the experience of objects, because they are *a priori* conditions for the possibility of objects as such. Thus Kant cannot look to experience to validate their use; he must warrant them by means of a deduction. The Transcendental Deduction, in particular, is meant to vindicate the claim that they are the formal rules according to which the manifold of sensible intuition is synthesized.[13]

Kant clarifies his project by relating it to a deduction in the legal sense:

> When teachers of law talk about rights and claims, they distinguish in a legal action the question regarding what is legal (*quid iuris*) from the question concerning fact (*quid facti*), and they demand proof of both. The first proof, which is to establish the right, or for that matter the legal entitlement, they call the *deduction*. (A84/B116)

Among Kant's contemporaries, a deduction had to do with vindicating one's legal right to something. This usually concerned property rights—for example, determining which principality owns a given piece of land, or how to disperse someone's property when he dies. Finding out who the oldest son is or which is the most recent will (the *quid facti*) does not by itself settle the question of who is entitled to a person's wealth (the *quid iuris*). To address the latter question, a lawyer must draw up a deduction exhibiting what is justified under the law. In the Transcendental Deduction, Kant attempts a similar thing: to demonstrate our entitlement to apply the categories to the content of experience.

Given what is required for a *quid iuris,* how successful would it be for Kant to look at how people have cognized over the course of human experience? What if he identified the categories with certain features of the human brain? Would this warrant their use? No. An empirical investigation can only explain how we *do* think, not how we *must* think: "The attempted physiological derivation concerns a *quaestio facti,* and therefore cannot properly be called a deduction at all" (A86–87/B119). Empirical psychology can give an account of why someone, for example, assumes causal necessity to be operative in experience. Hume provides just such an explanation by referring to habit. But this kind of approach can never show that such a causal claim is legitimate; it can never entitle us to the use of the categories. Only an *a priori* transcendental deduction, rather than an *a posteriori* generalization, can warrant our commitment to principles that are absolutely necessary and strictly universal—that is, that are conditions for the possibility of experience.

In organizing sensible intuitions according to *a priori* rules, we are not merely associating subjective states. Rather, we are making objective judgments that may be right or wrong, depending on whether we have properly construed what is given to us through the senses—that is, depending on whether we have brought our experience correctly under the proper categories. To reduce the *Critique of Pure Reason* to a set of empirical hypotheses about the way that the human brain does in fact work would be to lose the possibility of getting it right or wrong. We would return to subjective associations.

Thus we have to be careful not to think of Kant's epistemology as describing a pair of glasses (so to speak) through which we view things in experience. Kant's philosophy is often misunderstood in just this way. The categories are not physiological reflexes but "epistemic conditions," to quote one prominent Kant scholar.[14] Even though we are curious as to the ultimate basis of these functions of thought—what is the soul? what am I such that I can engage in the activity of judging?—inquiring into their basis would not only transform the *quid iuris* into a *quid facti,* but (as we will see) it would also transgress the limits of cognition by speculating about something that is not a possible object of experience.

Two Transcendental Deductions

As noted earlier, the Transcendental Deduction is the centerpiece of the entire *Critique*. If Kant succeeds here, he not only will have warranted the applicability of the categories to all possible experience but (once again) will have proven the truth of transcendental idealism.[15] The use of *a priori* concepts will be limited to appearances, and most importantly, the source of dialectical inferences will be explained. Kant will conclude that dogmatic metaphysics results from the improper use of pure concepts with regard to things in themselves. Showing how metaphysics ought to and ought not to proceed, the *Critique of Pure Reason* will have accomplished its primary task. The significance of this section was not lost on Kant:

> I know of no inquiries more important for exploring the power that we call understanding, and for determining at the same time the rules and bounds of its use, than those that I have undertaken in the second chapter of the Transcendental Analytic, under the title of *Deduction of the Pure Concepts of the Understanding*. They are also the ones that have cost me the greatest effort—but, as I hope, an effort not unrewarded. (Axvi)

Part of the difficulty is that such a thing had never been done before. Following the enumeration of the categories in the Metaphysical Deduction, Kant is inventing an argument form that depends on a new kind of demonstration.

The strategy of the deduction is to show that the categories are conditions for the possibility of experience. The central component of this analysis involves an account of the possibility of our representation of objects, as opposed to merely the subjective play of appearances. Kant believes that we must approach this from two directions:

> This study, however, which is designed to go to some depth, has two sides. The one side refers to the objects of pure understanding and is intended to establish and make comprehensible the objective validity of understanding's a priori concepts, and precisely because of this pertains to my purposes essentially. The other side seeks to examine pure

understanding itself as regards its possibility and the cognitive powers underlying it in turn, and hence seeks to examine it in a subjective respect. And although this latter exposition is of great importance for my main purpose, it does not pertain to it essentially. For the main question is always this: what, and how much, can understanding and reason cognize independently of all experience? rather than: how is our *power of thought* itself possible? (Axvi–xvii)

Kant must show that objective experience is only possible by means of the categories. This is the "main question," the "objective" part of the deduction. But since objects seem to be simply given to us, he will also give an account of what we do in order to arrive at objectivity. In short, he will deal with the understanding itself and how it works. This is the "subjective" part, which is not essential to the main problem. By addressing both sides of the demonstration, however, Kant will not only warrant our commitment to the categories as constitutive of objective experience but will explain how the understanding applies itself to our kind of sensible intuition.

This part of the *Critique* was so important to Kant's critical project that he largely rewrote it for the second (or B) edition. Although both subjective and objective elements are present in the each of the two deductions, their emphases are dramatically different. The A edition focuses on the subjective deduction, describing how the subject deals with what is given to it through the senses. It begins with the syntheses by which we construe experience as experience, moving from the subject to the object. In the A edition, then, the rules are said to apply to objects because objects are syntheses of experience. Concepts apply to objects because they constrain the ways that we put representations together.

The risk here, and the reason Kant revised the Transcendental Deduction so significantly, is that this seems, wrongly, to be a description of the psychology of the human mind, that this is just the way we happen to do things. As Kant notes in the B edition (and as I noted earlier), this could never get us to causal necessity and objectivity; it gets us only to subjective association:

the categories would in that case lack the *necessity* which belongs essentially to the concept of them. For, the concept of cause, e.g., which asserts the necessity of a result under a presupposed condition, would be false if it rested only on an arbitrary subjective necessity, implanted in us, to link certain empirical presentations according to such a rule of relation. (B168)

To correct this misinterpretation, the B edition stresses the objective part of the deduction. It focuses on the only possible ways that the elements in experience could count as objective content and then deduces the subjective conditions of such content. In other words, it primarily looks at what must be the case in order for sensible intuitions to be represented as objects. The Transcendental Deduction is supposed to establish the necessity of *a priori* constraints for making claims about the world. It is not merely supposed to describe how we make those claims. In the B Deduction, Kant emphasizes more clearly that this is a normative enterprise rather than a descriptive enterprise.

Nonetheless, both elements are essential to understanding the Kantian philosophy—it is hardly satisfying to see *that* the categories make objects possible without also understanding *how* they do so—so the A and B Deductions, though each is supposedly self-sufficient, are often treated together.

The (Subjective) A Deduction

The subjective part of the A Deduction focuses on how the mind functions in having a coherent experience. Integral to this account is the activity that synthesizes various sensations into a coherent whole:

If each singular presentation were entirely foreign to—isolated from, as it were—every other presentation and separated from it, then there would never arise anything like cognition; for cognition is a whole consisting of compared and connected presentations. Hence when I ascribe to sense a synopsis, because sense contains a manifold in its intuition, then to this synopsis there always corresponds a synthesis;

and thus *receptivity* can make cognition possible only when combined with *spontaneity*. (A97)

Kant begins by noting a particular feature of our experience, pointed out by Hume in the *Treatise:* Particular sensations do not cohere into an object, or into a series of related objects, by themselves (T 188–89). When we perceive a table in the center of the room on two different days, we have to relate those perceptions and conclude that we are seeing the same table, which exists independently of our perceptions of it. Any receptivity of sense impressions must be coupled with a spontaneity by which we synthesize our sensations in a manifold (a complex of particular presentations), relate sensations over time, and organize our sensations according to the categories. Sensibility must be coupled with the understanding:

> this spontaneity is the basis of a threefold synthesis that necessarily occurs in all cognition: viz., the synthesis of the *apprehension* of presentations that are modifications of the mind in intuition; the synthesis of the *reproduction* of these presentations in imagination; and the synthesis of their *recognition* in the concept. Now, these three syntheses guide us to three subjective sources of cognition that make possible the understanding itself and, through it, all experience, which is an empirical product of the understanding. (A97–98)

Kant distinguishes three syntheses as necessary conditions of such a unified manifold. The first, the synthesis of apprehension in intuition, is the activity of unifying concurrent intuitions into one representation; the second, the synthesis of reproduction in imagination, is the activity of forming a coherent representation over the course of successive intuitions; and the third, the synthesis of recognition in a concept, is the act of bringing the sensible manifold to concepts. As Kant will show, the objective unity of this manifold is possible only because it is united according to certain *a priori* rules—namely, the categories.

Imagine that you are looking at a painting. What you perceive is a collection of colors and shapes. These different (simultaneous) perceptions must be united into a common representation, or else the different sensations could not be related to one another. Similarly, the colors you see on the left side of the painting must be related to the colors you see on the right side, after you have turned your head. Many people, including Locke, would claim that the object itself constrains our representation of it. We know that the green and the blue are part of the same painting because a single object affects us in two different ways. We represent the object a certain way because the object *is* a certain way. The problem with this explanation is that, for us to understand how the empirical object constrains or regulates our perception of it, we would be making claims about that object ("the object *is* such and such"), representing it synthetically. Yet that is precisely what we are trying to explain. To say that certain characteristics inhere in a particular object because the object actually has such characteristics is to beg the question. This assumes that the object unites our sensations, without explaining how we come to attribute those sensations to an object in the first place.

Nothing inherent in the object itself brings together our sensations of its various properties. Nothing in a tablecloth, for example, tells us that it is on the table and not a part of the table. Rather, you must reproduce the first sensation and relate it to the second—either as a different thing in proximity to the other thing, or as two parts of the same thing. You make a judgment concerning the quantity of what you are seeing. For example, am I looking at two parts of one painting, or two different paintings? Of course, this is not something that one does consciously, like following a flow chart. Kant is not offering a genetic account of how we "work up" representations of objects. Rather, he is analyzing what must be the case for particular perceptions to be sufficiently like imaginatively reproduced perceptions, such that we judge them to represent a particular thing.

Kant is not unique in asserting our active contribution to experience. Even Hume had claimed that our belief in enduring objects is due to the imagination. And today it is commonly held that our beliefs and desires inevitably color our interpretation and memory of events, such that no unbiased account is ever possible. But Kant is making a more radical claim. The character of sensible intuitions themselves are partially dependent on the activity of the subject.

Against the empiricists, Kant argues that experience is not simply given to the mind, later to be interpreted. Rather, sensations themselves are organized by the mind into an experience, prior to the work of remembrance or interpretation:

> That the imagination is a necessary ingredient of perception itself has, I suppose, never occurred to any psychologist. This is so partly because this power has been limited by psychologists to reproduction only, and partly because they believed that the senses not only supply us with impressions, but indeed also assemble these impressions and thus bring about images of objects. But this undoubtedly requires something more than our receptivity for impressions, viz., a function for their synthesis. (A120n)

The common psychological thesis that we interpret given events differently is implicitly committed to an empiricism regarding the raw material for reinterpretation: We are given impressions and events that we then transform according to our preconceptions. Two people who witness a car accident may place the blame on different drivers. A dog may look like either a harmless fuzzball or a snarling beast, depending on your experiences with animals. Anyone would concede that experience depends on the subject in this way. However, we must not confuse what we personally associate with an experience and the formal conditions that make experience possible. Kant shows that even supposedly given impressions are the result of a synthesis on the part of the subject. Our representation of a dog or the collision of the two cars itself depends on our contributing something to experience in a way that transforms what we are given through the senses.[16]

Kant includes separate sections on the synthesis of apprehension in intuition (A98–100) and the synthesis of reproduction in imagination (A100–102), but these syntheses are primarily of interest insofar as they bring the manifold to the understanding and thus explain the applicability of the categories to experience. The fact that we must organize intuitions as a manifold (in space and time) is certainly important in its own right, but the fact that this organization can take place only if they are subject to the categories is what establishes the main thesis of the Transcendental Deduction: The pure concepts of the understanding are objectively valid.

Once Kant establishes that particular perceptions must be united and that the object itself cannot explain how to organize our perceptions, we are faced with a series of related questions: What constrains the unification of elements in a representation? Why is it that in discriminating objects in my visual field, I can only unify certain elements or properties as belonging to a given object? What guides our judgment when we make objective claims? Kant does not deny that sensations are relevant to what we can represent about the object—"thoughts without content are empty"—but he does claim that such information cannot account for objective representational unity unless it is organized according to *a priori* rules (A51/B75).

It is here, in his treatment of the synthesis of recognition in the concept, that Kant makes his crucial move. As Kant has already shown, we cannot explain our representation of an object by reference to the object itself, because that fails to explain how our various perceptions are united. Objectivity cannot have an *a posteriori* basis in our perceptions, so it must be grounded in "a function of synthesis that makes the reproduction of the manifold necessary a priori and makes possible a concept in which this manifold is united" (A105). We identify certain shared characteristics among our perceptions and, on that basis, organize them under pure concepts. To see this, we need only contrast non-rule-governed association of perceptions *a posteriori* with unification according to *a priori* concepts (for example, the category of causality): "I habitually associate heat with copper expanding" versus "Heat makes copper expand." I am able to represent an objective relationship by making a judgment that can be right or wrong. And this is not possible on the basis of *a posteriori* association.

But here we are faced with a problem. Unification according to a rule may well be a necessary condition of experience, but it cannot be a sufficient condition. If it were a sufficient condition, any rule would count as providing an objective representation. There would be no relationship among rule-governed unities. I may have conceived of the table I saw yesterday as a real thing, but unless I relate that judgment to the one I make today, then I cannot relate the two events as different experiences of the same table. In other words, unless there were something that allowed these different unities to be related, particular manifolds would count as objective unities as long as they were unified in a certain way, but different unities would be unrelated. To associate different representations over time, there must be a supreme condition under which we synthesize all of our representations. Kant calls this condition "the transcendental unity of apperception":

> there can take place in us no cognitions, and no connection and unity of cognitions among one another, without that unity of consciousness which precedes all data of intuitions, and by reference to which all presentation of objects is alone possible. Now this pure, original, and immutable consciousness I shall call *transcendental apperception.* (A107)

Particular perceptions cannot be related in rule-governed ways unless there is a "unity of consciousness" within which those perceptions are related. If I see the green part of a painting and someone else sees the blue part of the same painting, there is no way for these two separate impressions to be part of the same experience. But if *I* perceive the green and the blue, one after another, the three syntheses become possible. Perceptions must occur to an identical subject over time if they are to be unified as parts of a single, persisting object.

Kant thus rebuts the Lockean claim that objects can be given directly to the subject. Rather, experience is a matter of actively unifying (in consciousness) what is given to us through the senses. In addition, this sensible manifold must be governed by certain *a priori* rules in order to be properly synthesized. But none of this yet explains how objective representations are possible. Why do some representations seem to belong together?[17]

In the A Deduction, Kant initially calls this source for the "objective reality" of representations the "transcendental object", which provides the basis of our representations: "The pure concept of this transcendental object (which object is actually always the same, $= x$, in all our cognitions) is what is able to provide all our empirical concepts in general with reference to an object, i.e., with objective reality" (A109). This is what makes Kant an empirical realist. There must be some intelligible correlate of what I am given through the senses. Although I can have no cognition of such a thing, I must presuppose a transcendental object that gives me the marks that I relate to one another through concepts. The matter of experience is not merely a product of the imagination; it is "out there" and not just "in my head."

Appealing to the transcendental object explains the source of my sensations, but it cannot explain objectivity. What is given by the transcendental object does not settle the issue of what I make of my sensations. In order for those sensations to form an objective representation for me, they must be sorted according to the *a priori* conditions for the representation of the object: "this concept [of the transcendental object] cannot contain any determinate intuition whatever, and hence presumably pertains to nothing but that unity which must be encountered in any manifold of cognition insofar as this manifold has reference to an object" (A109). The objects that I experience are given in one sense, because I receive my sensations passively under the forms of space and time. But they are not given *as objects*. For them to become objective representations, I must unify what is given to me according to the categories.

The unified object of experience is not the transcendental object (which Kant sometimes equates with the thing in itself), and the rules that we use to make sense of our perceptions cannot be derived empirically. Rather, experience is possible only when sensible intuitions are synthesized according to *a priori* rules under the apperceptive unity of consciousness:

> This reference [to an object], however, is nothing but the necessary unity of consciousness, and hence also of the synthesis of the manifold brought about through the mind's concerted function of combining this manifold in one presentation. Now this unity must be regarded as necessary a priori (because otherwise cognition would be without an object); and hence the reference to a transcendental object, i.e., the objective reality of our empirical cognition, presumably rests on a transcendental law. This transcendental law says that all appearances must, insofar as objects are to be given to us through them, be subject

to a priori rules of the synthetic unity of appearances, a priori rules according to which alone their relation in empirical intuition is possible.
(A109–10)

Objective unity "must be regarded as necessary a priori" because it
cannot be merely associative, or derived from how the transcendental
object affects us through the senses. Furthermore, the necessary
conditions for the synthetic unity of appearances are also the necessary conditions for the representation of objects by means of those
appearances. This is what Kant calls a "transcendental law": Experience must be subject to the conditions for the possibility of (objective) experience, which in this case are *a priori* rules according to
which our sensations are synthesized as objects (A110). The imaginative synthesis, whereby the apperceptive I connects a number of
different representations, is governed by the only possible forms of
judgment—namely, the pure concepts of the understanding. By
means of these *a priori* rules, the manifold of sensible intuition is
synthesized into objective experience.

The (Objective) B Deduction

The basic claims of the A and B Deductions are very similar. In fact,
Kant insists in the preface to the B edition that he has made changes
only "as regards the [manner of] *exposition*"; there are no changes "in
the propositions themselves and in the bases used for proving them"
(Bxxxvii–xxxviii). In both deductions, Kant argues that in order for
given sensations to form a coherent experience, we must synthesize
them in space and over time, bring them under one consciousness (the
transcendental unity of apperception), and distinguish subjective
associations from objective cognition by means of the categories.
These elements are present in each version, and in each case they are
used to support the following conclusion: "The same function that gives
unity to the various presentations *in a judgment* also gives unity to the
mere synthesis of various presentations *in an intuition*" (A79/B104–5).
In other words, the understanding makes judgments when it organizes

experience (according to the concepts), just as when it reflects on that experience and conceptualizes it in language (according to the logical functions). The purpose of the Transcendental Deduction, then, is to warrant the applicability of the *a priori* concepts to experience.

The main problem with the A Deduction is that it sounds more like a psychological thesis than a transcendental deduction. Kant has shown *how* the understanding and its objectivity rules (the categories) are operative in experience, but he has not proven *that* they function this way with regard to actual representations. With his recognition of the need for synthesis, he has certainly demonstrated that our objective claims cannot be grounded in the transcendental object. But this negative claim does not by itself imply that the categories are a condition of synthetic unity per se. At the crucial point in the argument, Kant simply asserts that the categories make experience possible by making objectivity possible. But why should we believe this? The *quid iuris* has not been accomplished. Kant has not conclusively demonstrated the *necessary* applicability of intellectual conditions to what is given in sensibility.

To remedy this, the B Deduction proceeds differently, leading to its common label as the "objective deduction." As noted earlier, the B Deduction moves from the only possible ways that the elements in experience could count as objective content to the rules we must have as a condition for the possibility of experience; it moves from the object to the subject. Here he abandons the language of psychology and turns to a consideration of the object's appearance to consciousness and how that appearance is possible. This is a subtle difference, but one that is very important for establishing the necessary applicability of the categories to sensible intuition.

Synthesis (§15)

The B Deduction begins by considering the conditions of receptivity. We passively receive sensations according to the pure forms of sensible intuition: "The [uncombined] manifold of presentations can be given in an intuition that is merely sensible, i.e., nothing but receptivity; and the form of this intuition can lie a priori in our power of presentation without being anything but the way in which the subject is affected" (B129). In other words, independently of the concepts, objects are presented to us in space and time. Because space and time are *a priori*, any sensory manifold must have spatiotemporal unity.

In order for our different perceptions to be part of a coherent experience, we have to combine those perceptions. Particular perceptions are given in space and time, but the relationships among given perceptions in space and over time must be the result of my ordering them in a spatiotemporal manifold. When I am riding my bike and I see a child playing on the side of the road, I know that I can get by in the space I have, but I anticipate her chasing a ball into the street, and I am ready to adjust my path accordingly. We have to relate our particular perceptions to one another in space, and we have to relate our present sensible intuitions to our past and future intuitions. This is something that we actively carry out:

> a manifold's *combination* (*coniunctio*) as such can never come to us through the senses; nor, therefore, can it already be part of what is contained in the pure form of sensible intuition. For this combination is an act of spontaneity by the power of presentation; and this power must be called understanding, in order to be distinguished from sensibility. Hence all combination is an act of understanding . . . (B129–30)

Awareness of an object cannot be explained simply in terms of our having perceptions. Our ability to recognize certain perceptions as belonging together, or our representing an object in relation to other objects, is something we *do*. We synthesize the elements that we judge to be relevant to a particular object or series of objects:

> I would assign to this act of understanding the general name *synthesis*, in order to point out at the same time: that we cannot present anything as combined in the object without ourselves' having combined it beforehand; and that, among all presentations, *combination* is the only one that cannot be given through objects, but—being an act of the subject's self-activity—can be performed only by the subject itself. (B130)

Our unified experience of the world cannot be given immediately to the (passive) senses. Rather, unity is always the result of synthetic activity.

At one moment I see the top of the table, and then I shift my gaze and see the bottom of the table and the table legs. What I have is a succession of perceptions. But those perceptions are distinct and do not cohere on their own. I must relate them over time: The table leg I am seeing now is part of the table whose top I saw a moment ago. Or I see a chair, and then I close my eyes. When I open them, I conclude that it is the same chair—not one that looks similar to the one I saw previously (a subjective association), but that it *is* the same thing (an objective claim). When I perceive a table, I relate that perception to the chair that is next to it and the legs that are under it. In addition, I relate the perception of the chair that I had three seconds ago with the perception of the table I am having now. My experience of the table and the chair as objects means that they are bounded by and related to other things in space, and it means that they persist over time, independent of my particular perceptions of them at any given moment. This can result only from a judgment on my part.

What Kant emphasizes, here and in the A Deduction, is that nothing in our perception alone can get us to this point. If we approach the world merely empirically, then objects can never be given to us. We would have nothing but the habitual association of certain perceptions. This can never warrant objective claims, because (among other things) what we receive in sensation underdetermines the ways that we could take it up. In other words, how we make sense of our perceptions is not settled by the perceptions themselves. For example, why is the table leg part of the table but the tablecloth is not? Why is a painting not part of the wall where it is hanging? A mural, even a framed mural, is part of the wall, but a framed or unframed picture is not part of the wall. Such conclusions result from judgments that we make. To represent an object is to unify the elements by some constraint that cannot come from the object. It must come from the subject.

According to empiricism and rationalism, the object constrains us from without. Through the senses or through reason, we try to get to the object itself in order to correct our fallible perceptions and to discover the truth of what exists behind appearances. For Kant, however, the idea that the object in itself constrains our claim-making must be changed. The world as it exists apart from our representation

of it is outside our very activity of judging and is therefore nothing to us. It makes no sense for us to know things as they are apart from our conditions of knowing them. The transcendental object is merely a placeholder ("x") for the intelligible ground of the empirical representation. Claims about objects, however, are inside the normative dimensions of our own thinking, because any object, in order to be a thing about which we can make justifiable claims, must already be the product of a judgment. In short, we can never base the synthetic unity of the manifold on the way that we are affected through sensation. What we know depends on how we make objective claims. The perceptions do not relate themselves but are related as a result of the synthetic unity that we perform. The contents of consciousness do not represent an objective world distinct from our internal perceptions unless they are conceived by us as being representative.

Apperception (§§16–17)

As he does in the A Deduction, here Kant claims that the unification of the manifold (over time) is possible only if particular representations are brought under a single consciousness. Without this, there would be no way for the various representations to be related: "The *I think* must be *capable* of accompanying all my presentations. For otherwise something would be presented to me that could not be thought at all—which is equivalent to saying that the presentation either would be impossible, or at least would be nothing to me" (B131–32). Were I unable to bring what I perceive together as a complex whole, I would only have a series of isolated perceptions rather than objective representations. The representation of a spatiotemporal manifold depends on there being an identical subject who has these various perceptions.

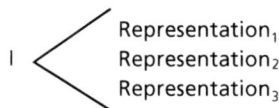

$$I \left< \begin{array}{l} \text{Representation}_1 \\ \text{Representation}_2 \\ \text{Representation}_3 \end{array} \right.$$

I must be able to conceive of my various perceptions as things that I have experienced or made judgments about ("I think"). What Kant calls *"pure apperception," "original apperception,"* or "the *transcendental* unity of self-consciousness" thus stands behind my experience as its supreme condition (B132). It is that within which I synthesize the manifold in space and time. Like Descartes, Kant says that the *cogito* is a condition for the possibility of having perceptions (or ideas) at all.

Transcendental apperception involves at least three related elements. First, for me to have experiences of any kind, the experiences must belong to me as a particular subject who persists over time, not to different centers of consciousness. Second, unity must be effected by the conscious subject. The "belonging together" of representations occurs for me because I actively unite representations into a manifold. Finally, the subject must be conscious of its own act of combining and discriminating its perceptions, or must take itself to be a subject in the act of synthesizing a manifold. The subject would not be the same throughout experience if such a subject "could not become conscious of the identity of function whereby it synthetically combines the manifold in one cognition" (A108). In order to be conscious of my experience, I have to be making judgments about it, which requires that I stand behind my judgments as claims that I am making.

The identity and unity conditions are clearly necessary if various perceptions are to be synthesized. When these elements are present, the I becomes a site within which the various perceptions come together— in relation to the subject spatially and over the course of the subject's existence in time. But why is consciousness of this (apperceptive) identity necessary for a unified subject who is capable of experience? Again, the answer can be found by scrutinizing the conditions of objective experience. If I could not become conscious of the rules I was applying in unifying my representations, then in attempting to represent objects, I would not be following rules or representing objects but merely associatively producing representations. The latter has no normative dimension. In other words, if I were not able to be conscious that I am making judgments, then I would not really be making judgments at all. I cannot get it wrong unless I can stand behind my judgment as a claim, and doing so requires an awareness of myself as a claim-maker. I *assert* that heat makes copper expand, and in doing so, I stick my neck out in a way that I would not if I merely associated the two.

Because transcendental apperception is not a matter of having particular representations but makes those representations possible as a whole under one consciousness, it must not be confused with what Kant calls "empirical apperception," the particular instances of reflecting on what I experience or the inner workings and ideas of my mind. As Kant describes it, "the faculty of inner sense" is "the faculty of making one's own representations the objects of one's thought."[18] The perceptions of inner sense—what is "in our heads," as opposed to "out there"—are internal cognitions that are psychologically grounded, whereas original apperception is a transcendental condition for the possibility of experience. The former is contingent on my intuiting myself; the latter is necessary for any intuition to be possible. All experience is a kind of apperception, acknowledging that you are making sense of it in a certain way. This is a formal condition of experience, not an instance of empirical cognition:

> in the transcendental synthesis of the manifold of presentations as such, and hence in the synthetic original unity of apperception, I am not conscious of myself as I appear to myself, nor as I am in myself, but am conscious only that I am. This *presentation* is a *thought*, not an *intuition*. Now *cognition* of ourselves requires not only the act of thought that brings the manifold of every possible intuition to the unity of apperception, but requires in addition a definite kind of intuition whereby this manifold is given. Hence although my own existence is not appearance (still less mere illusion), determination of my existence can occur only in conformity with the form of inner sense and according to the particular way in which the manifold that I combine is given in inner intuition. Accordingly I have no *cognition* of myself as I am but merely cognition of how I appear to myself. (B157–58)

Inner sense is a form of perception, for what I perceive when I introspect is given to me empirically. Because the ideas that I apprehend in inner sense are intuited as a sensory manifold in time, I can know myself only as I appear to myself. As we will see in Chapter 5, Descartes's claim that I am an immaterial thinking thing results from a dialectical inference, applying the categories beyond their limited applicability to appearances. These appearances can cohere only because the subject relates them to itself with the "I think," but what we are apart from our subjective conditions of knowing transcends our epistemic capacities.

As a condition of experience, all perceptions must be brought under a unified consciousness, an original apperception, by which my perceptions become mine. This act of self-attribution is not a judgment but a relating of sensible intuition to a unified self as a formal condition of my having experience. Thus we must strictly distinguish self-consciousness as an accompaniment to experience—the "I think"—from consciousness of our own internal representations—what I intuit about myself. The former is not identical with the latter but is a condition for the possibility of both outer and inner sense.

Were there only empirical apperception, there would be particular representations distinct from one another, and the different subjects (the different instances of inner sense) would also be distinct. There would be nothing to connect the different introspective moments. The subject would be dispersed over time, different I's corresponding to the different representations it receives.

This is all thinly disguised maximum skepticism

I_1 – Representation$_1$
I_2 – Representation$_2$
I_3 – Representation$_3$

Without original apperception, there would be one representation, then another representation, and then a different representation, but no subject would be carrying these things together. Nothing would connect the different introspective moments; there would be no "I" who is having an experience. There would just be a bunch of perceptions—"This. . . . This. . . . This. . . . I sense green. . . . I sense blue"—without any coherent subject. There would be different perceptions sensed at different unconnected moments, and different (distinct) perceivers along with it: "only because I can comprise the manifold of the presentations in one consciousness, do I call them one and all *my* presentations. For otherwise I would have a self as many-colored and varied as I have presentations that I am conscious of" (B134). Kant thus establishes a link between the possibility of temporal unity among representations and the possibility of being an identical subject of experience. I can have a coherent experience only if it is had by one consciousness, and I can have a particular consciousness only if I synthesize my various perceptions into a spatiotemporal manifold.

Only by relating my various perceptions in a unified consciousness, through an act of self-relation ("I think"), does subjectivity become possible. The succession of changing events that seems to threaten a cohesive identity is itself made possible by that very identity. Yet I can know myself only as a succession of perceptions, feelings, and volitions, only as an object of inner sense. Kant's claim that "thoughts without content are empty; intuitions without concepts are blind" has its parallel claim with regard to personal identity (A51/B75): Self-consciousness without perceptions is empty; inner sense without apperception is blind. Apart from inner sense, I have no knowledge of myself, only a pure thinking without reference. But such self-knowledge is possible only given a consciousness within which my various perceptions are synthesized. Both the stable "I" of apperception and the changing "me" of inner sense constitute my personal identity.

Concepts (§§18–21)

In the A Deduction, Kant argues that apperception is a necessary condition of cognition because only with an identical subject are the three syntheses possible. Here Kant arrives at apperception by showing that it is a condition for my having experiences *as a subject*. In order for objective judgments to be possible (as opposed to merely subjective associations), the manifold of sensible intuition must be held together as *my* experience. Claim-making requires that I stand behind my experience as a claim-maker. And I could not stand behind my experience in this way unless I were apperceptively aware of myself (or self-conscious) in every experience:

> For the manifold presentations given in a certain intuition would not one and all be *my* presentations, if they did not one and all belong to one self-consciousness. I.e., as my presentations (even if I am not conscious of them as being mine), they surely must conform necessarily to the condition under which alone they *can* stand together in one universal

self-consciousness, since otherwise they would not thoroughly belong
to me. And from this original combination much can be inferred.
(B132–33)

As noted earlier, apperception involves several different elements:
The subject must be identical throughout experience, representations
must be actively unified by the subject, and the subject must not only
make judgments about experience but also take himself to be making
such judgments. From this conclusion, that an apperceptive subject is
a condition for the possibility of experience, "much can be inferred."
Discovering the conditions under which a unified subject of experience is possible could help us to discover the conditions that govern
the unification of a manifold.

Indeed, Kant claims that this warrants the applicability of the
categories to experience. Why are such rules necessary? In the A
Deduction, Kant simply insists that concepts are a condition for the
possibility of objective unity. This is Kant's conclusion, but (as we
saw) there is little argument for why we should believe it. Here Kant
claims that transcendental apperception is a condition for the possibility of experience, and the categories are a condition for the possibility of transcendental apperception. The argument proceeds as follows:
Unless I can distinguish the variety of perceptions that I have from
unification according to a rule (an objectivity rule), then I could not
be said to be a single, unified subject of experience who has those
perceptions. If I could not make this distinction, "I" would just *be*
this state, then that state, then this state, simply produced by my having had those states—or, more properly, different perceptions would
occur, but there would be no "I" per se.

This is a difficult point. In order for the apperceptive subject to be
possible, I must be able to set my consciousness apart from the objects
it represents. If I could not distinguish how something seems to me
(subjectively) from what is the case (objectively), I would only have
particular, distinct perceptions rather than a coherent experience, and
"I" would be just a series of isolated subjects: "otherwise I would have
a self as many-colored and varied as I have presentations that I am
conscious of" (B134).

As we have already seen (in §§15–17), there must be an apperceptive subject behind the different representations for experience to be possible, because that is what makes synthesis possible. But there cannot be unified self-consciousness if the object is not distinguished from the subject; subjectivity would be as fragmented as these different perceptions are. Therefore, there must be some way to direct the required unification of experience and distinguish the object from the subject— again, because this is a condition for the possibility of apperception, which is a condition for the possibility of experience.[19]

How is this accomplished, that the object is represented *as* an object in opposition to the subject? We already examined (and dismissed) one possible answer: "The empiricists had it right. The object itself constrains our representation of it. We don't do it." As we noted, the object cannot constrain our perception of it unless we represent it synthetically, and this requires activity on the part of the knowing subject. Sensible intuition is relevant to what we can represent about the object, but receptivity alone cannot account for representational unity. Objectivity has a normative dimension. If it were just the way that we happened to combine things, then we could never be right or wrong about our objective claims; indeed, they would not be objective claims at all. Any unity is a claim for unity held together with a certain kind of warrant:

> [Presentations] belong to one another *by virtue of the necessary unity* of apperception in the synthesis of intuitions; i.e., they belong to one another according to principles of the objective determination of all presentations insofar as these presentations can become cognition—all of these principles being derived from the principle of the transcendental unity of apperception. Only through this [reference to original apperception and its necessary unity] does this relation [among presentations] become a *judgment*, i.e., a relation that is *valid objectively* and can be distinguished adequately from a relation of the same presentations that would have only subjective validity—e.g., a relation according to laws of association. According to these laws, all I could say is: When I support a body, then I feel a pressure of heaviness. I could not say: It, the body, is heavy—which amounts to saying that

these two presentations are not merely together in perception (no matter how often repeated), but are combined in the object, i.e., combined independently of what the subject's state is. (B142)

For objects and objective relations to be "out there"—that is, distinguished from the apperceptive subject, able to be true or false rather than merely subjectively associated—I must judge them in a certain way. I have to synthesize sensible intuitions according to objectivity rules. We already know that such rules cannot be derived empirically, because such rules are conditions for the very possibility of experience. They must be *a priori*. What are these rules? How do we discover the concepts by means of which we oppose objects to consciousness? The faculty of judgment by which I make such objective determinations— namely, the understanding—is the same faculty by which I make logical claims. Logic gives us a clue as to how we conceptualize experience. The categories allow us to recognize what we are given through the senses as objects rather than merely subjective states.

This is where the argument of the B Deduction goes beyond the A Deduction in demonstrating that the categories are conditions for the possibility of experience. Concepts are conditions for the possibility of distinguishing self-consciousness from objective representations, and because a unitary consciousness is necessary for experience to be possible, and a unitary consciousness is possible only given its distinction from objective representations, conceptual discrimination by the understanding is necessary for experience. Transcendental apperception is a condition of our making objective judgments, and there cannot be objective judgments unless we can distinguish arbitrary or associative unification from rule-governed, objectivity-conferring unification. The *a priori* concepts of the understanding are conditions of apperceptive unity, because they are rules by which the manifold is synthesized (in space and over time) and is distinguished from the "I think" that must accompany all my representations. In the B Deduction, then, not only is transcendental apperception necessary for a synthesis to take place, but it is the key to proving the necessity of the categories for experience.

This is obviously very complex reasoning. Many philosophers consider it the hardest part of the entire *Critique*. Just remember that this is a transcendental argument, which inquires into the conditions for the possibility of experience, and that in the B Deduction, Kant is working from the object of experience to the activity of the subject. From these general strategies follows the basic outline of the deduction: Experience depends on apperception, apperception depends on distinguishing the subject from the object, and making this distinction depends on judging by means of the categories.

Transcendental Idealism and Empirical Realism (§§22–23)

In the first part of the Transcendental Deduction (§§15–21), Kant has shown that in order for experience to be possible, representations must be distinguished from the apperceptive subject according to objectivity rules. These rules can only be the categories, because they cannot be derived empirically, and the table of logical functions provides us with a clue to discover the *a priori* concepts used by the understanding. Because transcendental apperception is a condition for the possibility of experience, and discrimination according to the categories is a condition of apperception, nothing could be given to us or any other kind of discursive intellect that contradicts them. Any being who depends on intuitions that are given independently of his thinking must synthesize them according to these concepts:

> The categories are only rules for an understanding whose entire power consists in thought, i.e., in the act of bringing to the unity of apperception the synthesis of the manifold that has, in intuition, been given to it from elsewhere. Hence such an understanding by itself cognizes nothing whatever, but only combines and orders the material for cognition, i.e., the intuition, which must be given to it by the object. (B145)[20]

The categories can tell us about the way things are only if they are supplemented by what we are given through the senses. But sensations can constitute an objective experience only if they are organized according to the categories. Thus Kant has shown that, in order to make meaningful claims about the world, sensible intuitions must be given intelligible form *and* conceptual discriminations must be given content from without.

In §§22–23, Kant pauses to explain what follows from this conclusion. One implication of the givenness of sensations and the need to synthesize them according to *a priori* concepts is that the world as it is in itself can never be known to us. We cannot know things apart from the way that we organize our perceptions, and we cannot use the concepts to obtain knowledge beyond what is given to us in sensation, because without sensibility they lack cognitive content. Therefore, we only know the world as it appears to us. Transcendental idealism is true.

By focusing only on the categories apart from a particular sensory manifold, however, we cannot know anything about the content of actual judgments. For this reason, Kant also describes his position as empirical realism. From the side of intuition—that is, the way that the senses are affected—there is a unity to the givenness of the object. It is not the case that we merely take a mess of stuff and impose order on it. Rather, there must be some objective guidance, some marks by which we classify our perceptions under concepts. The transcendental object gives us sensations, and there is a right way to synthesize what we are given into a spatiotemporal manifold. But the empirical constraints are impossible to discuss philosophically because they are not known *a priori*. We must encounter the world to determine what exists or what causes what.

Kant is not doing away with the world as a thing that is distinguishable from our perception of it. This is where Kant's transcendental idealism differs significantly from the immaterialism of Berkeley. But he does conclude that the matter of experience cannot be incongruent with conceptual forms. The thing in itself does affect us, but the formal conditions of experience allow us to represent sensible intuitions as objects. Kant is a transcendental idealist because he claims that we have knowledge of the world only as it appears to us, subject to our epistemic conditions. He is an empirical realist because he also argues that we have knowledge of an external world that we directly intuit by means of the senses. The judgments that we make about the world are right or wrong depending on whether we have properly organized what we are given, but the resulting representations are not things in themselves. There is no object for us except as it appears according to the pure forms of sensible intuition and the categories. This is why the understanding and sensibility are both necessary parts of experience: "Thoughts without content are empty; intuitions without concepts are blind" (A51/B75). The world guides our construals of it, but it must also be unified in some way so that we have experience that is consistent with our subjective conditions of knowing.

Is the Thing in Itself Un-Kantian?

At the risk of interrupting the flow of the Transcendental Deduction, we need to pause here and consider the thing in itself. Kant says that the categories we use to make sense of experience have no content without sensible intuitions to which we apply them. In order to have experience, then, something has to be given to us from without; the mere forms of thinking have no application apart from what is given to the senses. Therefore, although representations must be had by a self-consciousness in order for them to be represented, they are not entirely the product of consciousness. They are also the result of some thing in itself that is completely independent of consciousness. In this sense, Kant is a realist.

Many of Kant's philosophical successors in the late eighteenth and nineteenth centuries criticized Kant for his commitment to something that, from their perspective, violated the very principles of the critical philosophy. According to F. H. Jacobi, it is impossible to enter the Kantian system without the thing in itself, but it is impossible to remain a Kantian with it.[21] In other words, Kant claims that to know anything, we must be given the matter of cognition by the thing in itself, yet he also concludes that objects exist only as representations for consciousness, that they are "mere appearances" (A46/B63). G. E. Schulze insisted that Kant illegitimately applies the category of causality to the thing in itself when he claims that it affects us through the senses, or causes sensible intuitions.[22] Arthur Schopenhauer repeated this objection and, further, claimed that talk of a thing in itself or things in themselves extends the categories of unity or plurality beyond their proper use.[23] The common theme here is that given the rest of his philosophy,

Kant cannot make sense of a thing in itself. Saying anything about things in themselves, or even conceiving of them as possible entities, would involve applying our concepts to something that, by definition, exists apart from our formal conditions of knowing.

Such objections, however, rest on a misunderstanding of the thing in itself as a separate entity that causes appearances.[24] Appearances and things in themselves are not two different things. Rather, they are the same thing considered from two different perspectives. In Kant's own words, the Copernican turn necessitates "the distinction . . . between objects of experience and *these same objects* as things in themselves" (Bxxvii, emphasis added). There are not two objects—a transcendental object and a represented object—but one object that is either subject to our conditions of knowing or conceived of apart from those conditions.

Furthermore, the thing in itself does not involve the category of unity, because Kant is not making any claims about it as a thing with properties. Instead, "thing in itself" is just a label for whatever is left when we abstract from the categories and the pure forms of sensible intuition. Kant writes that "*noumena* . . . are nothing but representations of a problem" (Pro 316) and that "the concept of a noumenon is . . . only a *boundary concept* serving to limit the pretension of sensibility, and hence is only of negative use" (A255/B310–11). In a late manuscript, Kant says that "the thing *in itself* is not an existing being but = x, merely a principle."[25] So, the thing in itself is not a thing per se but rather reality as it exists apart from our epistemic conditions. Schulze and Schopenhauer are right that attempts to attribute some special agency to it or to give it a quantity would apply the categories beyond possible experience. But Kant makes no such attributions, nor does he need to given his understanding of how appearances are related to things in themselves—that is, as two different ways of considering things.

A second, related objection to the thing in itself is that it is a holdover of a certain kind of dogmatic materialism, and that taking the *Critique* to its logical conclusion would reveal that the idea of a thing with no relation to consciousness is contradictory. The German idealists who followed Kant—most notably Fichte, Schelling, and Hegel—claimed that Kant had not given a complete explanation of experience. He had reduced experience to the activity of the understanding and the passivity of the sensibility as it is affected by a thing in itself, but these are very different things. Kant did not account for their relation, except to say that they may ultimately have the same basis: "Human cognition has two stems, viz., *sensibility* and *understanding*, which perhaps spring from a common root, though one unknown to us" (A15/B29). We are left with the problem of how to account for their connection.

The philosophers who followed Kant tried to discover this unitary ground of the subject and the object, and they concluded that for something to be an object, it must be related to consciousness. We posit the object as distinct from the subject (Fichte), nature produces the subject that limits itself in relation to the object (Schelling), or the object is a result of the alienation of consciousness from itself (Hegel). Kant's thing in itself is in principle unknowable. Kant can only conceive of such a thing by thinking of it as standing behind perceptions. But that means that the idea of an independent thing as the cause of our experience is the result of our conceiving of our representations *as* caused by a thing in itself. The object and the subject are distinguished within some unitary ground—the I, nature, or Spirit (*Geist*)—in which the two are actively related to one another.

Although these philosophers sometimes claimed only to be extending or transforming the Kantian project, Kant thinks that the thing in itself is necessary in order to make sense of experience, "otherwise an absurd proposition would follow, viz., that there is appearance without anything that appears" (Bxxvi). This makes possible Kant's claim that he is an empirical realist rather than an empirical idealist—that is, someone who doubts or denies the existence of mind-independent objects. In addition, by inquiring into what the thing in itself is, the post-Kantian idealists have been accused by some of practicing a kind of metaphysical speculation that Kant himself shows to be impossible. If things in themselves are defined as things apart from our conditions of knowing them, then reducing them to elements in consciousness transgresses the limits of human cognition.

Obviously, whether the thing in itself is inconsistent with the spirit of the critical philosophy is a difficult issue, with historical and philosophical significance. Weighing the various arguments on both sides would go beyond the scope of this book.

The Spatiotemporal Manifold and the Categories (§§24–26)

Having considered the thing in itself, we can now return to the Transcendental Deduction. Beginning with §24, Kant shifts his focus to demonstrate that the categories are conditions for the possibility of a spatiotemporal manifold in particular. It is conceivable that not every discursive intellect experiences things in space and time, so Kant sets out to demonstrate that we must use the categories with regard to our kind of sensible intuition.

Although Kant calls this the second half of an incomplete deduction—he says that, in the first part, he has only made "the beginning of a *deduction*" (B144)—what he says here seems redundant on the face of it. He has already shown that the categories are necessary for *any* sensibly affected discursive intellect to have experience. That the categories provide unity for our kind of manifold, or constitute a kind of space- and time-consciousness, would seem to follow logically from what he has already demonstrated. According to some commentators, the *quid iuris* has been accomplished.

But this interpretation misses an important point. There is more at work in §§24–26 than merely a specification of how we use the categories. Early in the Transcendental Deduction, Kant worries about the possibility that the understanding cannot organize what is given to us in space and time, that there is a fundamental disjunction between the receptive and discursive faculties, sensible intuition and the understanding:

> For, I suppose, appearances might possibly be of such a character that the understanding would not find them to conform at all to the conditions of its unity. Everything might then be so confused that, e.g., the sequence of appearances would offer us nothing providing us with a rule of synthesis and thus corresponding to the concept of cause and effect, so that this concept would then be quite empty, null, and without signification. But appearances would nonetheless offer objects to our intuition; for intuition in no way requires the functions of thought. (A90–91/B123)

Kant has demonstrated that for something to be an experience of an object, it must meet the conditions of the categories. However, at this point Kant has to address the apparent possibility that there could be things that appear to us in space and time but that are opaque to the understanding. Objective claims are subject to the categories, but are the categories valid for the manifold of sensible intuition? The first half of the deduction abstracted from our form of sensibility, but not sensibility in general. In the second half, Kant drops this abstraction and demonstrates that for something to be a spatiotemporal manifold, it must be subject to the categories; or, to put it another way, the unity of our form of intuition and the unity governed by the categories are two aspects of a single, unifying faculty of cognition. Thus, as Kant claims, there is both an objective and a subjective part of the larger proof (Axvi–xvii): He first investigates the understanding and how it functions in making a coherent experience possible (§§15–23), and then he explains how the categories are related to representations as they are given to us in space and time (§§24–26).

Kant begins this part of the deduction by claiming that the activity of the imagination allows us to anticipate what events in the world will be like. As opposed to Kant's description in the A Deduction, where the imagination is portrayed as an independent faculty, here the productive imagination is an organ of the understanding:

> the synthesis of imagination is an exercise of spontaneity, which is determinative, rather than merely determinable, as is sense; hence this synthesis can a priori determine sense in terms of its form in accordance with the unity of apperception. To this extent, therefore, the imagination is a power of determining sensibility a priori; and its synthesis of intuitions *in accordance with the categories* must be the transcendental synthesis of *imagination*. This synthesis is an action of the understanding upon sensibility, and is the understanding's first application (and at the same time the basis of all its other applications) to objects of intuition that is possible for us. (B151–52)

Because it is the understanding in another guise, the imagination forms expectations about our experience based on what we require of it conceptually. For example, we expect the table not to disappear suddenly because we judge it to be a substance that persists over time.

The ability to anticipate what is given to us in sensible intuition, to require a certain formal consistency in space and over time, depends on a connection between the productive imagination and space- and time-consciousness. If Kant can establish that they are necessarily related, then he will have succeeded in demonstrating the interdependence of spatiotemporal unity and conceptual unity.

Kant first notes that space and time are not just forms of sensible intuition; they are also pure intuitions. Not only are space and time the subjective conditions under which experience is possible, but, as Kant demonstrates in the Metaphysical Expositions of the Concepts of Space and Time, they are also singular wholes within which we represent things. There is one space in which all particular spaces occur, and one time in which all particular times occur. This is the linchpin of the argument, because if space and time are themselves intuitions, then they must be subject to the unity of the categories. And if space and time are subject to the categories, then any sensible intuition we have must be subject to the categories, because every sensible intuition must be apprehended by us in space and time.

This may sound confusing. Space and time do not appear to us as particular objects do. However, we do apprehend things *in* space and time. For example, a kid occupies a certain amount of space, but I also intuit the kid as part of an all-encompassing space within which she is related to other things, such as my bike, her ball, and the street. As formal intuitions (and not just forms *of* intuition), then, space and time contain manifolds that require a unity, which, as we have seen already, is possible only as a rule-governed synthesis. And as Kant shows in the Metaphysical Deduction, the only possible rules for such a synthesis are the pure concepts of the understanding.

Kant gives two examples to illustrate that spatial and temporal relations essentially involve the application of the categories. First, to illustrate the necessity of concepts in spatial consciousness, Kant uses the example of a representation of a house:

> when I turn the empirical intuition of a house into a perception by apprehending the intuition's manifold, then in this apprehension I use as a basis the *necessary unity* of space and of outer sensible

intuition as such; and I draw, as it were, the house's shape in con-
formity with this synthetic unity of the manifold in space. But this
same unity, if I abstract from the form of space, resides in the understanding, and is the category of the synthesis of the homogeneous in
an intuition as such, i.e., the category of *magnitude*. Hence the synthesis of apprehension, i.e., perception, must conform throughout to
that category. (B162)

When I picture the various parts of a house, I synthesize my sensations
according to a specific category of quantity. In order for an object to be
a single thing with a certain magnitude, it is not enough for it to be
bounded by space. I have to unite my various perceptions into a spatially designated unity by means of a concept. I apprehend the house in
space—it is taking up space, it is in relation to other things, it is here
rather than somewhere else, and so on—but even if I remove from the
experience the spatial orientation that is contributed by the form of
sensibility, its unity still must conform to the categorical constraints
that the mind imposes—in this case, having a given magnitude. In order for an object of possible experience to be related to a unitary space,
I must already know what could count as a distinct object (that is
extended in space). I must represent it as a distinct object through
the categories.[26]
We can also think about spatial consciousness by imagining a
framed picture that is nailed to the wall. It is not part of the wall, but it
is related spatially to the wall. In perceiving the picture on the wall, we
make a discrimination: This is an object distinct from the wall. To
conceive of an object in relation to another object, however, we must
do something. Specifically, we must apply the category of plurality to
our perceptions: There are two things here rather than one. The picture is related to the wall spatially, but that spatial relation is possible
only given a rule-governed synthesis: "this unity [of presentation]
presupposes a synthesis; this synthesis does not belong to the senses,
but through it do all concepts of space and time first become possible"
(B161n). Things are related in space not only because of the conditions of receptivity (the pure forms of sensible intuition), but because
of the way that we cut up our experience according to the categories.

Kant's second example illustrates the necessity of concepts in temporal consciousness. He has us imagine that we are observing water slowly freezing:

> When (to take a different example) I perceive the freezing of water, then I apprehend two states (fluidity and solidity) as states that stand to each other in a relation of time. Since the appearance is inner *intuition*, I lay time at its basis. But in time I necessarily present synthetic *unity* of the manifold; without this unity, that relation could not be given *determinately* (as regards time sequence) in an intuition. However, this synthetic unity, as a priori condition under which I combine the manifold of an *intuition as such*, is—if I abstract from the constant form of *my* inner intuition, i.e., from time—the category of *cause*; through this category, when I apply it to my sensibility, *everything that happens is, in terms of its relation, determined* by me *in time as such*. Therefore apprehension in such an event, and hence the event itself, is subject—as regards possible perception—to the concept of the *relation of effects and causes*; and thus it is in all other cases. (B162–63)

The two states of the water (fluidity and solidity) could not be connected to one another in time unless I synthesized those two states, relating my current experience to a previous experience. But Kant has already shown in the first part of the Transcendental Deduction that this synthesis can occur only through the application of certain *a priori* rules. In this case, the current state is taken to be the effect of a previous state and the cause of a future state. I anticipate the future state through the productive imagination, and this anticipation is made possible by applying the category of causality. Time is only given determinately through the relation of perceptions according to the categories.

Because we know (from the Transcendental Aesthetic) that space and time are formal conditions for the possibility of experience (and intuitions in any experience), and because we know that conceptual unity is necessary for things to appear determinately in space and time, we know that conceptual unity is a condition of our kind of sensible intuition—that is, for spatiotemporal consciousness. For different perceptions to be related in space and time, they need to be related by some objectivity rules; for example, a thing that takes up a certain space needs to be distinguished by the concept of magnitude, and particular events temporally related need to be related through the concept of causality. To see a house as a spatially distinct object (sensible unity) and to see the shape of the house as a magnitude (intellectual unity) are two aspects of the same unity. To see water and ice before and after in time (sensible unity) and to see the first event as causing the second (intellectual unity) are two aspects of the same unity. In order to see determinate things in space and time, we need to make conceptually informed judgments. Therefore, the categories are conditions for the possibility of a spatiotemporal manifold; or, as Kant phrases it, "the categories contain the bases, on the part of the understanding, of the possibility of all experience as such" (B167).[27]

The Schematism

At this point, Kant has shown that objective experience is possible only when the sensible manifold is synthesized according to the pure concepts of the understanding. Kant spends the next chapter of the Transcendental Analytic explaining how the categories are applied to sensible intuitions, given that they are such different things. In other words, how do we apply *a priori* concepts to what is given to us *a posteriori*? This strikes Kant as a problem that needs to be solved:

> Whenever an object is subsumed under a concept, the presentation of the object must be *homogeneous* with the concept. . . . Pure concepts of understanding, on the other hand, are quite heterogenous from empirical intuitions (indeed, from sensible intuitions generally) and can never be encountered in any intuition. How, then, can an intuition be *subsumed* under a category, and hence how can a category be *applied* to appearances . . . ? (A137/B176–A138/B177)

The understanding and sensible intuition contribute very different elements to experience. Yet to understand something means that we make use of a concept with regard to what is given to us spatiotemporally. So, Kant asks, how are concepts given content through the senses?

Again, some critics claim that such an explanation is superfluous. Kant has already shown that a spatiotemporal manifold must be organized according to the categories. Indeed, the Transcendental Deduction (especially §§24–26) has as its primary purpose to break down the strict division between sensible intuition and the categories. Having already shown *that* they go together, it seems unnecessary to understand *how* they do. As in the A Deduction, Kant seems to be formulating nothing more than a psychological thesis.

Kant's worry, however, is that skepticism could creep in about how the categories are applied. It is not enough to understand what a concept means. For the concept to be constitutive of experience, we also need to know how the concept is related to intuition. As noted in Chapter 2, I may understand the concept of a triangle as a three-sided figure, and I may know how to use the word 'triangle' in a sentence, but it is quite another thing to be able to recognize a triangle presented to me in experience or to be able to construct a triangle in accordance with this concept. In this part of the *Critique*, then, Kant introduces a third element, a faculty whereby the understanding and sensibility are brought together: "If the understanding as such is explicated as our power of rules, then the power of judgment [*Urteilskraft*] is the ability to *subsume* under rules, i.e., to distinguish whether something does or does not fall under a given rule . . . " (A132/B171). Judgment is the mental capacity to put together concepts and intuitions, and it does so by means of what Kant calls "schemata."

Kant explains it as follows: Concepts provide us with the criteria whereby individual objects are distinguished and related according to perceived marks. When these marks are recognized, we connect them in certain ways, according to the *a priori* rules for the unification of sensible intuitions—that is, according to the categories. This is clear enough. However, simply having such a rule is not sufficient for understanding how experience is brought under this rule. There must be a talent for applying the rule, and this talent must be independent from the rule itself. Otherwise, there would have to be a rule for its application, a rule for how to follow the rule for its application, and so on *ad infinitum* (which would not make sense). The imagination (as the faculty of judgment) helps us to relate the general rule with particular instances by recognizing similarities among intuitions. The work of judgment is thus to apply concepts to the world. To have synthetic *a priori* knowledge, the mind must judge in a way that is not explained by the manifold or by the concept, or by both together. The concepts must be applied to the manifold in order for us to make substantive claims about objects. This requires an interpretation, an act of judgment, using schemata that allow the imagination to synthesize intuitions over time.

In keeping with his attempt to formulate a systematic account of how the understanding functions—and he is nothing if not systematic!—Kant lists the schemata that correspond to the different kinds of judgments and the different categories (quantity, quality, relation, and modality). For example, an affirmative judgment corresponds to the category of reality, which is related to the manifold schematically as a filling up of time (A143/B182). In other words, we judge that something is real by recognizing its persistence over time. A hypothetical judgment corresponds to the category of causality, which is related to the manifold schematically as a necessary succession (A144/B183). Different events are given to sensible intuition, and the imagination brings them together both by synthesizing them as a succession of events and by judging them to be a necessary succession under the category of causality. In this way, the schema of necessary succession forms the third element that bridges the gap between the intuition and the concept. Sensations are unified as successive events within a spatiotemporal manifold, and these events are judged to be necessarily related according to the category of causality, but this is possible only because of a transcendental schema "that must be homogeneous with the category, on the one hand, and with the appearance, on the other hand, and that thus makes possible the application of the category to the appearance" (A138/B177). Kant has already demonstrated that objective claims about the world are possible only according to the categories and that the categories include the concept of causality and dependence (cause and effect). With the Schematism, he demonstrates that the categories are modes of human time-consciousness and that, therefore, even our perception of successive events requires that they be causally related.

The Pure Physiological Table of the Universal Principles of Natural Science

After addressing the problem of how the categories are related to the sensible manifold, Kant goes on to specify rules for their application to experience. These "synthetic principles of pure understanding"— "synthetic principles" because they tell us something about experience, beyond what is discovered merely by analyzing the concept itself, and "of pure understanding" because they are schematized versions of the categories—determine how things must appear to us in time (A158/B197). Kant lists these principles systematically in what he calls elsewhere the "pure physiological table of the universal principles of natural science" (Pro 303), a third table that corresponds to the table of logical functions and the table of categories (A161/B200). With the table, Kant claims to give a complete list of the kinds of *a priori* ("pure") principles that must be assumed in any scientific investigation ("universal principles of natural science") into nature or the physical world ("physiological"). (See Figure 4.3.) Comparing the three tables shows that the concepts they list become progressively less abstract. The table of logical functions lists the forms of thinking in general, the table of categories lists the categories that are relevant to experience, and the pure physiological table of the universal principles of natural science lists the concepts as they are relevant to our kind of sensible experience (in space and time).

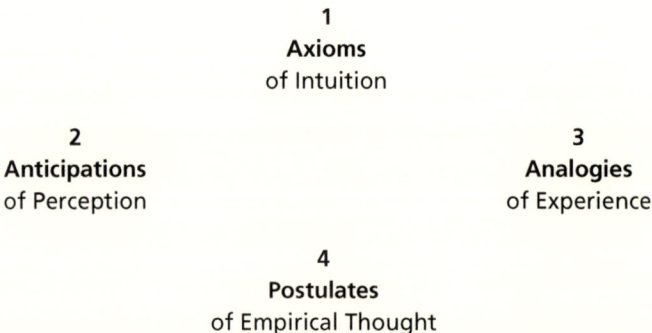

1
Axioms
of Intuition

2
Anticipations
of Perception

3
Analogies
of Experience

4
Postulates
of Empirical Thought

FIGURE 4.3 The pure psychological table of the universal principles of natural science (A161/B200)

Kant organizes the universal principles of natural science into four kinds of principles, corresponding to the four groups of categories: quantity, quality, relation, and modality. Corresponding to the categories of quantity are the Axioms of Intuition, according to which a plurality of appearances must be synthesized over time into *"extensive magnitudes,"* or unified objects of intuition (A162/B202). Corresponding to those of quality are the Anticipations of Perception, which allow the imagination literally to anticipate the *"intensive magnitude"* of appearances as they are given to us, that is, to make it possible for us to perceive them as real and persisting over time (A166/B207). This is where we assign things degrees of reality: real, nothing, or in the process of coming to be or disappearing. Corresponding to the categories of relation are the Analogies of Experience, which connect appearances as causally related instances of a permanent substance (A176/B218). The final principles, the Postulates of Empirical Thought, correspond to the categories of modality, but they are different from the other three in that they govern not only how appearances are related to one another but how they are related to the knowing subject. Possible experiences or empirical concepts are consistent with the formal conditions of experience (the forms of sensible intuition, the categories, and the Analogies of Experience), actual experiences are given sensations received according to these formal conditions, and necessary experiences are those that must follow actual experiences, given what our judgement requires of the world (A218/B265–66). A deeper treatment of the first *Critique* would explore all of these different principles in more detail, but Kant's discussion of the Analogies of Experience is the clearest and most interesting. For our purposes, focusing on them will allow us best to understand this particularly difficult section of the book.

The Analogies of Experience

When Kant discusses the Analogies of Experience, he is using the term *Analogie* more or less in its traditional sense. An analogy compares two things that are otherwise different, usually to imply something that is not immediately evident. Kant probably had mathematical analogies in mind. Such analogies use ratios to discover missing terms. For example, the mathematical analogy 'six is to twelve as eight is to x' allows us to discover that the value of x is sixteen. The Analogies of Experience similarly dictate how our experiences are related to one another. According to the Second Analogy (which I discuss below), every event must be related to another event as an effect is related to its cause. Because of this, we are justified in expecting certain future events on the basis of what has happened in the past. The Analogies of Experience are thus at the heart of Kant's proposed solution to the problem of induction, because here he explains why our perceptions must be causally related in order for experience to be coherent.

First Analogy: Principle of the Permanence of Substance

Kant has already shown that a representation must be located in time in order to exist as an object for us. He has also shown that its persistence as an identical thing through time is only possible because we organize our representations according to the categories. Here Kant lists three Analogies, corresponding to the three categories of relation, by which we associate our experiences and warrant our expectations about what will happen next. The First Analogy concerns inherence and subsistence and dictates that "*in all variation by appearances substance is permanent, and its quantum in nature is neither increased nor decreased*"; that is, matter is neither created nor destroyed in any chemical reaction (A182/B224).[28] Kant claims that this is a pure principle. We know this *a priori*, because it is necessary for our experience to make sense.

Secondary materials on Kant disagree about how to interpret his arguments for the Analogies of Experience, and many think that they are hopelessly confused. They are certainly confusing to Kant's readers. But here he seems to have something like this in mind: Events happen along one time line. Objects that coexist do so in the same (singular) time, and other objects appear either earlier or later in relation to that time. There are not separate times, but one time in which all material things exist and all physical events take place. Kant demonstrates as much in the Transcendental Aesthetic. This permanent time forms the backdrop against which things change and affect one another. Without this unchanging element of our experience, we would never be able to relate different events, because they would appear at different, distinguishable times. We know, for example, that the Chicago Cubs last won the World Series (1908) before Neil Armstrong walked on the moon (1969) because both events can be located on the same time line.

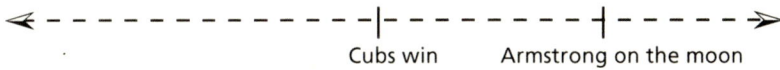

Cubs win   Armstrong on the moon

It is hard for us to imagine, because it contradicts the form of our sensible intuition, but if there were self-contained times within which events happened, one event would not occur before the other. They would occur at different times, but the two times could not be related.

Cubs win   Armstrong on the moon

For events to be relatable, there must be some persisting field within which they can be situated. However, "time cannot in itself be perceived"—we do not see or hear time—so there must be something besides time that allows us to relate different events in time (A183/B226). This is the key point. Duration over time is possible only if there is a "*substratum* of the empirical presentation of time itself*" (A183/B226). In other words, we can relate successive events only if there is some permanent element within which changes take place over time. We know that, in order to have a coherent experience, we must be able to relate successive events. Therefore, there must be a permanent substratum, and such a substratum is traditionally called substance. So, Kant shows that if we apply the categories to our experience in space and time, we must assume that there is an underlying, permanent substance in order to make sense of experience—specifically, how different events are related in time.

The argument of the First Analogy is very important for positioning Kant in the history of early modern philosophy. Kant has demonstrated that objects are composed of a substance that under-lies all existing things, which seems to accord with common sense, Locke's appeal to primary qualities, and the claims of Newtonian science. This also distinguishes his position from Berkeley's ideal-ism and overcomes Hume's skepticism. There are things that persist whether or not they are being perceived. Indeed, such things are a condition of our perceiving objects at all. Kant's position is thus a form of realism.

However, the substance that is a condition of experience (over time) is not to be strictly distinguished from what the senses give us, as such diverse figures as Descartes and Hume had claimed. The perma-nent substance is not the thing in itself but results from a judgment that the physical objects we experience—that is, phenomena—must in principle be distinguished from those qualities that change based on the particular perceiver. Considered empirically, Kant's distinction echoes Locke's distinction between primary and secondary qualities, but we must remember that, considered transcendentally, even the ob-jects themselves are mere appearances. A permanent substance is a condition for the possibility of temporal relations, but that substance is the result of our application of an *a priori* principle—specifically, the First Analogy of Experience—to the sensible manifold and thus is only an appearance.

Second Analogy: Principle of Temporal Succession According to the Law of Causality

The Second and Third Analogies are closely related: The former principle (concerning causality and dependence) demands that every event be caused by a prior event, and the latter principle (concerning community) demands that all events be related not only to a prior event but to a future event as well. More generally, the upshot of the Third Analogy is that all natural events are related in a web of causal relationships. As we will see, the proof of this claim depends on the proof of the Second Analogy, which will receive our fuller attention. The Second Analogy is very important, because it explains how causal claims follow necessarily from our kind of time-consciousness. This is Kant's most direct response to the problem of induction.

The Second Analogy asserts that the world is governed by natural laws: "*all changes occur according to the law of the connection of cause and effect*" (B232). For every change in the world, for everything that happens—either the creation of an object or the alteration of an already-existing object—that change follows necessarily from some prior state. If a bridge collapses, something had to have caused it to collapse; given the existence of some prior event—for example, the tremors of an earthquake, which put too much stress on the structure—its collapse had to follow.

Kant argues for the Second Analogy by reminding us of what he has already demonstrated in the Transcendental Deduction—namely, that apperceptive unity is a condition for the possibility of experience. As we saw there, for a coherent experience to be possible, rather than merely separate and unrelated events, there must be an "I think" that accompanies all of my representations. And for there to be an apperceptive subject, I must be able to distinguish subjective perceptions from objective representations. The categories are the *a priori* rules that allow us to do so. Here, in his argument for the Second Analogy, Kant extends this to a consideration of time-consciousness: We must distinguish objective from subjective succession over time, and we can do this only because of the category of cause and effect. Only such an *a priori* rule allows us to distinguish subjective association from causal necessity. Therefore, we must presuppose the Second Analogy if experience is to be possible.

To make his case, Kant uses the example of a ship traveling downstream (A192/B237). I perceive it first upstream, then downstream, and I could not have perceived it otherwise. This is in contrast to my perception of a particular object, like a house, the parts of which I may perceive in any order: from the basement to the roof or from the roof to the basement, from right to left or from left to right (A192/B237–38). Here I am taking in one object over time, and the order in which I perceive its parts is not determined in any way. But when I perceive a succession (or change) of events in time, the order of my perceptions is constrained: "this rule is always to be found, and through it the order of the perceptions succeeding one another (in the apprehension of this appearance) is made *necessary*" (A193/B238).

When one billiard ball hits another one and makes it roll along the table, I could not have perceived the motion of the second ball before the motion of the first. When I watch the ship, I can see it downstream only after I have seen it upstream. There is a certain necessary order to the succession of these appearances. But necessity cannot be derived *a posteriori* from our experience of things. I am making a judgment about my perceptions of the ship that I am not making about my perceptions of the house. Beyond the mere succession of perceptions, I must relate my perceptions in time according to an *a priori* rule. The movement of the second billiard *must* occur after the first one hits it. Experiencing them in this way depends on my applying the categories to the events.

The necessary succession cannot result from the nature of things themselves. As noted earlier, appealing to the object itself in order to explain how our various perceptions are united begs the question; for us to make such a claim about the object, we must already be representing it synthetically. Similarly here, we must judge two events to be necessarily related if we are to make an objective, causal claim, beyond how we associate events subjectively. Necessity cannot be derived merely from the empirical apprehension of objects. Hume has demonstrated as much. But we must relate our perceptions in certain ways if we are to experience one event as effecting the other. How are such causal relationships possible?

At this point, Kant reminds us that objects are sensible intuitions synthesized according to *a priori* rules. In other words, objects result from our making judgments about what is given to us through sensation. Part of our representing an event in the world as a particular thing involves our distinguishing it from those prior times when it did not exist. Given the conclusions of the Transcendental Aesthetic, the event becomes possible for us as an object of experience only by setting it in the context of a certain time. It is a particular thing because it exists at this particular time, *after* the events that preceded it: "when I perceive that something occurs, then this presentation contains, first, [the presupposition] that something precedes; for precisely by reference to this preceding something does the appearance acquire its time relation, viz., its existing after a preceding time in which it was not" (A198/B243). When I see a billiard ball roll across the table, it can be an object for me only if it is situated in time. And if it is situated in time, then it is represented as happening now, in contrast to the events that came before.

This is where we see an important illustration of why the categories are necessary for objectivity claims. If I am to get beyond merely subjective representations—"I feel heat; I see copper expand"—then I must think that my representations occur in a certain temporal order *necessarily*. I could just as easily see the copper expand before noticing the change in temperature, but to make the objective claim that heat makes copper expand, I must order my perceptions according to a rule of irreversibility:

> how is it that in addition to the subjective reality that they have as modifications [of the mind], we also attribute to them who knows what sort of objective reality? . . . Suppose that we inquire what new character is given to our presentations by the *reference to an object*, and what is the dignity that they thereby obtain. We then find that this reference does nothing beyond making necessary the presentations' being combined in a certain way and being subjected to a rule; and we find, conversely, that only through the necessity of a certain order in the time relation of our presentations is objective signification conferred on them. (A197/B242–43)

Objective representations are possible only if the succession of events is taken to be necessary. Yet Kant and Hume both have shown that such necessity cannot be derived from experience. The events must be organized according to an *a priori* rule—namely, the category of causality—that makes objectivity possible. Of course, we cannot determine *a priori* any particular cause of a particular event, but we can know *a priori*, as a condition for the possibility of experience (beyond merely subjective associations), that every event has a cause.

Third Analogy: Principle of Simultaneity According to the Law of Interaction or Community

Kant's argument for the Third Analogy, which deals with mutual causality among coexisting things, is a bit harder to reconstruct and is more problematic than either of the first two. He seems to say that if there were no reciprocal influences among objects, then they would be isolated from one another and separated by empty space. But this would preclude objective experience, because we would be unable to relate our successive perceptions of things. In order to represent objects as coexisting in space—that is, as objective things, apart from my subjective perceptions—I must be able (over time) to pass from one thing to another through a continuous series of perceptions: "Without community every perception (of appearance in space) would be severed from any other; the chain of empirical presentations—i.e., experience—would begin entirely anew with each new object, and the previous chain could not in the least cohere with it or stand to it in a time relation" (A213/B260–A214/B261). For object A and object E to coexist, I must move from A to B to C to D to E over successive moments. Without such a continuous series, there would be empty space between A and E, and I could only have a perception of A and a subsequent perception of E, without being able to relate them. I see the roof of a house, then the upper story, the lower story, and the basement. Through this progression, I can recognize that the roof and the basement coexist. But if the two perceptions (of the roof and the basement) were not united by other perceptions between them, I would have no way to relate them as coexisting things. They would be merely different perceptions. Therefore, given the argument of the Second Analogy—that a succession of representations must be related causally if they are to constitute objective experience—every coexisting event must be connected causally to every other event in a relation of "*thoroughgoing interaction*" (B256).

With the Analogies of Experience, Kant is giving us the beginnings of what he calls a metaphysics of nature, the *a priori* foundation of Newtonian mechanics (A841/B869). He is also directly responding to previous philosophers' characterizations of the world. The Second Analogy is clearly an answer to Hume. Every event must have a cause if we are to have objective experience, as opposed to merely the subjective play of appearances. The Third Analogy counters Leibniz's contention that causal relations among individual substances is impossible.

But the First Analogy is particularly important in the section that follows, in which Kant differentiates his brand of idealism from the positions of Descartes and Berkeley.

The Refutation of Idealism

Kant calls himself a transcendental idealist, and he is at pains to distinguish that position from "*problematic* idealism," which he attributes to Descartes, and "*dogmatic* idealism," which he attributes to Berkeley (B274). For Descartes, the most certain thing is my existence as a thinking thing. Objects in general can be derived logically from the existence of God as a nondeceiver, but the existence of any specific object is always dubitable, because we can never know with certainty that a particular sensation actually corresponds to a particular object. Berkeley goes beyond this to claim that the very concept of material objects is self-contradictory; there is nothing that can be characterized completely independently of our perception of it. Thus he denies the existence of mind-independent objects and claims instead that all objects are merely subjective ideas that we take to be regularly related. Kant worried that his readers would wrongly equate his transcendental idealism with the positions of Descartes and Berkeley. This fear was not unfounded. Many people still interpret Kant as something of a Berkeleyan idealist. But Kant neither denies nor doubts the existence of external objects.

As we saw, Kant shows with the First Analogy of Experience that there must be some permanent substance (within which changes take place) if we are to relate successive events in time. Because time itself cannot be perceived, and because we must be able to relate successive events in order to have coherent experience of the world, a condition for the possibility of experience is a permanent substratum that underlies apparent change. Therefore, in order for us to have experience at all, we must perceive objects as instances of this substance, outside of us, or intuited in space.

Kant is thus not a dogmatic (or Berkeleyan) idealist, because my having experience at all depends on there being things distinguishable from my perception of them. He is also not a problematic idealist, because the external world is no more doubtful than the existence of the I. Indeed, as Kant shows in the Transcendental Deduction, in order to have a series of related perceptions, they must be held together by a unified apperceptive subject; and in order for such a subject to be possible, I must be able to distinguish my subjective perceptions from what is the case objectively. The *cogito* is possible only if I have the direct experience of an external world that I set in opposition to the "I think." Thus Kant argues for the existence of external objects: as a condition of our experience of successive events and as a condition of a unified subject that is capable of having such an experience.

What Is True If the World Is Merely an Appearance?

Some people find Kant's "Refutation of Idealism" less than satisfying. We are used to thinking that we truly experience reality when we perceive it as it actually is, apart from how we or anyone else happens to take it in. However, the Copernican turn transforms how we understand the world. The world is merely an appearance for consciousness. Kant says that conceiving of our perceptions in objective terms is enough to demonstrate that there is a world out there, but this is not what we usually mean when we talk about objects. Kant may have demonstrated that this kind of (transcendental) realism is mistaken, but it is unclear what it means for an empirical claim to be true if we can know things only as they appear to us. If knowledge is possible—and Kant insists that only his philosophy can show how knowledge is possible, by validating synthetic *a priori* judgments—then it cannot involve correspondence to mind-independent reality. But what is the alternative? If Kant is right, what does it mean to say that an empirical claim is true?

Because experience involves making judgments about our perceptions, the short answer is that an empirical claim is true when we make the right judgment. Such a circular explanation is clearly unsatisfactory. Kant says that objective cognition must accurately reflect the world as it is, but this is indicated by consensus: "Truth . . . rests on agreement with the object; consequently, in regard to the object, the judgments of every understanding must be in agreement" (A820/B848). In other words, a claim is true if it reflects what actually exists, and people agree with the claim because of its correspondence to the object. Anyone in the same position must make the same judgment that I do or else be mistaken. Kant describes this in terms of the difference between conviction (*Überzeugung*) and mere assent (*Fürwahrhalten*, literally "considering-true"). To have conviction, we must believe that what we are claiming is true, *and* it must in fact be true.

As an example, Kant considers the judgment that a body is heavy. The 'is' here marks it as a claim about the world, that heaviness and the body are related to one another in the object. Rather than merely associating these qualities subjectively—I lift it, then feel the pressure of heaviness—my representation corresponds to qualities possessed by the thing itself. My perceptions of the body and its heaviness "are combined in the object" rather than merely in my particular consciousness (B142). This is why publicity is a characteristic of objective claims. If these qualities correspond to qualities had by the object, then the unity of these perceptions is "necessary and universally valid" for everyone (B140; see also Pro 298). Kant does not ascribe to the so-called consensus theory of truth, according to which whatever is agreed upon is true. Instead, people agree only because we live in a world of shared objects to which our judgments must correspond. This is a correspondence theory of truth.

There is a problem with Kant's explanation, however: Because we can never know things in themselves, we have nothing outside of our experience to compare our judgments to. Therefore, even if Kant demonstrates that we must use concepts in organizing sensible intuitions and that we must regard some of our experiences as perceptions of external things, one may object that it is impossible to know if we are applying the concepts correctly. This question plagued Kant's predecessors as well as Kant himself, who posed this as one of philosophy's fundamental questions: "What is the ground of the relation of that in us which we call 'representation' to the object?"[29] Kant answers this with the Copernican turn. However, given the limits of human cognition, we can never in principle compare the world that we organize according to the categories (that is, the world as an appearance) against the thing in itself. That led philosophers like Hegel to claim that Kant has deprived us of truth altogether and relegated us to mere opinion: "This is like attributing to someone a correct perception, with the rider that nevertheless he is incapable of perceiving what is true but only what is false."[30] The correspondence between our representation and the object can be known, but that is because the object *is* a representation. We can never know how our representation of the object is related to the object as it is in itself—whether it is accurate or true, or whether those terms even make sense given our inability to conceptualize the thing in itself.

Thus there is a tension between Kant's transcendental idealism and his empirical realism. Kant is at once saying that any experience involves intuitions (in space and time) and concepts, and he is saying that the world is not illusory because there is a mind-independent world, a thing in itself, that gives the material of cognition to us. However, Kant cannot make any such (realist) claims because of the limits of our cognition. The only thing we have to work with is the world as it appears to us. Therefore, we can never know what is true about the world itself, or even if there is such a thing apart from consciousness.[31]

One traditional response to such an all-encompassing skepticism is that we often do distinguish between the correct and incorrect use of concepts. If I point out a desk in the classroom, all of the students would agree that there is a desk there. Someone who disagrees may not see it from his vantage point, he may have forgotten to wear his glasses, or he may be hallucinating because of lack of sleep. But that means that we can explain his failure to see it. He did not see the desk even though there is a desk there.

The possibility that all of our experiences are false would mean that everyone is deceived even under ideal conditions. There would be no way to tell when someone is mistaken. But if there is no way to distinguish between the proper and improper use of concepts in principle, then there is no distinction to be made. An illusion makes sense only in opposition to a veridical experience. The idea of a universal illusion is nonsense.

Therefore, to show that we are able to make true claims, Kant does not need to rule out the possibility that nothing exists and that all of our claims are false. He only needs to show that there are better and worse judgments to be made, better and worse ways of applying the concepts to reality as it appears to us. And that does not depend on some view from nowhere from which we compare our judgments to the thing in itself. It depends only on public agreement within a common theoretical framework and on a shared world against which to test our empirical judgments.

Phenomena and Noumena

Although Kant asserts the existence of things apart from human consciousness, his empirical realism does not commit him to transcendental realism, the view that we know things as they are in themselves. The substance that Kant describes in the First Analogy is not the Lockean thing, a bearer of primary qualities that roughly corresponds to our ideas of it. According to Kant's transcendental idealism, we do perceive objects, but only subject to our conditions of experiencing them. In a transcendental sense, then, the objects that stand behind our changing perceptions are themselves appearances. Remember the example of the rainbow in Chapter 3. Things are given to us in certain ways, subject to certain epistemic conditions— namely, the pure forms of sensible intuition and the categories. That means that we can never know things as they are apart from these conditions. As Kant phrases it, we can only know phenomena and never noumena:

> certain objects as appearances are called by us beings of sense (phenomena), because we distinguish the way in which we intuit them from the character that they have in themselves. But if this is so, then our concept of beings of sense already implies that these objects regarded in that character (even if we do not intuit them in that character)—or, for that matter, other possible things that are not objects of our senses at all—are, as it were, contrasted by us with the beings of sense, viz., as objects thought merely through understanding, and that we may therefore call them beings of the understanding (noumena). (B306)

Although it should be fairly clear by now what phenomena are—objects as they are understood under transcendental idealism, as appearances— Kant claims that there is a fundamental ambiguity regarding the concept of a noumenon. Considered in a negative sense, noumena are identical with things in themselves, and Kant often uses the terms synonymously (see Pro 312). It is whatever things are apart from space, time, and the pure concepts of the understanding. For us, who can only experience the world under these conditions, it is merely "an unknown something" (A256/B312).

If a being were capable of intuiting things non-sensibly, however, then such a being could understand noumena in a positive sense (B307). For example, God knows things as they are in themselves. God does not have to look around like we do to know what is going on. He is not subject to the conditions of space and time, so he does not have a particular perspective. Instead, God perceives things immediately through thought. He has the capacity for what Kant calls "intellectual intuition" (directly intuiting things in themselves) and "divine intuition" (producing things through thinking alone, rather than receiving them). Kant uses the Greek/Latin terminology here for a reason. 'Noumena' literally means things that are thought or things accessible only to thought, as opposed to 'phenomena', things that appear or things as they are seen. Objects as they are known by a divine being are noumena, because God intuits things intellectually, not sensibly.[32]

We are not gods, so our knowledge is restricted to things as they appear to us through the senses—in space and time, and subject to the categories. As Kant shows in the Transcendental Aesthetic, space and time are inapplicable beyond things as they appear to us. And because "the categories have signification only in reference to the unity of intuitions in space and time," they have no transcendental application; that is, they cannot be used to know things in themselves (B308). Therefore, we can never have knowledge of a noumenon, because doing so would make it no longer a noumenon; we would be subjecting it to the categories by which we make sense of spatiotemporal objects.

For us, then, noumena can be understood only in a negative sense, as things considered apart from our subjective conditions of knowing.

A noumenon in this sense is merely what we call the limit to what we can know, rather than a thing per se: "The concept of a noumenon is, therefore, only a *boundary concept* serving to limit the pretension of sensibility, and hence is only of negative use" (A255/B310–11). Kant says that the thing in itself can be *thought* through the categories, but any knowledge claims about noumenal entities necessarily transgress our epistemic limits. We can never represent such things in consciousness.

How the Transcendental Idealist
Conceives of *Vorstellungen*

The scope of what we can represent and the ways that perceptions become representations for us will be the key to Kant's analysis of metaphysics in the Transcendental Dialectic. In fact, understanding what Kant means by representation (*Vorstellung*) is central to understanding his entire theoretical philosophy, and at this point in our exposition, the philosophical import of the term should be clear. In the *Critique*, Kant identifies two kinds of conscious representations, or perceptions (*Perzeptionen* or *Wahrnehmungen*): A sensation (*Empfindung*) "refers solely to the subject, viz., as the modification of the subject's state," but a cognition (*Erkenntnis*) refers to objects (A320/B376). In the *Prolegomena*, Kant uses a slightly different vocabulary but essentially makes the same distinction, calling subjective associations "judgments of perception" and objective claims "judgments of experience [*Erfahrungsurteile*]" (Pro 297–305). Both sensations and cognitions are empirical claims, because they are about experience. But subjective perceptions are merely about what I feel or what I associate, without any claim to objectivity. For example, when I say that "the room is warm, sugar sweet, and wormwood nasty," I am describing internal states that you may not share (Pro 299). It is possible that the room seems cool to you, or that your taste is different from mine. But when I say that an earthquake caused the bridge to collapse, I am making an objective claim about the world. I am saying that this is how two events in the world are in fact related and that you must agree with me, or else be wrong. As we have seen, the ability to make such claims depends on organizing what I am given through the senses by means of the categories. Therefore, Kant says, both intuitions and concepts are species of the genus *Vorstellung*.

At A320/B376, Kant gives a detailed taxonomy of the different kinds of representations in order to clarify the term and eliminate confusion. (See Figure 4.4). Given everything that is involved in having a representation, understanding what Kant means by *Vorstellung* is arguably the key to understanding the entire *Critique*. Here we see the upshot of the Transcendental Deduction: Objective perceptions are the result of our bringing sensible intuitions to consciousness in a

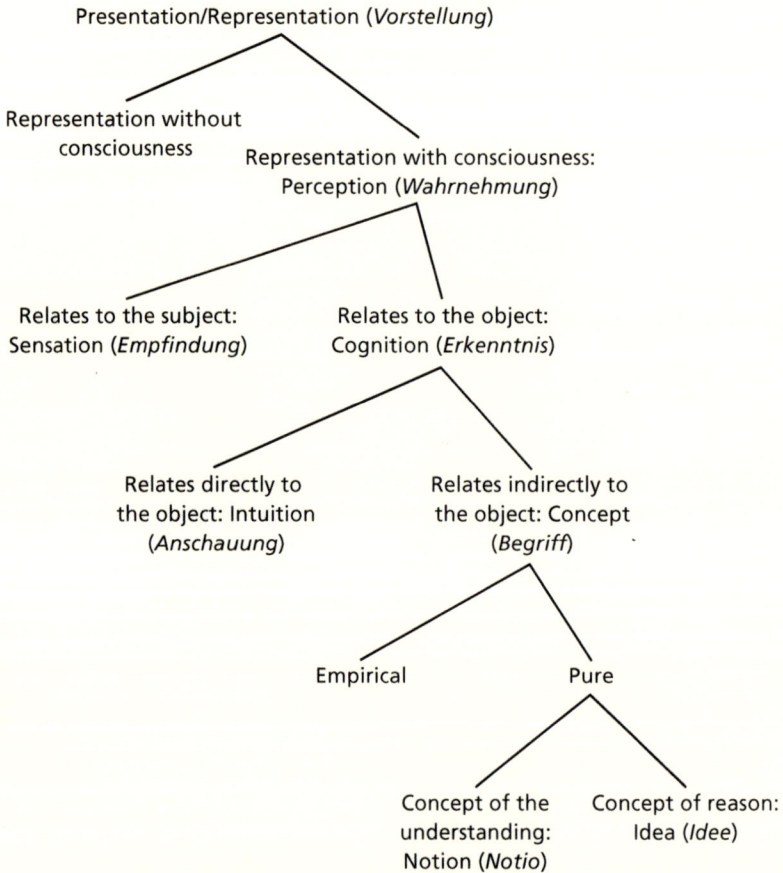

Figure 4.4 Kant's articulation of *Vorstellung*

rule-governed synthesis. We may also make empirical generalizations based on experience and represent a class of things to ourselves—for example, calling a particular animal a dog because of its relation to other dogs—but the representations that make such generalizations possible are the result of notions. And as we will see in the next chapter, dialectical illusions result from our making objective claims on the basis of ideas, or concepts of reason, rather than pure concepts of the understanding. Such mistaken applications of the categories are precisely what has led to groundless metaphysical speculation.

CHAPTER FIVE

The Transcendental Dialectic

HAVING ESTABLISHED the applicability and necessity of the categories for normatively governed experience, Kant can now address the kinds of questions that have plagued philosophy since its beginning and that have led to the confusion and aimlessness that he hopes to correct. Kant thinks that his conclusions regarding the basis of objectivity and the scope of human knowledge will allow him to explain our prior errors and to approach metaphysics in a new way:

> as soon as I had succeeded in solving Hume's problem, not merely in a particular case, but with respect to the whole faculty of pure reason, I could proceed safely, though slowly, to determine the whole sphere of pure reason completely and from universal principles, in its boundaries as well as in its contents. This was required for metaphysics in order to construct its system according to a sure plan. (Pro 260–61)

As Kant has demonstrated, things in themselves do not determine how we think about objects of experience. Even to be attended to as objects, intuitions need to be synthesized according to the categories. Because *a priori* concepts are conditions for the possibility of experience, however, our knowledge can extend only to nature as "the sum of all appearances," limited to experience subsumed under the categories (B163).

Kant's purpose, remember, is to make sense of how metaphysics is possible as a science. As we saw in Chapter 2, metaphysics consists of synthetic *a priori* claims, so he has been explaining how such claims are possible: They are possible because the world conforms to our way of understanding it (according to the categories) and our way of receiving it (in space and time). This is the Copernican turn in philosophy, and the result is transcendental idealism. We can only know things as they appear to us, because we can only make judgments of experience—that is, objective claims about the world—by using the categories.

Because the formal conditions of experience are applicable only to what is given to us through the senses, they do not apply to the supposed objects that transcend possible experience. This means that if we did apply the categories to things in themselves, we would be using them in the wrong way. Any such claims would be unjustified: "as soon as we leave this sphere, these concepts retain no meaning whatever" (Pro 315).

At this point, we can see why metaphysics has not made any progress: Metaphysical questions are solved only by going beyond the boundaries of experience, metaphysical claims are synthetic *a priori*, and the concepts used to make such claims are applicable only to experience. Therefore, given the conclusions of the Transcendental Aesthetic and the Transcendental Analytic, it is impossible to establish metaphysics as a science: "the proud name of an ontology that pretends to provide, in a systematic doctrine, synthetic a priori cognitions (e.g., the principle of causality) of things in themselves must give way to the modest name of a mere analytic of pure understanding" (A247/B303). In other words, previous metaphysicians had assumed that *a priori* judgments could elucidate the nature of mind-independent reality. Once Kant demonstrates that this is a misuse of the categories, we are left with nothing but an investigation into how the understanding represents things. The thing in itself is in principle unknowable.

So, at this point in the book, Kant comes back to his original question: "How is metaphysics possible as a science?" And he answers, "It's not." He has shown that all of the metaphysical speculation going on for thousands of years has just been a big mistake and that we cannot know the answers to such questions. This is why Heine called the *Critique of Pure Reason* an "executioner's sword." Metaphysics had been going along just fine—without making progress, of course, but with the belief that progress could be made—and Kant killed it. By explaining the basis and scope of synthetic *a priori* judgments, he demonstrates that we can never know whether there is a God, freedom, or immortality.

To be a science, a field of thought must be based on necessary first principles that are discoverable *a priori* and from which we can justify a system of beliefs that achieve rational consensus (see Bvii, B109, A832/B860, A849/B877–A850/B878). In other words, a science gives us the means by which certain questions can be answered. The fact that philosophy had not reached consensus on metaphysical questions reveals that a scientific path to certainty had not been reached. The *Critique* explains why: Synthetic *a priori* judgments cannot warrant metaphysical propositions. However, it has also shown how knowledge of the world is possible. It has shown us the *a priori* basis of objective claims—indeed, it has revealed the formal conditions that must be true of the world (as an appearance)—and thus has formed what Kant calls a metaphysics of nature: "The metaphysics of nature contains all pure principles of reason, based on mere concepts (hence excluding mathematics), of the *theoretical* cognition of all things" (A841/B869). Metaphysics as the inquiry into God, freedom, and immortality has given way in theoretical philosophy to metaphysics as a science that deals with the *a priori* concepts that are applicable to experience. This is the only metaphysics of which we are capable, at least in a theoretical sense.

Dialectical Illusion

Kant directly addresses metaphysical claims in the Transcendental Dialectic. In calling this a dialectic, Kant is drawing on Aristotle's distinction between demonstrative reasoning and dialectical reasoning, the latter of which uses apparently good argument forms but bases its premises on mere opinion. The purpose of such an argument is not necessarily to arrive at the truth but to convince people of the conclusion.[1] Like Aristotle, Kant focuses on judgments that seem convincing, but he does so in order to expose them as illusions. Specifically, Kant uncovers the false presuppositions on which seemingly good arguments for metaphysical claims are based, and he finds that they all make the same kind of mistake: applying the categories to things in themselves. Thus Kant defines dialectic as "a critique of understanding and reason as regards their hyperphysical use" (A63/B88).

If we cannot pursue metaphysics without transcending the limits of what we can know, why have philosophers endlessly occupied themselves with such questions? Kant says that despite these limits, we are led by the nature of reason itself to engage in metaphysical speculation—to discover the ultimate basis of what we perceive, or the unconditioned ground of the conditioned in experience. For example, if I were curious about the cause of a rock slide on the California coast, a scientist may tell me that it was caused by erosion. But what caused the erosion? The tides. And what causes the tides? The gravitational pull of the moon. What caused the moon? Probably a collision between the young earth and another large, planetary body. But what caused the planets and all of the things that were floating around then? The Big Bang. And what caused the Big Bang? We can go on and on, postulating causes indefinitely, but inevitably we have to wonder not what caused a particular event but how anything came to be in the first place. What is the cause of all of the events in the world, the totality of things that exist and affect one another? Must there have been an uncaused cause that began the process, or not?

Answers to these kinds of questions, about the totality of experience or the ultimate basis of what we know, are what Kant calls ideas (or concepts) of reason.[2] The categories of the understanding are only applicable to appearances. The problem is that asking about the totality of experience is not the same thing as asking about a particular event. Just as the baseball season, which contains all of the baseball games in a given year, is not itself a baseball game, "the absolute totality of all possible experience is itself not experience" (Pro 328). When reason tries to make sense of the totality of experience, that is different from asking how experience is possible in general, with regard to our sensible intuition of the world. Metaphysicians have been using the categories to solve the transcendent problems set out by reason.[3] The extension of those forms of thought to the totality of experience applies them beyond their proper sphere, to things in themselves, and results in dialectical illusion.

Kant claims that we make such improper inferences in three different ways, by misusing the three traditional forms of syllogistic inference—categorical, hypothetical, and disjunctive:

> There are likewise three kinds of syllogisms, each of which proceeds by prosyllogisms to the unconditioned: one proceeds to the subject that is itself no longer a predicate; another to the presupposition that presupposes nothing further; and the third to an aggregate of those members of a division which require nothing further in order to complete the division of a concept. (A323/B380)

A categorical proposition, with the form 'A is B,' concerns the relationship between subject and predicate. In its effort to discover the unconditioned basis of original apperception, reason commits itself to a kind of absolute subject that cannot be predicated of other things—the self as a substance or soul. A hypothetical proposition, with the form 'If A, then B,' concerns the relationship between a consequent and its antecedent. In its effort to discover the unconditioned basis of the history of particular events, reason commits itself to the existence of an absolutely first cause. A disjunctive proposition, with the form 'A or B,' concerns our ability to understand conceptual oppositions. In order to make such oppositions possible, reason commits itself to a singular basis for all of our concepts of things in general. On the basis of these syllogisms, three kinds of dialectical inferences follow:

> all transcendental ideas can presumably be brought under *three classes*, of which the *first* contains the absolute (unconditioned) *unity of the thinking subject*, the *second* the absolute *unity of the series of conditions of appearance*, the *third* the absolute *unity of the condition of all objects of thought as such*. (A334/B391)

The apperceptive subject, the class of natural events, and our concept of things in general prompt us to search for the unconditioned bases of all of these things. The ideas that arise from these faulty inferences are the claims that metaphysicians have made in the so-called sciences of psychology, cosmology, and theology. (See Table 5.1.)

Misused syllogism	Categorical (subject-predicate)	Hypothetical (if-then)	Disjunctive (either-or)
Misapplied category	Inherence and Subsistence	Causality and Dependence	Community
Branch of metaphysics	Psychology	Cosmology	Theology
Idea of reason	Immortal soul	Freedom	God
Transcendental illusion	Paralogism	Antinomy	Ideal of pure reason

Table 5.1 Classification of dialectical inferences

This probably sounds confusing. To put it more plainly, what is happening is that, in our attempt to answer the kind of ultimate metaphysical questions that haunt us—that is, in reason's attempt to discover the unconditioned—we commit ourselves to the existence of a soul, freedom, and God. Because of the limits to what we can know, however, we can never justify such theoretical claims. They are "transcendental illusions," which, although they are "natural and unavoidable," result from the misapplication of the categories to things in themselves (A297–98/B354). In the Transcendental Dialectic, Kant shows why reason cannot justifiably make these inferences and explains how these metaphysical questions ought properly to be addressed.

The Paralogisms

First Kant explains the Paralogisms of Pure Reason. Generally speaking, a paralogism is an instance of fallacious reasoning. In the Transcendental

Dialectic, Kant addresses transcendental paralogisms in particular, or cases where we draw invalid conclusions on the basis of a transcendental ground (A341/B399ff.). Kant claims that the "I think," which is a formal condition of experience, is erroneously used to justify metaphysical claims concerning the soul's substantiality, simplicity, identity, and relations. In each case, reason improperly brings this transcendental ground under a general rule (or category) that does not apply to it.

Here, for the first time, we get a clear sense of how Kant will attempt to reform metaphysics. Kant uses his conclusion concerning the limits of inner sense and its distinction from transcendental apperception to criticize rational psychology, which is typified by Descartes. As we saw in Chapter 4, Kant insists that for a complex of thoughts to be thought together (as a unified cognition), there must be a simple subject as its formal condition. But this is only a formal condition. The apperceptive I introduces a logical unity to our various perceptions, a subject that stands behind and combines sensible intuitions, but rational psychologists wrongly invest this with metaphysical significance:

> the formal proposition of apperception *I think* remains the whole basis on which rational psychology ventures to expand its cognitions. But this proposition is, of course, not an experience, but is the form of apperception. Although this form attaches to and precedes every experience, it must still always be regarded only as concerning a possible cognition as such, viz., as *merely subjective condition* of such cognition. (A354)

The apperceptive subject is a necessary condition for any experience, but by making claims about what the subject is in itself, rationalists misapply the categories beyond experience to a transcendental condition of experience. Apperception makes experience possible and thus cannot itself be an object of experience. It stands behind the categories rather than being subject to them.

Descartes's contention that the subject is a substance, for example, is true in one sense. According to Aristotle's influential definition, a substance is a kind of thing that is not simply a property of another thing; rather, things are predicated of it.[4] For example, we can say "The door looks open" but not "The table looks door." The door is a substance, so it can have characteristics; it is not itself a characteristic of another thing, as openness (which is not a substance) is. The apperceptive subject is like this in that it cannot be represented as the determination of another substance. However, Descartes wrongly takes this to be a metaphysical claim about what the subject is in itself. He concludes that the fact of my thinking intuitively implies my existence as an immaterial thinking thing. As a substantial being, I am the ground or basis of predication. Things can be true of me, but I cannot be true of other things.

In the Second Paralogism, Kant explains why, even though the apperceptive subject cannot be predicated of other things, we must reject Descartes's inference to the I's substantiality. As a condition of experience, the "I think" can never be an object of experience: "This *presentation* is a *thought,* not an *intuition*" (B157). We can think about the metaphysical basis of the "I think" through the pure concepts of the understanding, because there is no other way we can think about it. All of our thinking is necessarily bound by the categories, so just as a matter of course, we tend to talk about self-consciousness as a thing. However, such thinking can never have cognitive content, because the I as it is in itself—apart from our subjective conditions, including time—can never be intuited. We can know nothing about the soul, even whether there is such a thing, despite Descartes's claim to the contrary.

The Antinomies

As noted in Chapter 2, metaphysical speculation into the unconditioned also leads to a conflict within reason itself—specifically, the assertion of contradictory and apparently unresolvable positions. In the Antinomy of Pure Reason, Kant discusses four cosmological ideas (corresponding to the four titles of the categories) that lead to such a conflict: questions about whether the world has a beginning in time and boundaries in space (Quantity), whether there are simple parts in nature that cannot be further divided (Quality), whether there is a first (uncaused) cause of all things (Relation), and whether a necessary being (God) exists (Modality). In each case, reason attempts to discover the absolute ground of every hypothetical ('if x, then y') or causal ('x causes y') claim. It attempts to think the unconditioned condition of experience and, in doing so, affirms seeming contradictories—for example, that there are simple parts in nature *and* that everything is divisible.

If Kant has succeeded, transcendental idealism will allow us to resolve these problems. To see how it does so, we will focus once again on the Third Antinomy, which is particularly important for understanding how Kant addresses metaphysical questions in his practical philosophy. According to Kant, in questioning the basis of events in nature, reason comes to an impasse: Either events in nature are caused by an uncaused cause, a free act that begins the causal series; or every event in nature is caused by a previous, caused event, such that freedom is impossible. These two positions, which Kant labels the thesis and the antithesis, respectively, are seemingly irreconcilable, and there is an argument against each position that seems to support the other.

Defenders of the thesis claim that the causal connections that determine events in the world must have been initiated by an original cause, one that is absolutely free. To justify this position, they contend that the opposite position—the idea that all events must some prior cause—does not explain what it needs to explain. Scholars disagree about how to interpret the thesis argument, but Kant seems to be saying that if every event has a cause, then the cause of every event must fully explain the effect: "the law of nature . . . consists precisely in this: that nothing occurs without a cause sufficiently determined a priori" (A446/B474). Yet if every cause must also have a cause that preceded it (and so on *ad infinitum*), then there is no ultimate explanation for *any* event. An infinite regress of conditioned causes would not explain to us why this particular causal chain exists rather than some other. In short, a complete causal explanation that is supposed to make events intelligible actually makes it impossible to explain the series of causes and effects that led to this moment.

Think about it like this: A series of prior events has led to your sitting here right now, reading this book. If someone asks why you are reading this book, you may offer a causal explanation: You are reading because of your desire to learn, which was instilled in you by your parents, who were influenced by their parents, and so on, all the way back to the Big Bang, and all of the events that led up to that event. But if someone asks why that series of events occurred rather than some other, no explanation can be given. Things could just as easily have occurred differently, such that you were not reading, or you were not even born. But this would mean that no explanation can be given for why you are reading right now, because there is no explanation—no complete explanation—for the series of events taken as a whole. What is happening now is not "sufficiently determined" by prior events. We can always ask why a certain event came about, or what caused it, but not every event can be conditioned, because if this were so, the "why" question could never be answered in principle. This is one of the classic arguments for the existence of God, first formulated by Aristotle and later by Aquinas: There must be an "unmoved mover" or a "first cause."[5] And if there is such an unmoved mover, then there is at least one instance of free action, undetermined by any prior cause.

Defenders of the antithesis claim the contrary position, that freedom is impossible because every event in nature must follow necessarily from a prior event. If a supposedly unmoved mover causes something, why does it do so? To explain this action, we would have to refer to something that moved it to act; something must have caused it to actualize its potential. Indeed, the truth of this conclusion has already been demonstrated in the Transcendental Analytic. Objects of experience are subject to a rule-governed synthesis, and one of those rules is the category of causality. The idea of an uncaused cause contradicts the conditions for the possibility of experience—specifically, that every event has a cause—because such an absolutely free act "disrupts the guidance of rules that alone makes possible an experience having thoroughgoing coherence" (A447/B475). Something that is not caused by a preceding state does not make sense.

The thesis and antithesis are opposite views on the ultimate source of natural events, but it later becomes clear that Kant's overriding concern is how to reconcile the causal necessity required by theoretical reason (by which we achieve knowledge) with the capacity for free choice required by practical reason (by which we decide how to act). Although here Kant is considering a first cause of all things, a similar contradiction results when we consider human action as a particular case of uncaused causation *and* as part of a natural world that is governed by causal laws. How is it possible for us freely to decide how to act, even though everything in the world, including our actions, would seem to be the result of prior circumstances? According to the category of causality, determination by a prior cause is a condition of any possible experience, yet "if our will is not free . . . ; then the *moral* ideas and principles also lose all validity" (A468/B496). How can the belief in freedom, to which we are committed to our moral lives, be consistent with the belief that there is no such thing as a first cause? Proving the thesis would support the existence of a particular case of uncaused causation and would (at least) rule in the possibility of human freedom.

As we saw earlier, Kant hopes to establish a firm foundation for metaphysics to be advanced as a science. Yet even if Kant succeeds in proving the correctness of transcendental idealism, you may be wondering how this helps us to address metaphysical questions more successfully. If we can know things only as they appear to us, then how could we possibly understand God, human freedom, or the soul, none of which we can experience?

We necessarily ask metaphysical questions, but doing so has led to rampant speculation. The first step in setting metaphysics on the right path is to recognize the limits of human cognition. We cannot adjudicate among the different answers to these metaphysical questions by appealing to experience, because the questions themselves transcend our powers to know. In addition, we cannot draw metaphysical conclusions on the basis of *a priori* concepts, because such concepts apply only to possible experience. Kant's first step, then, is to rule out metaphysics as a kind of theoretical investigation. The objects of metaphysics cannot be objects of cognition.

As noted earlier in the chapter, this sounds like a failure. If Kant has succeeded in demonstrating the limits of our knowledge, he seems to have shown that these metaphysical questions are unanswerable. He has not helped us to advance at all, only to recognize our inability to advance. This is the "destructive, world-crushing thought" to which Heine referred.

But Kant's project also has the effect of resolving the conflict that reason has with itself. Considering the thesis and antithesis of the Third Antinomy to be contradictories depends on a realist presupposition: By maintaining the impossibility of an unconditioned cause of appearances, the antithesis dogmatically construes everything—both objects of experience as well as the thing in itself—to be subject to the category of causality. But under transcendental idealism, the categories are relevant only to nature as the sum of appearances. Within nature, all things must be caused. However, because the categories have a limited use, only with regard to appearances, then the concept of causal necessity is not applicable to things in themselves. Hence, the antinomy results from misapplying the categories.

Both the thesis and the antithesis can be affirmed if causal mechanism is referred to the empirical perspective (appearances) and freedom is ascribed to the intelligible perspective (the thing in itself). We can ultimately hold people responsible for what they do, but we can also explain their actions by looking at social, psychological, and physiological causes. Human action can be considered as causally determined insofar as it takes place in nature, but apart from such a consideration—that is, considered in itself, apart from the concept of causality—human action may be free. Therefore, the transcendental idealist concludes "that this antinomy rests on a mere illusion and that nature at least does *not conflict* with the causality from freedom" (A558/B586). Without contradiction, Kant can both assert that all natural events are causally determined *and* that freedom from prior empirical constraints is possible. Whether we are actually free, however, is beyond our capacity to know.

Of course, it is difficult to understand what it means to say that freedom and necessity are compatible. Kant scholars continue to debate this. According to the compatibilist interpretation, saying that freedom and necessity are compatible is the same thing as saying that, with human action, we can explain it in terms of natural causes, *or* we can also explain it as the result of a free choice. There are two different ways of considering events, as appearances or as things in themselves,

*or I could see a multi-dimensional, [illegible]
3-headed alien both outside of time & space,
but perception of me must be conditioned
by natural causality.*

so human actions (as events) are subject to causality when they are understood as appearances, and they are free when they are considered apart from the category of causality. For example, you can say that you attend college because of your upbringing and how it shaped your desires that motivated you to learn, *or* you can say you went to college because you decided to go. Both explanations are equally good. They are just approaching the action in different ways.

By contrast, according to the incompatibilist interpretation, actions are free only if they actually affect the world; free actions must actually change events as appearances. If we are free, our practical reasoning is undetermined by prior events, but it begins a chain of events in nature. So, for example, there is only one way to understand actions for which you are responsible: You decided whether to give in to your desires or to do what is right. As a thing in itself (a rational agent who stands apart from natural causes), you have an effect on yourself as an appearance (the actions of your body).

Although it is important to decide which interpretation is more plausible, for our purposes it is enough to know how Kant demonstrates that freedom and determinism are not inconsistent. Causal determinism is limited to the world as it appears to us, so it is at least conceivable that, as things in themselves, rational beings are free.

The Ideal of Pure Reason

Toward the beginning of this chapter, I mentioned that the three kinds of transcendental illusion result from mistaken categorical, hypothetical, and disjunctive inferences. The Second Paralogism, for example, results from wrongly claiming that the soul is a simple substance based on apperceptive unity as a formal condition of experience. The Third Antinomy results from assuming that an uncaused (free) cause must ultimately end the regress of conditional explanations. But how God is related to the disjunctive form of inference is not immediately clear.

A disjunctive proposition is simply an 'or' claim, such as 'Today is Wednesday or today is not Wednesday.' For every predicate—that is, for every quality that a thing can have—we know that either it or its contradictory is true of every substance that exists. For example, my dog is either brown or not brown. Mercury either is or is not the planet closest to the sun. Elvis is either alive or not alive. He cannot be both living and nonliving, because these predicates are contradictories; only one can be true of any particular thing.

Kant claims that negative predicates—nonbrown, not-closest-to-the-sun, nonliving—can be understood only if the positive predicates—brown, closest-to-the-sun, living—are understood: "no one can think a negation determinately without using as a basis the opposed affirmation" (A575/B603). So, when reason tries to conceive of "the possibility and thoroughgoing determination of all things"— that is, when it tries to understand how all existing things, which have at least some negative predicates, are possible—it must conceive of something that has all and only positive predicates (A575/B603). In other words, to understand things that are limited or are characterized by negative predicates, we must conceive of an unlimited something in terms of which our understanding of all the limited things is possible. I and everything in the world have some positive predicates, but because we are all finite, we also have some negative predicates. I know that I am imperfect, for example, because I pale in comparison with perfection. The concept of such a perfect being, with only positive predicates, without limitation, is the concept of God. Therefore, in order to understand the negative predicates that form half of every possible disjunction (concerning predicates), I must have a concept of God as an absolutely perfect being. God is an ideal of reason in the sense that God's existence depends on no other being—it is "determined thoroughly through itself"—and God is the source of all existing things—that is, all things to which we can apply predicates (A576/B604).[6]

On the basis of this concept alone, a number of philosophers have concluded that God must exist. In the Ideal of Pure Reason, Kant lists three kinds of arguments that metaphysicians have used to establish the existence of God—the ontological argument, the cosmological argument, and the argument from design—and he explains why such inferences can never legitimately be made. The most important argument, and the one that the other two depend on for support, is the ontological argument. We will focus our attention there.

The ontological argument for the existence of God was first formulated by Saint Anselm,[7] but it is also used by Descartes in the Fifth Meditation. There Descartes claims that because existence is a positive attribute, and because the concept of God is the concept of a perfect being, God must exist. If God did not exist, God would not be perfect, which is a contradiction:

it is quite evident that existence can no more be separated from the essence of God than the fact that its three angles equal two right angles can be separated from the essence of a triangle, or than the idea of a mountain can be separated from the idea of a valley. Hence it is just as much of a contradiction to think of God (that is, a supremely perfect being) lacking existence (that is, lacking a perfection), as it is to think of a mountain without a valley. (M 46)

The concept of God and the concept of a triangle are similar in that each includes certain predicates as part of its essence. The interior angles of every triangle must total 180 degrees, and God must be perfect. But they are dissimilar in that triangles may not exist, because existence is not part of the essence of a triangle. By contrast, God's essence includes his existence. Nonexistence is a lack, or a negative predicate that can be understood only in relation to the positive predicate of existence, so the very concept of God as a perfect being means that God necessarily exists. In short, because the idea of God is the idea of an absolutely perfect being, and because existence is a perfection, it is contradictory to think of God as nonexistent. And the opposite of any contradictory proposition must be true: God exists.

Kant mounts two related criticisms of the ontological argument based on his understanding of what it means to assert something's existence. First, Kant appeals to the analytic/synthetic distinction in order to challenge Descartes's claim that God's nonexistence is self-contradictory. As we know, the predicate of any analytic claim is implicit in the subject. 'All bachelors are unmarried males' is true because what it means to be a bachelor is to be an unmarried male; the proposition merely unpacks the meaning of the term ' bachelor'. By contrast, a synthetic claim adds to our understanding of the subject.

'Sam is a bachelor' tells us something new about Sam, and 'Every event has a cause' goes beyond the bare definition of what an event is. The two kinds of claims are clearly different: Analytic claims amount to tautologies, whereas synthetic claims expand on what we know.

In the main premise of the ontological argument, it is assumed that existing is part of what it means to be a perfect being, which would make 'A perfect being exists' analytic. However, such an existential judgment does not merely explicate what a perfect being is. Rather, it asserts that there is such a being. The assertion may or may not be true. Experience is necessary to determine whether something exists—that is, whether we ought to apply the category of reality to it (A373). Therefore, 'A perfect being exists' must be synthetic, because its truth-value is conditional on our experience of what is the case. Of course, Kant concludes that the question of whether God exists, like all metaphysical questions, is beyond the bounds of possible experience. We cannot know whether God exists. However, we can know that that the mere concept of a perfect being does not necessarily imply God's existence. Consequently, Descartes contradicts himself by treating a synthetic proposition as if it were analytic (A597/B625). He brings the concept of existence into the idea of God, thus casting 'A perfect being exists' as an analytic claim; and because existential judgments are not mere tautologies, he must also assert it as a synthetic statement of fact.

One characteristic of synthetic claims is that the predicate can be "annulled without contradiction" (A598/B626). To say that a bachelor is not an unmarried male is a contradiction in terms because of what it means to be a bachelor. However, denying that Sam is a bachelor is not uttering nonsense. It is simply false given the facts. Because 'A perfect being exists' is also synthetic, it may be true or false, but negating it cannot result in a contradiction. Therefore, even though God may exist, it is not necessarily the case that God exists.

Kant concedes that were there an absolutely perfect being, his existence would be necessary. However, the predicate in this case is conditional on the subject: *If* there were a God, denying his existence *would* result in a contradiction. If the subject were denied—if there were no God—then the predicate, his necessary existence, could also be denied:

> If in an identical judgment I annul the predicate and retain the subject,
> then a contradiction arises, and hence I say that the predicate belongs
> to the subject necessarily. But if I annul the subject along with the
> predicate, then no contradiction arises, for *nothing is left* that could be
> contradicted. To posit a triangle and yet to annul its three angles is
> contradictory; but to annul the triangle along with its three angles is
> not a contradiction. And with the concept of an absolutely necessary
> being the situation is exactly the same. If you annul the being's exis-
> tence, then you annul the thing itself with all its predicates. Whence,
> then, is the contradiction to come? (A594/B622–A595/B623)

The interior angles of any triangle must total 180 degrees. But that
does not mean that there ever was a triangle. *If* there is a triangle, *then*
its interior angles total 180 degrees. The predicate is conditional on
the subject. In the case of 'A perfect being exists,' we must accept
God's necessary existence if there is such a thing as God. In other
words, were God to exist, then he could not have come about contingently, as a result of the way the world happens to be. Rather, if God
exists, then he must always have existed and must be incapable of
nonexistence (death). If God exists, it would not make sense for such a
being not to exist. However, Kant says that we can without contradiction "annul the subject along with the predicate." Descartes merely
presupposed the existence of God and then "discovered" his necessary
existence in the concept of God. But if we deny that God exists from
the outset—if we reject Descartes's initial (unjustified) assumption
that God exists—then there is no such being whose nonexistence is
self-contradictory; everything exists only contingently. Thus we can
deny both that there is a God and that he exists necessarily.

Kant's second, better-known objection to the ontological argument
is to claim that existence is not a property of a thing: "*Being* is obviously not a real predicate. . . . it is merely the copula of a judgment"
(A598/B626). When I say that the door is open, I am adding to what
you know about the door and distinguishing it from closed doors. If I
say that the door does not exist, however, I am not telling you anything about the door, because there is no door. If I say instead that the
door does exist, I am still not telling you any of its properties. I am

merely saying that it is the kind of thing that can have properties. Because it exists, it may be open or closed, it is made of a certain material, it has a certain color, and so on. One cannot prove God's existence by saying that existence is a perfection, because it is not the sort of thing that can be a perfection. It is neither a perfection nor an imperfection, because it is not an attribute at all.

For these two reasons, the ontological argument fails. A thing's existence cannot be established by means of definitions—for example, 'God is a perfect being.' God may exist or may not exist, but we cannot deduce rationally that God necessarily exists. Instead, existence is a category that we apply to sensible intuitions, and using that concept to make claims about something that transgresses possible experience is misguided.

Making Room for Faith

Kant's transcendental inquiry into the conditions for the possibility of experience demonstrates that our knowledge is limited to things as they appear to us. In the Transcendental Dialectic, he shows that reason attempts to transgress this boundary by improperly applying the categories to metaphysical questions. We cannot know whether we have souls, whether we are free, or whether God exists in the same way we can know that the door is open or heat causes copper to expand. The former subjects are not matters of empirical cognition. Thus we cannot justify such claims theoretically; that is, they cannot be discovered empirically and cannot be derived rationally using the tools of the understanding. The negative project of the first *Critique* is to reveal these limitations to us.

By distinguishing phenomena from noumena, however, Kant has also provided for the possibility of things that are beyond our experience or that contradict natural laws:

> I cannot even *assume God, freedom*, and *immortality*, [as I must] for
> the sake of the necessary practical use of my reason, if I do not at the
> same time *deprive* speculative reason of its pretensions to transcendent

insight. . . . I therefore had to annul *knowledge* in order to make room for *faith*. (Bxxix–xxx)

With regard to freedom, for example, the *Critique of Pure Reason* has shown that nature is wholly governed by causal laws because it is synthesized by the understanding according to the categories. But causal necessity does not apply to things in themselves. Uncaused causation is possible apart from the categories. Kant's transcendental idealism thus resolves the antinomy of pure reason and allows for the compatibility of freedom and determinism.

Of course, this limitation on the applicability of the categories does not prove that we are in fact free. Theoretical reason cannot overstep its proper bounds. It can demonstrate only that God, freedom, and immortality are possible. However, it does serve an important positive role in spelling out how metaphysics ought to be approached: It "make[s] room" for the "practical use of my reason." In other words, Kant understands the world in terms that preclude certain kinds of metaphysical speculation, but this allows us to pursue metaphysics in a different way. Rationalists and empiricists who attempted to answer metaphysical questions not only extended concepts such as causality beyond their lawful employment (with regard to appearances) but addressed them as theoretical questions rather than practical questions.

The Domain of Practical Reason

Kant identifies two primary objects of philosophical investigation: "The philosophy of nature concerns everything that *is*, the philosophy of morals concerns only what *ought to be*" (A840/B868). Nature and morals are studied, respectively, by reason in its theoretical use and reason in its practical use. In the *Critique of Pure Reason*, Kant is investigating theoretical cognition (*Erkenntnis*)—that is, our experience of the world subject to our epistemic conditions.[8] As we have seen, any objective experience consists of our conceptually discriminating what is given to us in sensible intuition according to the pure concepts of the understanding. If we judge what we are given correctly, we have knowledge (*Wissen*) of the world, an experience that not only conforms to the concepts but to the way the world is. It is not only something I believe but something that is verified by experience and thus should convince other experiencers of its truth (A822/B850).

In addition to theoretical cognition, Kant also recognizes something called practical cognition, which involves an understanding of what ought to be the case (A633/B661). Specifically, through practical cognition, we become aware of the moral constraints that govern our behavior and the conditions under which such constraints are possible. It is only with regard to our lives as moral beings that metaphysical propositions are warranted. As we will see, Kant argues that in order for the moral law to make sense as something that binds us, we must presuppose not only that we are free but that God exists and we have immortal souls.

God, Freedom, and Immortality
in the Second *Critique*

Not until the second *Critique*, the *Critique of Practical Reason* (1788), does Kant show that the beliefs in God, freedom, and immortality are rationally warranted—although only as matters of practical faith (*Glaube*). Kant's arguments for what he calls "the postulates of pure practical reason" deserve their own book, but a cursory examination here will help us to understand how, in light of the Copernican revolution in philosophy, Kant attempts to address the metaphysical questions we must ask given the nature of reason itself (CPrR 132ff.).

With regard to freedom, Kant's argument (briefly stated) is that we must be free if we are bound to act morally, and we know that we are so bound because of our immediate sense of moral constraint:

> the moral principle . . . itself serves as the principle of the deduction of an inscrutable power that no experience was able to prove but that speculative reason had to assume as at least possible (in order to find among its cosmological ideas what is unconditional in terms of its

causality, so as not to contradict itself): viz., the power of freedom, the freedom of which the moral law, which itself needs no justifying grounds, proves not only the possibility but the actuality in beings who cognize [*erkennen*] this law as obligating for them. (CPrR 47)

Theoretical (or "speculative") reason demonstrates the possibility of freedom by limiting causal necessity to nature as the sum of appearances.[9] Practical reason then extends faith beyond the boundaries of theoretical cognition to assert the reality of freedom. Although theoretically freedom can be neither affirmed nor denied, "the power of freedom" is a condition for the possibility of obligation to the moral law—we cannot be required to choose rightly if we are unable to choose at all—and consciousness of the moral law (what Kant calls "the fact of reason") demonstrates that we can act on its basis. In short, I am morally necessitated ("I *ought to* do x"), and a condition for its possibility is my being free ("I *can* do x"). The unjustified theoretical pronouncements of dogmatic metaphysics are thus replaced with practical faith: "their possibility can and must in this practical reference be *assumed* even without our theoretically cognizing and having insight into them" (CPrR 4).

Proving the practical reality of God and immortality requires an additional assumption: Actions must aim not only at doing what is right—that is, acting as I ought to act regardless of the consequences—but also at achieving what is good. For Kant, the condition of all other goods is adherence to the moral law; this is the *supreme* good. But for morality to make sense to us, for it to be complete, happiness and virtue must be united somehow. It would strike us as wrong if Hitler had lived out the remainder of his life in the lap of luxury. The goodness even of happiness depends on the person's acting rightly. Yet we know that bad people often live happy lives. After World War II, Josef Mengele escaped to South America, where he lived comfortably until 1979. He died of a stroke while swimming. Something is wrong with that. Given the atrocities he committed at Birkenau, he deserved to be punished, not to die more than thirty years later while frolicking in the surf. Right action is not the only good thing. It is also good for people to get what they deserve, or to be happy in proportion to their virtue. This is the *highest* good.

Pursuing happiness is not what makes actions virtuous.[10] For the highest good to be possible, for these two things to correspond to one another, virtue must be the cause of happiness. If we act rightly, we must be rewarded. But as we know, a lot of good people live miserable lives. Often good people suffer while evil people are happy—in this life. For virtue and happiness to be properly related, I must be able to pursue absolutely perfect virtue (to move toward the supreme good), and happiness must be doled out in proportion to how virtuous I am. There are thus two conditions of the highest good: There must be infinite progress, which is possible only if I have an immortal soul (if this life is not the only life), and there must be a just distribution of happiness, which is possible only if God serves as a divine apportioner. God fulfills the demands of justice by giving people what they deserve.

Our practical lives make sense to us only if our moral considerations are consistent with our interest in happiness. We must rationally hope that there will eventually be this coincidence between happiness, which is the essential end we have as human beings, and virtue, which is the essential end we have as rational agents. This requires that we accept God and immortality as practical postulates—that is, not merely as probable hypotheses, but as "absolutely necessary" objects of faith (A633/B661–A634/B662).

The practical faith in freedom, God, and immortality "rests on subjective bases (of the moral attitude)" (A829/B857), so faith could never constitute knowledge (*Wissen*), which is "assent that is sufficient both subjectively and objectively" (A822/B850). Yet because Kant can establish that the moral law obligates us to act in a way that presupposes our freedom, as well as the possibility of achieving happiness in proportion to virtue (which requires God and immortality), we must postulate their objective reality in a practical sense because of what is morally required of us:

> those concepts, which are otherwise problematic (merely thinkable), are now assertorically declared to be concepts to which objects actually belong, because practical reason unavoidably requires the existence of

these for the possibility of its object, the highest good, which moreover is absolutely necessary practically, and theoretical reason is thereby entitled to presuppose them. (CPrR 134)

The distinction between an empirical claim and a practical postulate rests on the different ways of supporting them. For example, we cannot have an experience of freedom to justify our belief in its reality, because we cannot represent freedom to ourselves. We can make no theoretical claims without the pure concepts of the understanding, including the category of causality. Any uncaused cause is possible only apart from those conditions. However, our belief in freedom is justified as a necessary condition for the possibility of our being bound by the moral law, which is recognized through the fact of reason. Freedom, along with God and immortality, thus must be presupposed as matters of practical faith in our moral lives. Kant is not simply asking us to give in to old prejudices. He is not just saying that we believe it, and that is good enough. This is practical faith, which means that it is justified by moral reasoning.[11]

I do not know that God exists like I know that a table exists; it is not known theoretically. However, Kant claims that it would be positively irrational not to believe in God, freedom, and immortality, given that they are necessary for our moral lives to make sense. This means that the aims of a science—justifying a system of beliefs based on first principles—are achieved for metaphysics in Kant's practical philosophy. Of course, none of this would be possible without the *Critique of Pure Reason*, which restricts reason in its theoretical use, diagnoses the failure of speculative metaphysics, and makes room for a different kind of inquiry that warrants the postulates of pure practical reason.

Given the state of metaphysics at the end of the first two *Critiques*, Kant has accomplished what he set out to do. He has established a firm ground for metaphysics by examining the nature of cognition, but he has done so by setting narrow limits on both. Not only has he advanced the aims of philosophy, but he has given it the tools to progress by formulating a rational approach to self-understanding.

Kant's Legacy

Enlightenment is man's emergence from his self-incurred immaturity. . . . The motto of enlightenment is therefore: Sapere aude! Have courage to use your *own* understanding.

—Immanuel Kant, "An Answer to the Question: 'What Is Enlightenment?'"

Enlightenment cannot be bestowed upon us, and it cannot be forced upon us. Unlike Plato's image of the prisoner dragged violently out of the cave, Kant depicts a journey we must have the daring to undertake deliberately and for the sake of our own freedom. Fundamentally, the project of the Enlightenment interrogates the nature of authority. Are we content to be carried along by the beliefs of others, or do we cultivate our own understanding? The possibility of self-determination emerges in taking responsibility for what we believe. In this sense, Kant's project serves as the point of departure for an ongoing endeavor: to live up to the central promise of our humanity.

During the Enlightenment period, the rejection of dogmatism in all its forms—in science, in religion, in philosophy—inspired rationalists and empiricists alike, who shared the belief that humanity's intellectual progress could take place only by scrutinizing our own epistemic capacities. These philosophers examined the world in terms of how we relate to it, recognizing reality as a reflection of our rational concepts, or deriving those concepts from what is grounded in the senses. The innovation here, initiated by Descartes, is the radical turn inward. The animating question of philosophy becomes "What can I know?" rather than "What exists?" We arrive at knowledge of the truth by evaluating the grounds of our beliefs and setting them on a firm foundation.

For many, Kant is the paradigmatic Enlightenment philosopher. His most important work examines our own capacity to know. It is a critique of pure reason, an exercise in self-cognition. And he concludes that the epistemological question and the ontological question cannot be so easily distinguished. What is the case can be understood only in terms of how we make judgments about what is the case. Objectivity is possible only subject to our epistemic conditions, so the external world is as much a reflection of our own faculties as it is of anything given from without.

This Kantian insight has shaped the trajectory of modern and contemporary philosophy. The method of attending to how we experience the object as a way to get at the object itself was taken up by European phenomenology in the late nineteenth and twentieth centuries. And the animating question in Anglo-American epistemology and philosophy of mind is, arguably, how to understand the relationship between content and form, sensibility and the understanding, passivity and activity. The terms that guide their inquiries were largely formulated by Kant, and their approaches to these issues—studying consciousness or language to know what is true or to understand what truth is—borrow a great deal from Kant's own attempt at self-cognition.

But Kant may also have sown the seeds that would subvert philosophy as a rational enterprise. The "executioner's sword" is not only a death blow to speculative metaphysics but an empowering statement of our own free capacities. Although our knowledge is limited, nature exists for us only as we relate it to ourselves. Truth is defined in terms that we require of it. The distinction between phenomena and things in themselves, and our ability to transcend the limits of the understanding through faith, inspired the German and British Romantics to embrace the artistry of world-creation and to exalt the power of intuition over reason.[1] Nietzsche later claimed that the scientific will to truth was ultimately undermined by Kant's critique, which exposed our inability ever to transcend the subjective point of view. By reinterpreting the true and the false in terms of our own judgments about the world, the Copernican revolution both opened up the possibility of relativism and paved the way for a new kind of humanistic philosophy. Ironically, then, Kant's attempt to synthesize rationalism and empiricism caused a much greater schism than the one between Descartes and Locke.

It would be misleading to think that the *Critique*'s epistemological focus restricts its influence to narrow philosophical problems. The idea that philosophy begins with a critique of our ways of thinking has far-reaching implications. Understanding ourselves as rational beings is the foundation for becoming self-governing, rather than finding ourselves controlled by existing prejudices, irrational desires, or others' positions. In this sense, the implications of Kant's philosophical work radiate outward to the most concrete manifestations of the Enlightenment—the conception of the individual as naturally self-determining and the political revolutions that emerge from that commitment.

After Kant, the fundamental philosophical questions no longer concern primarily the source(s) of knowledge but explore the limits and value of knowledge in the wider human experience. In pursuing this broader critique of the Enlightenment, post-Kantian philosophers substantially take on Kant's Enlightenment project—the desire for truth and freedom—while recognizing the extent to which truth and freedom are conditioned by our way of understanding, by history, by language. Kant's power to inspire such divergent strains of thought attests to his important place in the history of philosophy, but it should also serve as a cautionary note: Never accept any interpretation of the *Critique* as the final word.

Notes

Chapter 1

1. In a circular or question-begging argument, the premise does not warrant the conclusion. The conclusion is already being assumed in the premise, so the argument would not convince someone who did not already agree with the conclusion. The classic illustration of a circular argument is from Richard Whately's *Elements of Logic*: "'to allow every man an unbounded freedom of speech must always be, on the whole, advantageous to the State; for it is highly conducive to the interests of the Community, that each individual should enjoy a liberty perfectly unlimited, of expressing his sentiments'" ([London: Mawman, 1826], 181). The premise and conclusion here say the same thing: that freedom of speech is "highly conducive to the interests of the Community" and that it is "advantageous to the State." Therefore, the argument proves nothing.

2. In the twentieth century, the logical positivists would develop these themes more systematically.

Chapter 2

1. Heinrich Heine, *Zur Geschichte der Religion und Philosophie in Deutsch-land*, in *Heinrich Heines sämmtliche Werke: Bibliothek-Ausgabe* (Hamburg: Hoffman und Campe, 1885), 7:96–97.

2. Leibniz states his version of the principle of sufficient reason in the *Monadology* (1714): "Our reasoning is based upon two great principles: first, that of Contradiction, . . . [a]nd, second, the principle of Sufficient Reason, in virtue of which we believe that no fact can be real or existing and no statement true unless it has a sufficient reason why it should be thus and not otherwise" (PE 217). In other words, there must be a reason why each thing is as it is, or a ground of its existing. Kant adopted this idea with minor changes in his *New Exposition of the First Principles of Metaphysical Cognition* (1755).

3. Leibniz identifies the law of identity as one of the primary truths from which all other truths can be derived (PE 30).

4. Immanuel Kant, *Gedanken von der wahren Schätzung der lebendigen Kräfte*, in *Kants gesammelte Schriften*, ed. Königlichen Preußischen Akademie der Wissenschaften (Berlin: de Gruyter, 1902/10), 1:17.

5. Immanuel Kant, *Correspondence*, trans. and ed. Arnulf Zweig (Cambridge: Cambridge University Press, 1999), 10:130. This is from Kant's famous letter to Marcus Herz of February 21, 1772.

6. Kant focuses on cognition (*Erkenntnis*) more than knowledge (*Wissen*). When he talks about cognition in the *Critique of Pure Reason*, he usually is looking at how we experience or make claims about the world rather than the subclass of things that we are able to justify (to others) as true. In this narrower sense of what knowledge is, what we know is *based on* what we cognize; they are not equivalent. Recently, translators of the *Critique of Pure Reason* have emphasized this distinction. Norman Kemp Smith's long-standard translation of the first *Critique* renders *Erkenntnis* (usually) as "knowledge," but Paul Guyer & Allen W. Wood and Werner S. Pluhar (whose translation I am using) have adopted the more appropriate "cognition." This helps to clarify an important distinction in Kant's philosophy. Were they to be equated, practical cognition could wrongly be construed as knowledge, when it is only a matter of faith (*Glaube*).

When it comes to cognition in the theoretical sense, Kant sometimes identifies the two. Cognition is equated with knowledge rather than merely what justifies a claim to know. Similarly, colloquial English uses 'knowledge' broadly to include what we experience of the world. Talk of "cognition" or what we "cognize" sounds stilted, and the meaning of the English term does not clearly capture what Kant means by *Erkenntnis*. I spell out the distinction between *Erkenntnis* and *Wissen* in "The Domain of Practical Reason" section of Chapter 5, but throughout the remainder of the book, talk of "knowledge" or what we "know" should be understood in this more general sense.

7. At times, Kant seems to make a claim's analyticity dependent on contingent psychological facts. For example, he says that "the question is not what we *are to* add in thought to the given concept, but what we *actually* think in the concept, even if only obscurely" (B17). If this were the case, then analytic truths would not be necessarily true; they would be contingently true, depending on how words are used. This actually bolsters W. V. O. Quine's claim that even analytic truths could in principle be falsified, and that analytic and synthetic truths are not different kinds of claims. See Note 8 below.

8. Recently, Kant's distinctions have been challenged by a number of philosophers. Quine, for example, says that the analytic-synthetic distinction is untenable, because no noncircular definition of analyticity can be given. Instead, analytic claims are just statements about reality that lie so close to the core of our understanding of reality—at the center of a web of belief— that it would be difficult to imagine experiences that challenge them. By contrast, synthetic claims are more readily doubted and prone to falsification. Therefore, analytic and synthetic assertions are not distinct kinds of truths. Both are contingent claims to which we assent with different degrees of confidence. See Willard Van Orman Quine, "Two Dogmas of Empiricism," in *From a Logical Point of View: Nine Logico-Philosophical Essays*, 2d ed. (Cambridge: Harvard University Press, 1980), 20–46.

Other philosophers, such as Saul Kripke, have questioned the distinction between *a priori* and *a posteriori* judgments. According to Kripke's causal theory of reference, things are named through an initial act of naming. A bachelor is called a bachelor as a matter of convention. Contingently, speakers come to refer to things by particular names. But that means that identity assertions such as 'All bachelors are unmarried males', although necessarily true, are knowable only *a posteriori*, within a given linguistic community. In addition, some sentences are *a priori* yet are true only contingently: for example, 'The standard meter bar in Paris is one meter long'. Because this bar defines the length of a meter, it seems to be true *a priori*. It is contingent, however, because it is conceivable that the bar could be broken. See Kripke, *Naming and Necessity* (Cambridge: Harvard University Press, 1980).

Both of these objections would undermine Kant's characterization of synthetic *a priori* judgments because it would make them contingent rather than necessary conditions for the possibility of experience.

9. "Things in themselves" and "noumena" are not always synonyms for Kant. I explain how these ideas are related in the "Phenomena and Noumena" section of Chapter 4.

10. Aristotle, *De Anima*, bk. II.

11. This directly contradicts a traditional argument for God's existence, the ontological argument, which I discuss in Chapter 5.

12. Although we tend to use the word 'aesthetic' more narrowly, Kant uses the word in its traditional sense, to refer to an inquiry that deals with sensibility generally, rather than to describe the effect of the beautiful in particular on the faculty of sensation. The term 'aesthetic' has a long history, and Kant's use of it follows philosophical tradition more closely than we do. Kant's contemporary A. G. Baumgarten is credited with redefining the term in his *Aesthetica* of 1750. See A21/B35–36.

Chapter 3

1. Kant uses the word 'concept' (*Begriff*) loosely here and in the title to the second section of the Transcendental Aesthetic to mean our understanding of what space and time are. In fact, Kant argues that space and time are not concepts, but intuitions.

2. Isaac Newton, *The Principia*, trans. Andrew Motte (Amherst, N.Y.: Prometheus, 1995), 13–14.

3. Leibniz's argument runs something like this: There cannot be two things that are exactly alike; otherwise, they would not be distinguishable as two things. If there were empty spaces between things, then those particular spaces would be identical, because nothing distinguishes one empty space from another. But this would mean that they are both different (space here and space there) and the same (because they are identical), which is a

contradiction. Therefore, empty space is impossible. The argument turns on what Leibniz calls the "identity of indiscernibles."

4. Newton, *Principia*, 13.

5. Immanuel Kant, *The Jäsche Logic*, in *Lectures on Logic*, trans. and ed. J. Michael Young (Cambridge: Cambridge University Press, 1992), 9:91.

6. Ibid., 9:94.

7. Kant here anticipates Albert Einstein's own challenge to Newtonian space in the special theory of relativity. According to Einstein, time and distance are perceived differently, depending on the observer's own movement. And because there is no absolute or well-defined state of rest, there is no absolute space and time independent of variable perception. Still, we must not overlook the differences between their views. Although space and time are forms of sensible intuition, Kant believes that we represent only one space and one time. For Einstein, there are many different spaces and times, because there are many different frames of reference.

8. In the *Prolegomena*, Kant gives a parallel example involving arithmetic. When we say that seven plus five equals twelve, we are not arriving at the sum simply by analyzing the initial concepts. Rather, we are *constructing* the concept twelve *by means of* the concepts seven and five (Pro 272):

> The concept of twelve is by no means thought by merely thinking of the combination of seven and five; and, analyze this possible sum as we may, we shall not discover twelve in the concept. We must go beyond these concepts by calling to our aid some intuition corresponding to one of them, i.e., either our five fingers or five points (as Segner has it in his *Arithmetic*); and we must add successively the units of the five given in the intuition to the concept of seven. Hence our concept is really amplified by the proposition $7 + 5 = 12$, and we add to the first concept a second one not thought in it. Arithmetical judgments are therefore synthetic . . . . (Pro 268–69)

As was already noted, when Kant says that we use an intuition, he just means some representation in thought, and this representation—our fingers, or points—helps us to figure out what seven plus five amounts to. We do not analyze the meaning of those terms. We use them to arrive at something that goes beyond what they mean. Thus, although we join twelve together *with* the concepts of seven and five, twelve is not discoverable *in* seven and five (Pro 271). This represents a major break with Hume, who claims that math is analytic. Kant is claiming that it is *a priori* but synthetic.

9. It was mentioned earlier (in Note 7) that Kant's approach to space anticipates Einstein's own rejection of Newton's absolute space. However, in his general theory of relativity, Einstein undermines the Euclidean geometry that Kant claims to characterize space as a pure form of sensible intuition. Euclid and Kant assume a flat space in which the distance between two parallel lines would remain constant. According to Einstein, however, bodies impose curves on space; space curves toward matter. But that means that parallel lines within a space are parallel only within that space. They curve as the lines are measured away from the body. Thus, according to general relativity theory, space is only locally Euclidean. Globally, it is hyperbolic.

10. Some critics have claimed that mathematical theorems such as 'The interior angles of any triangle must total 180 degrees' follow analytically from the basic axioms of a given calculus. If this were the case, then the theorems could be derived without having to construct the figures in intuition, and the argument from geometry could not justify space as a pure form of sensible intuition. In addition, mathematical theorems about the world could be false if the axioms from which they are derived do not properly relate to the world. Mathematical systems become merely different ways of interpreting reality, with no claim to necessity.

11. Kant makes note of this divergence in the Transcendental Exposition of the Concept of Time, where he writes: "I may refer for this exposition to No. 3, where, for the sake of brevity, I put among the items of the metaphysical exposition what in fact is transcendental" (B48). Strictly speaking, an inquiry into the conditions for the possibility of axioms about time should be considered a transcendental investigation, not a metaphysical exposition. In section one (on space), the discussion of geometry is in its proper place.

12. For a similar claim regarding space, see A28/B44.

13. Even if we grant that space and time are pure forms of sensible intuition, it is unclear what the implications are for things in themselves. Scholars disagree about what follows from Kant's arguments in the Transcendental Aesthetic. Does he demonstrate that things in themselves are *not* in space and

time, or does he show simply that we *cannot know* whether things in themselves are in space and time? The latter position is known as the "neglected alternative," according to which our intuition of space and time is subjective, but things in themselves also have inherent spatial and temporal properties.

14. Kant's contention that introspecting on the contents of our minds can give us ourselves only as we appear to ourselves is demonstrated by the fact that the thoughts of which we are conscious occur in time, which is a pure form of sensible intuition. What Kant calls inner sense is considered in more detail in the section on "Apperception (§§16–17)" in Chapter 4.

Chapter 4

1. Kant refers to the pure concepts of the understanding as categories in order to distinguish these primary concepts both from empirical concepts, which are derived from experience (*a posteriori*), and from predicables, which are pure (*a priori*) but are derived from the categories. We will discuss all three kinds of concepts later in the chapter. See A81/B107–A82/B108.

2. As noted in Chapter 3, Kant's philosophy should not be understood as a psychological investigation into how our particular brains happen to function in making sense of the world. However, Kant often describes the way that we know the world in terms of certain faculties or "cognitive powers [*Erkenntnisvermögen*]" that we have: The "lower" faculties of sensibility and the "higher" faculties of reason, judgment, and the understanding are related but can be distinguished by the functions they serve. See, for example, Immanuel Kant, *Critique of Judgment*, trans. Werner S. Pluhar (Indianapolis: Hackett, 1987), 20:201–8. Kant's reference to powers or faculties has often been used to support a psychologistic reading of the critical philosophy. However, they can also be understood merely as labels for our capacities to receive sensible intuitions and to make sense of what is given.

3. Immanuel Kant, *The Jäsche Logic*, in *Lectures on Logic*, trans. and ed. J. Michael Young (Cambridge: Cambridge University Press, 1992), 9:92–95.

4. Kant also distinguishes the categories and empirical concepts from a third kind of concept, which he calls a predicable. Predicables result "when the categories are combined either with the modes of pure sensibility or with one another" (A82/B108). In other words, concepts that are nonetheless pure can be derived by relating basic concepts, which we will examine later,

with other basic concepts or with the pure forms of sensible intuition (space and time). For example, the predicable of force is derived from the category of causality. Kant claims it is unnecessary to give a complete list of predicables in the *Critique* (A82/B108) but says that they can be found in "any good ontology." He mentions A. G. Baumgarten's *Metaphysica* (1739) in particular (Pro 325n).

5. Immanuel Kant, *Correspondence*, trans. and ed.. Arnulf Zweig (Cambridge: Cambridge University Press, 1999), 12:370. This appears in Kant's "Public Declaration concerning Fichte's *Wissenschaftslehre*," August 7, 1799.

6. There have been a number of objections to Kant's conception of logic. The idea that logic is purely formal and abstracts entirely from experience has been questioned by Quine and others. Quine claims that logical rules, like all analytic claims, are subject to revision based on empirical data. See Chapter 2, Note 8. Furthermore, Kant's conception of logic is at odds with much of contemporary propositional logic. Although Kant's logic deals with predicative relations in a way that is similar to first-order monadic predicate logic, it is still limited in that, among other things, it cannot handle multiplace predicates. One could defend Kant by saying that he misidentified the *a priori* rules of thought and that different categories would follow from those. However, this is a lot to concede.

7. Most translators, including Kemp Smith and Guyer & Wood, render *Allheit* as "totality," such that the categories of quantity are unity, plurality, and totality. Pluhar translates *Allheit* as "allness," reserving "totality" for *Totalität*.

8. Kant, *Correspondence*, 12:370.

9. Aristotle, *Topics*, 103b20–25; and Aristotle, *Categories*, 1b25–2a4.

10. See G. W. F. Hegel, *Hegel's Logic*, trans. William Wallace (Oxford: Clarendon, 1975), §42; and Georg Wilhelm Friedrich Hegel, *Lectures on the History of Philosophy: The Lectures of 1825–1826*, trans. R. F. Brown and J. M. Stewart, ed. Robert F. Brown (Berkeley: University of California Press, 1990), 3:225, 229. Arthur Schopenhauer says that the clue to the table of categories is not the table of logical functions but Kant's own "love for architectonic symmetry" (*The World as Will and Representation*, trans. E. F. J. Payne, vol. 1 [New York: Dover, 1969], 448).

11. Even though Hume's empiricism cannot justify our commitment to mind-independent objects, he seems to differentiate objects from appearances. Beliefs that we cannot help falling into are called "fictions," a term

that relies on the distinction between how things are and how they seem. In the *Treatise*, Hume lists a number of different fictions, including the fiction of the continued and distinct existence of perceptions (T 209) and the fiction of personal identity (T 254, 259). In the *Enquiry Concerning Human Understanding*, Hume says that causal necessity is a belief rather than a fiction only because we *feel* differently about it (EHU 47–50).

12. When Pluhar refers to presentations and I refer to representations, we are both referencing the same word in Kant's original German: *Vorstellungen*. For a discussion of this important term, see the section on "How the Transcendental Idealist Conceives of *Vorstellungen*" at the end of this chapter. As I explain there, intuitions are presented to us, but we represent them to ourselves according to the concepts.

13. Here Kant continues the structure of explanation begun in the Transcendental Aesthetic: He begins by outlining the character of space, time, or the categories (a metaphysical exposition or deduction) and then goes on to warrant their applicability to us in particular by showing them to be conditions for the possibility of experience (a transcendental deduction). The first part of the Transcendental Analytic is called a metaphysical deduction rather than a metaphysical exposition because the agreement between the forms of logical judgment and the table of categories is meant to justify this particular list of categories.

14. Henry E. Allison, *Kant's Transcendental Idealism: An Interpretation and Defense* (New Haven: Yale University Press, 1983).

15. The Transcendental Aesthetic also establishes the truth of transcendental idealism. Because space and time are pure forms of sensible intuition, and because all of our perceptions of the world must occur in space and time, we can know things as they are only subject to these conditions, not as they are in themselves.

16. As we saw in Chapter 3, this is one of the dangers in saying that the pure forms of sensible intuition and the categories are subjective. 'Subjective' is ambiguous. Kant does not mean that they are personal or variable among individuals. Instead, he means that they are contributed by the subject to experience. Similarly, when Kant talks about objective experience, he is talking about the representation of objects. He is not talking about eliminating bias.

17. Fichte calls this the "feeling of necessity" that accompanies some of our representations. What he means is that we do not have a say in how they affect

us. You come through the door and you see a table there, whether you want to or not. So, the question becomes: How does the transcendental idealist explain the feeling of necessity, since the world as it appears to us results from the judgments we make about our perceptions, rather than the object as it is given empirically? See J. G. Fichte, "[First] Introduction to the *Wissenschaftslehre*," in *Introductions to the Wissenschaftslehre and Other Writings (1797–1800)*, ed. and trans. Daniel Breazeale (Indianapolis: Hackett, 1994), 7–35.

18. Immanuel Kant, *The False Subtlety of the Four Syllogistic Figures*, in *Theoretical Philosophy, 1755–1770*, trans. and ed. David Walford (Cambridge: Cambridge University Press, 1992), 2:60. See also A107.

19. The idea that consciousness must distinguish the object from itself through its own activity had a tremendous impact on the other German idealists (Fichte, Schelling, and Hegel), as we will see later in the chapter.

20. God is not bound by the categories, because a divine intellect does not depend on a given manifold for knowledge. Kant says of God that "all his cognition must be intuition rather than *thought*, which always manifests limits" (B71). If God can be said to think, it is entirely different from the thinking that we have, because our judgment is necessarily related to the world of appearances. As we will see later in the chapter, God intuits things intellectually, not sensibly.

21. Friedrich Heinrich Jacobi, "On Transcendental Idealism," in *The Main Philosophical Writings and the Novel "Allwill,"* trans. George di Giovanni (Montreal and Kingston: McGill-Queen's University Press, 1994), 331–38.

22. Gottlob Ernst Schulze, *Aenesidemus oder über die Fundamente der von dem Herrn Professor Reinhold in Jena gelieferten Elementar-Philosophie*, ed. Manfred Frank (Hamburg: Meiner, 1996), 203–14. Schulze is drawing on Humean skepticism, which he claims has not been refuted by Kant. As we saw in Chapter 1, Hume argues that we cannot infer that objects are the cause of our impressions without begging the question. Schulze is making a related objection here, that attributing causality to the thing in itself is nonsensical on Kant's own terms.

23. Schopenhauer, "Criticism of the Kantian Philosophy," in *The World as Will and Representation*, 413–534. On illegitimately applying the category of causality to the thing in itself, see esp. 436, 447, 502–3, 505, 506.

24. Kant is partly responsible for this misreading, since he often writes as if the thing in itself causes sensations. For example, in the *Prolegomena*, Kant

claims "that things as objects of our senses existing outside us are given, but we know nothing of what they may be in themselves, knowing only their appearances, i.e., the representations which they cause [*wirken*] in us by affecting [*affizieren*] our senses" (Pro 289). See also A19/B33, B69, A50/B74, A247–49, and Pro 315.

25. Immanuel Kant, *Opus Postumum*, trans. Eckart Förster and Michael Rosen, ed. Eckart Förster (Cambridge: Cambridge University Press, 1993), 22:34.

26. There are three categories of quantity listed on the table of categories: unity, plurality, and allness. Kant's reference to the category of magnitude anticipates the axioms of intuition, where these categories are related to our space- and time-consciousness as extensive magnitudes.

27. Because spatiotemporal unity already involves conceptual discrimination on the part of the knowing subject, we cannot interpret Kant's model of cognition as a two-stage process in which sensations are first brought under the forms and then are cut up according to the concepts. There is no manifold of sheer receptivity that the understanding subsequently "takes up." Many interpreters of Kant mistakenly identify these as two separable events in the formation of experience.

28. This is the Law of Conservation of Mass (or Matter), which is attributed to Antoine Laurent Lavoisier (1743–1794), who formally proposed it in the *Traité Élémentaire de Chimie* (*Elementary Treatise of Chemistry*, 1789). Even though it was assumed by many others before then, including Anaxagoras, Bacon, Galileo, and Kant himself, Lavoisier was the first to have proven it experimentally and to have explicitly stated it in print.

29. Kant, *Correspondence*, 10:130.

30. G. W. F. Hegel, *Hegel's Science of Logic*, trans. A. V. Miller (New York: Humanities, 1969), 46.

31. This problematic idealism is what Descartes is left with at the end of the First Meditation. As we saw in Chapter 1, he argues that we must appeal to a nondeceiving God to get beyond the contents of the mind. But as we will see in the next chapter, we cannot know whether there is such a being. Thus Kant can never in principle get beyond the objects of consciousness.

32. See Immanuel Kant, *On the Form and Principles of the Sensible and the Intelligible World* (Inaugural Dissertation), in *Theoretical Philosophy, 1755–1770*, 2:396–97; B72 and B307–9 in the first *Critique*; and Immanuel

Kant, *Lectures on the Philosophical Doctrine of Religion*, in *Religion and Rational Theology*, trans. and ed. Allen W. Wood and George di Giovanni (Cambridge: Cambridge University Press, 1996), 28:1051ff.

Chapter 5

1. Aristotle, *Topics*, 100a25–101a3. See also Aristotle, *Posterior Analytics*, 81b18–20; and *Topics*, 105b30–31. Like Kant, Aristotle claims that the purpose of dialectic is to expose merely apparent deductions from real deductions (*Rhetoric*, 1355b15–18).

2. As we saw at the end of Chapter 4 (with Kant's analysis of *Vorstellungen*), the word 'idea' [*Idee*] has a technical meaning in the critical philosophy. It is "a concept of reason whose object simply cannot be met with in experience." See Immanuel Kant, *The Jäsche Logic*, in *Lectures on Logic*, trans. and ed. J. Michael Young (Cambridge: Cambridge University Press, 1992), 9:92. See also A319/B376–A320/B377.

3. 'Transcendent' here is not to be confused with 'transcendental.' Transcendent ideas transcend experience. 'Transcendental' just means having to do with conditions for the possibility of experience. Kant realized that this would (and did) cause confusion, which is why in the *Prolegomena* he says that he would like to start calling his position critical idealism rather than transcendental idealism (Pro 375).

4. Aristotle, *Categories*, 5; and *Metaphysics*, bk. VII (Z).

5. Aristotle, *Physics*, bk. VIII, 4–6; Aristotle, *Metaphysics*, bk. XII (Λ), 1–6 Saint Thomas Aquinas, *Summa Theologica*, I,q.2,a.3; and Saint Thomas Aquinas, *Summa Contra Gentiles*, bk. I, ch. 13.

6. The *ideal* of pure reason is one of the *ideas* of reason that transcend possible experience. The ideas have to do with the unconditioned basis of what is conditioned in experience. As the source of all being, God is one of these unconditioned entities. Therefore, God is an ideal because God is an archetype for all other existing (imperfect) beings.

7. Saint Anselm, *Proslogion*, ch. 2.

8. Understood broadly, *Erkenntnis* is an objective perception. We can see this by its place on the *Vorstellung* diagram at the end of Chapter 4. Given Kant's analysis of what makes experience possible, we can identify several different kinds of theoretical cognition. Conceptual cognition

analyzes some concept in its relation to experience. Kant focuses on the pure concepts of the understanding, as *a priori* conditions for the possibility of objective experience (A320/B376–77). Other cognitions, or elements of objective experience, involve what is given to us through sensible intuition. Such cognitions are *a priori* if they concern the pure forms of sensible intuition (space and time) or are *a posteriori* if they relate to actual perceptions as they are given to us through the senses (A176/B218). Most often, however, when Kant refers to cognition, he is referring to experience proper: sensible intuitions that have been organized according to the categories.

9. Usually, Kant calls reason speculative when it transcends the boundaries of what we can know and pursues metaphysics. However, sometimes 'speculative reason' is a synonym for 'theoretical reason.' That is the case in this passage.

10. Of course, philosophers continue to debate this claim. To understand how Kant argues for it and whether his argument is successful would require an extensive discussion of his moral philosophy, particularly the *Groundwork of the Metaphysics of Morals* (1785).

11. Accordingly, Kant thinks that traditional metaphysics should be restricted and that religion itself should be reformed in accordance with rational principles—hence the title of one of his books, *Religion within the Limits of Reason Alone* (1793). Because of how our faith is justified, Kant's religion is reduced to something like a superstructure primarily to support moral progress. Any beliefs that are not essential to our moral lives are unnecessary and perhaps even misleading. Pure religion requires no dogma beyond God and immortality. Christ is the son of God only metaphorically, as an ideal of moral perfection. To have a religious attitude means nothing but to look on our moral duties as divine commands. Religion merely represents morality. The moral law is self-legislated through our own reason, so were we to act on the basis of others' commands—from the church bureaucracy, from the Bible, or even from God—our actions would be heteronomous, and thus without moral value.

Conclusion

1. Kant's own philosophy of art in the *Critique of Judgment* (1790), the third *Critique*, also had a profound influence on the Romantic movement.

Glossary of Technical Terms

Kant's text is filled with technical terms, some that were common among his philosophical contemporaries and some that he substantially redefined. The meaning of these terms can best be understood in context, so I encourage you to look at how they are used in the *Critique of Pure Reason* and the relevant sections of the *Companion*. The following glossary is provided as a quick reference when the jargon gets a little too thick. After each entry, I indicate where in the *Critique* Kant most clearly explains the term.

A posteriori/a priori: A priori claims are distinguished from *a posteriori* claims based on how they are warranted as well as their modal status. First, an *a posteriori* claim is proven or disproven by appealing to experience. We prove or disprove an *a priori* claim without appealing to experience. Second, because we have to look at the world to determine whether an *a posteriori* claim is true, the claim is only contingently true. It depends on the way that the world is, and it could have been otherwise. But anything that is true *a priori* is necessarily and universally true. For example, I know that seven plus five equals twelve without actually going out and counting things. And I know that adding seven and five will always equal twelve no matter what. But I know that the door is open only because I see that it is open, and I know that it could very well have been closed, or that it may be closed later. See B2–4.

A priori   See "*a posteriori/a priori.*"

Analytic (*analytisch*)   An analytic statement is true by definition, because of the way that the subject and the predicate are related. 'All bachelors are unmarried males' is true because that is what it means for someone to be a bachelor. Kant describes this as the predicate's being "contained in" the subject. See A6/B10–A7/B11.

Apperception (*Apperzeption*)   In order to have experience, I must use certain rules to combine what is given to me through the senses. Such a combination depends on my being an identical subject over time who can become conscious that I am making such judgments. Kant calls this the transcendental unity of apperception, pure apperception, or original apperception. This is not a case of reflecting on the contents of my mind (inner sense) but rather a formal condition of any experience, either inner or outer. It is not an intuition but a thought or immediate self-consciousness, the "I think" that accompanies my representations. See A106–7 and B131–32.

Category (*Kategorie*)   Also known as the pure concepts of the understanding, the categories are the *a priori* rules that the understanding uses to organize what is given to it through the senses. They allow us to make judgments about the world that can be right or wrong. They are conditions for the possibility of experience, because through the categories we distinguish objective claims from subjective associations. For example, using the category of causality, we can claim that heat makes copper expand, rather than merely associating the feeling of heat with expanding copper. See B128, B143, A244–46.

Cognition (*Erkenntnis*)   Sometimes translated as "knowledge," *Erkenntnis* in the theoretical sense is an objective perception. It involves both a passive element (sensible intuition) and an active element (the understanding); we must confront an object immediately through the senses, and we must make judgments about what we are given by means of the categories. See A320/B376–77.

Concept (*Begriff*)   There are two kinds of concepts: empirical (or derivative) concepts and pure (or basic) concepts. Empirical concepts are drawn from experience by means of comparison, reflection, and abstraction. We know what a dog is because we have seen a lot of dogs and recognize some common attributes. Pure concepts, which Kant also calls categories, are *a priori* rules that make experience possible. Thus we can form empirical concepts only after we have empirical data, and we have experience (in part) only because of the application of pure concepts. See A95–96 and A320/B376–77.

Dialectic (*Dialektik*)   The Transcendental Logic is divided into two parts: the Transcendental Analytic, which explains how the understanding functions in making sense of the world, and the Transcendental Dialectic, which explains and criticizes errors we make by improperly applying the categories beyond possible experience. Dialectical illusion results when reason transcends the limits to what we can know in its attempt to achieve epistemic completeness and makes theoretical claims concerning God, the world, freedom, and the soul. See A60/B85–A64/B88 and A293/B249.

Empirical realism (*empirischer Realismus*)   As opposed to transcendental realism, according to which we know things in themselves, empirical realism is the view that our sensibility is directly affected by things that exist apart from consciousness. Space and time are empirically real in the sense that they relate to objects, even though such objects are not things in themselves. See A28/B44 and A35–36/B52.

Experience (*Erfahrung*)   Kant uses this term in two different senses. Usually he is referring to sensible intuitions that have been organized by the understanding according to the categories. This is also called cognition or empirical knowledge. However, sometimes he refers to sensible intuition itself as a kind of experience. Experience in the latter sense is immediate—it is more properly called simply an intuition—as opposed to what has been mediated by our judgment. See B147–48 and B218–19.

Idea (*Idee*)   An idea is a kind of representation that results from the misuse of the categories in ways that transcend possible experience.

Transcendental ideas are pure concepts of reason (rather than the under-standing) that refer to the totality of possible experience rather than experience itself. This is what yields metaphysics—most importantly, the be-lief in God, freedom, and immortality as theoretical propositions (and thus dialectical illusions). See A311/B368 and A320/B377–A321/B378.

Imagination (*Einbildungskraft*)   The imagination is the intermediary between sensibility and the understanding. It performs the three syntheses (apprehension, reproduction, and recognition), organizing our sensations and bringing them to the categories. See B151–52.

Inner sense (*innerer Sinn*)   When we reflect on the contents of our own minds, we are using the faculty of inner sense. Through inner sense, the perceptions and ideas that we have become objects of consciousness. Inner sense is opposed to outer sense, which is our experience of external objects. The objects of inner sense are in time but not in space. Kant also strictly dis-tinguishes inner sense from apperception (self-consciousness). The former is a kind of experience, whereas the latter is a condition for the possibility of experience. See A22–23/B37 and B156.

Intuition (*Anschauung*)   Kant uses *Anschauung* sometimes to mean the capacity to represent things and sometimes to mean what is represented in space and time. When we intuit something, we are in some kind of direct re-lationship with that thing. Kant says that space and time are pure intuitions because they are singular (one space, one time) and immediately had by us. They do not result from any kind of judgment on our part. We also intuit objects through the senses. This is called sensible intuition. Intuitions are visualizations—*Anschauungen*, literally "at-lookings"—although presum-ably there are counterparts with the other four senses. This means that we have particular representations of things that are distinguished from more general concepts of things—my perception of a particular dog, as opposed to my understanding of what dogs are. Kant also mentions the possibility of an intuitive faculty that does not depend on sensations, which he calls "intel-lectual intuition." God, for example, does not have a receptive faculty by which objects are given to him. Rather, God knows objects—and, indeed, creates them—directly through thought. See A19/B33.

Judgment (*Urteil*)   In the *Critique of Pure Reason*, Kant focuses on the-oretical judgments, or judgments concerning what exists. The power of judgment (*Urteilskraft*) is the ability to apply concepts to experience. See B141–42 and A132/B171.

Knowledge (*Wissen*)   A claim about the world is known when it is not only something I believe but something that is verified by experience, such that others should be convinced of its truth. Kant contrasts knowledge with mere opinion, where even I am uncertain of its truth, as well as faith, which convinces me but may not convince other people. See A822/B850.

Manifold (*Mannigfaltiges*)   A manifold is simply an organized group of intuitions. It may be pure, as it is when we consider space and time themselves or we study geometry; or it may be empirical, as it is when we experience the world. When we organize and relate the various sensations that we receive, the unified whole that results is called the empirical manifold of sensibility. It can also be described as a spatiotemporal manifold, because, as beings who intuit the world sensibly, we receive sensations under the forms of sensible intuition (space and time). See A99.

Noumena   Kant sometimes identifies noumena as things in themselves, which he defines negatively as things as they are apart from our subjective conditions. Of course, we can in principle know nothing about them. Kant also defines noumena positively, as things as they would be perceived by a being with a nonsensible (intellectual) intuition. See B306–7.

Object (*Gegenstand, Objekt*)   The two German words that are both translated as 'object' have different meanings for Kant. Most often, Kant uses *Gegenstand*, by which he means the object as it appears to us in space and time, and subject to the categories. This is what we refer to when we talk about an external object, "out there." It is what our empirical judgments are *about*. Sometimes, however, Kant uses *Objekt* to describe the relationship that the understanding has to an object in abstraction from the forms of sensibility. In other words, this is our internal conception of the object as it is *thought* through the categories. *Gegenstände* are objects of possible experience, but *Objekte* are (more generally) objects of possible judgments. For our purposes, it is more crucial to understand what Kant means by *Gegenstand*. See A92/B124–A93/B126.

Phenomena   Phenomena are things as they appear to us, subject to the categories and the pure forms of sensible intuition. See B306.

Practical (*praktisch*)   A practical claim concerns our moral obligations. Practically, we recognize our obligation to the moral law, and we have faith in freedom as a condition of being so obligated and in God and immortality as conditions for the possibility the highest good. As opposed to theoretical reason, practical reason concerns itself with questions of what ought to be the case rather than what is the case. See A633/B661 and A841/B869.

Presentation (*Vorstellung*)   See "representation."

Pure forms of sensible intuition (*reine Formen sinnlicher Anschauung*)   We are affected by sensations in such a way that we perceive them in space and time, which Kant calls the pure forms of sensible intuition. They are pure because they are not derived from experience (*a priori*), and they are formal features of our receptivity because they characterize how things are given to us. They are not actively contributed to experience by the understanding. See B41 and A26/B42.

Reason (*Vernunft*)   Reason abstracts completely from sensibility in its attempt to unify thought. While the understanding unifies appearances by means of rules, reason attempts to unite the rules of the understanding under unconditioned principles. The fact that reason is not tied to possible experiences leads to dialectical inferences. See A302/B359 and A326/B382–83.

Receptivity (*Rezeptivität, Empfänglichkeit*)   This is our capacity to be affected by objects. When what we are given through the senses is brought together with the categories, we are able to make claims about the world. Sensibility is what we call our capacity for receptivity. See A44/B61 and A50/B74.

Representation (*Vorstellung*)   This is a broad term to mean any perception that the (conscious) subject has. This includes both sensations, which relate only to the subject ("I feel cold"), and objective perceptions or cognitions, which relate to the object ("The door is open"). Objective perceptions can be further subdivided into intuitions, which refer immediately to the object, and concepts, both empirical and pure. *Vorstellung* is sometimes translated "presentation" and sometimes "representation," but no single translation seems appropriate. See A320/B376–77.

Schema (*Schema*)   A schema is a rule that the imagination uses to relate intuitions to the pure concepts of the understanding. The plural of 'schema' is 'schemata.' See A139/B178–A140/B180.

Sensibility (*Sinnlichkeit*)   Sensibility is the mind's receptivity for intuitions, or its capacity to be affected by objects. In outer sense, we are affected by external, physical objects; and in inner sense, we are affected by the mind itself, or its ideas. See A15/B29 and A19/B33.

Speculative (*spekulativ*)   Speculative philosophy is a kind of theoretical inquiry into things that transcend human experience. Speculative philosophers engage in metaphysics. See A634/B662–A636/B664.

Spontaneity (*Spontaneität*)   Spontaneity is the active counterpart to receptivity. The understanding acts spontaneously because it contributes something to experience. It is not simply determined by what is given to it empirically. The understanding actively combines the sensible manifold according to *a priori* rules (the categories). See B129–30.

Synthesis (*Synthesis*)   Our experience forms a coherent whole only because we unify what is given to us through the senses. In the A Deduction, Kant distinguishes three syntheses that make possible a unified manifold: the synthesis of apprehension that unites the manifold into one presentation, the synthesis of reproduction that relates preceding representations to current representations, and the synthesis of recognition in a concept. See A77/B102–3.

Synthetic (*synthetisch*)   A synthetic statement is not analytic, which means that its truth-value does not depend only on the meanings of its terms and how they are related. Synthetic statements include empirical claims about the world ("The door is open") but also such things as mathematical truths. See A6/B10–A7/B11.

Theoretical (*theoretisch*)   A theoretical claim concerns objects of cognition, or what is the case. As opposed to practical reason, theoretical reason concerns itself with epistemic questions (what we know) rather than moral questions (how we ought to act). See A633/B661 and A841/B869–A842/B870.

Thing in itself (*Ding an sich*)   If we abstract space, time, and the categories from experience, we are left with the thing as it is in itself. By definition, we can know nothing of the thing in itself because it is the object considered apart from our subjective conditions of knowing. It is not an object of possible experience and thus serves as a limit to the extent of our cognition. See A42/B59 and B164.

Transcendent (*transzendent*)   Transcendent principles are claims about (noumenal) objects that cannot be sensibly intuited. Such principles are unfounded because they transcend possible experience, thus yielding transcendental ideas. See A295/B352–A296/B353.

Transcendental (*transzendental*)   A transcendental inquiry is concerned with the *a priori* conditions for the possibility of experience. It distinguishes objective cognitions, which are subject to these conditions, from speculative claims about things as they are in themselves. "Transcendental" should not be confused with "transcendent." Transcendental philosophy rules out transcendent claims as theoretically unjustifiable. See A11–12/B25 and A56/B80–81.

Transcendental idealism (*transzendentaler Idealismus*)   According to transcendental (or critical) idealism, we can know only appearances and never things in themselves. Kant is careful to distinguish his position from dogmatic idealism, which states that the world is nothing but ideas in the mind. Transcendental idealism does not deny the existence of an external world. Rather, it says that we can never know the world as it is apart from our subjective conditions of knowing it. See A369.

Transcendental object (*transzendental Objekt*)   The thing in itself, noumenon, and transcendental object are closely related; in fact, Kant sometimes equates them. However, they are distinguishable by the functions they serve in the critical philosophy. The transcendental object is the intelligible cause of appearances, the thing that affects the senses but itself cannot be known. See A494/B522–A495/B523.

Understanding (*Verstand*)   In contrast to sensibility, which is receptive, the understanding is the faculty of judgment by which we actively apply the categories to experience. See A51/B75, A67/B92–A69/B94, and A126.

Annotated Bibliography

A complete list of books and articles on the *Critique of Pure Reason* would fill several volumes. The following selected bibliography contains a number of recommended further readings, what I take to be the most important English-language scholarship accessible to an audience of undergraduate and graduate students.

Allison, Henry E. *Kant's Transcendental Idealism: An Interpretation and Defense*. New Haven: Yale University Press, 1983.
Allison criticizes the "metaphysical" interpretation of Kant (proposed by Strawson and others), according to which we can know only subjective appearances, or the contents of our minds. Instead, Allison argues for an epistemological conception of the distinction between appearances and things in themselves, asserting that they are not two kinds of things but two ways of considering the world, either subject to our epistemic conditions or not.

Beck, Lewis White. *Essays on Kant and Hume*. New Haven: Yale University Press, 1978.
This book collects a number of Beck's influential essays on Kant, including (among other things) his interpretation of transcendental idealism as an attempt to synthesize rationalism and empiricism, a brief history of the analytic/synthetic distinction, an analysis of the categories as conditions for the

possibility of coherent experience in general, his claim that Kant's and Hume's responses to the problem of causation are more similar than most historians of philosophy would have us believe, and several brief essays on the Second Analogy.

Bennett, Jonathan. *Kant's Analytic*. Cambridge: Cambridge University Press, 1966.

_____. *Kant's Dialectic*. Cambridge: Cambridge University Press, 1974. Bennett's books differ from other commentaries in their selective focus; they cover important themes rather than proceeding according to the order of the text. Furthermore, Bennett's primary purpose is to assess rather than merely to explicate Kant's arguments, and he is more critical of Kant than most commentators. *Kant's Dialectic* is especially important because it is one of the only book-length studies on the second half of the *Critique*.

Caygill, Howard. *A Kant Dictionary*. Oxford: Blackwell, 1995. Caygill provides an alphabetically arranged list of Kant's key technical terms, with definitions that make reference to the whole of Kant's oeuvre, as well as the historical background from which many of the terms made their way to the eighteenth century. This is particularly useful for clarifying certain ideas. However, some familiarity with Kant is essential, as many of the definitions themselves are steeped in Kantian jargon.

Guyer, Paul. *Kant and the Claims of Knowledge*. Cambridge: Cambridge University Press, 1987. Using a historical investigation into how the *Critique* was composed, Guyer claims that the published version contains a fundamental problem that Kant never adequately resolves. The method that we see in the Transcendental Deduction assumes that we know certain necessary truths about the world, and it arrives at transcendental idealism through a deduction of *a priori* principles that make such truths possible. Elsewhere Kant seems to assume that even our contingent judgments depend on certain principles, but that such judgments more or less conform to the world as it is in itself. Guyer concludes that Kant never fully succeeds in his attempt to portray these approaches as two parts of one argument.

Guyer, Paul, ed. *The Cambridge Companion to Kant*. Cambridge: Cambridge University Press, 1992.

_____, ed. *The Cambridge Companion to Kant and Modern Philosophy*. Cambridge: Cambridge University Press, 2006.
These collections include expository essays by a number of leading Kant scholars. They cover several elements of the theoretical philosophy, including the pre-critical period; the different sections of the *Critique*; Kant's terminology and methods of argumentation; and the implications of the critical philosophy for psychology, mathematics, natural science, and metaphysics. Essays also cover Kant's ethics, aesthetics, religion, and political philosophy.

Henrich, Dieter. "Identity and Objectivity: An Inquiry into Kant's Transcendental Deduction." Trans. Jeffrey Edwards. In *The Unity of Reason: Essays on Kant's Philosophy*, ed. Richard L. Velkley, 123–208. Cambridge: Harvard University Press, 1994.
Henrich's interpretation of the Transcendental Deduction focuses on Kant's understanding of judgment, particularly the idea that objective claims are possible only when perceptions undergo a rule-governed synthesis. Central to this account is an understanding of the relationship between the categories and an identical self-consciousness.

_____. "The Proof-Structure of Kant's Transcendental Deduction." *Review of Metaphysics* 22, no. 4 (June 1969): 640–59.
According to Henrich, the B Deduction is composed of two different argumentative steps, each of which is essential to the overall proof: a proof of the categories' validity and an explanation of how they relate to sensible intuition. Against those who insist on the superiority of the A Deduction as well as those who dismiss the second part of the B Deduction as superfluous, Henrich claims that the B Deduction more closely adheres to the structure of the *Critique* as a whole and that it is more consistent with Kant's philosophical methodology, namely, his use of a synthetic rather than an analytic method.

Hintikka, Jaakko. "On Kant's Notion of Intuition (*Anschauung*)." In *The First Critique: Reflections on Kant's* Critique of Pure Reason, ed. Terence Penelhum and John James MacIntosh, 38–53. Belmont, Calif.: Wadsworth, 1969.
Hintikka sets Kant's use of the term *Anschauung* in its historical context and concludes that Kant understood intuitions in two different ways: both as particular and immediate ideas, and as necessarily related to sensibility. He then examines how this affects Kant's treatment of space in the Transcendental Aesthetic as well as his philosophy of mathematics.

Kemp Smith, Norman. *A Commentary to Kant's* Critique of Pure Reason. Rev. ed. New York: Humanities, 1962.
Originally published in 1918, this was the first English-language commentary and for many years was (along with Paton) the standard secondary text on the *Critique of Pure Reason*. Many of Kemp Smith's theses, including his claim that the book was assembled as a kind of patchwork, are now generally accepted. Kemp Smith follows the structure of the *Critique* carefully, although he also draws on Kant's published and unpublished writings to illuminate the text, and he includes critical assessments along with his interpretations.

Kuehn, Manfred. *Kant: A Biography*. Cambridge: Cambridge University Press, 2001.
In this first full-length biography of Kant in more than fifty years, Kuehn gives a thorough account of his life and places his writings in their historical context. Of particular interest are Kuehn's detailed description of Kant's "silent decade" leading up to the publication of the first *Critique* and his claim that the critical philosophy emerged gradually rather than as a result of some sudden inspiration.

Longuenesse, Béatrice. *Kant and the Capacity to Judge: Sensibility and Discursivity in the Transcendental Analytic of the* Critique of Pure Reason. Trans. Charles T. Wolfe. Princeton: Princeton University Press, 1998.
Many philosophers reject the idea that Kant discovered the exhaustive table of categories (derived from the table of logical functions), but they accept the general thrust of the Copernican turn. Against this selective

endorsement of Kant, Longuenesse argues that the validity of the Transcendental Deduction depends essentially on a certain conception of mental activity and the specific rules that Kant claims govern discursive thought.

Paton, H. J. *Kant's Metaphysic of Experience: A Commentary on the First Half of the* Kritik der reinen Vernunft. 2 vols. London: George Allen & Unwin, 1936.
Along with Kemp Smith, this is one of the first step-by-step commentaries on the Transcendental Aesthetic and the Transcendental Analytic, and its interpretation remains highly influential, particularly its explication of the Transcendental Deduction.

Pippin, Robert B. *Kant's Theory of Form: An Essay on the* Critique of Pure Reason. New Haven: Yale University Press, 1982.
Pippin understands Kant's philosophy as a "formal idealism," and he investigates how the forms of sensibility and the categories are related to the matter of experience. He also assesses Kant's specific arguments and his epistemology in general.

Sellars, Wilfrid. *Science and Metaphysics: Variations on Kantian Themes*. London: Routledge & Kegan Paul, 1968.
Sellars begins by offering an interpretation of Kant. Like Strawson, he strictly distinguishes between experience and things in themselves. Then he adopts a Kantian perspective to address current issues in analytic philosophy regarding meaning, existence, and truth, as well as objectivity in ethics. Although the book is most appropriate for those who already have a firm grasp on the *Critique of Pure Reason*, it makes a strong case for Kant's contemporary relevance.

Strawson, P. F. *The Bounds of Sense: An Essay on Kant's* Critique of Pure Reason. London: Methuen, 1966.
Strawson's influential account of the critical project brings Kant firmly into the analytic philosophical tradition. According to Strawson, Kant limits what is intelligible to mind-dependent appearances, which he (like Berkeley) equates with the whole of nature. Thus the way that our minds work—our psychology—fundamentally separates us from reality.

Wolff, Robert Paul. *Kant's Theory of Mental Activity: A Commentary on the Transcendental Analytic of the* Critique of Pure Reason. Cambridge: Harvard University Press, 1963.
Wolff reconstructs the argument of the Transcendental Analytic, emphasizing the A Deduction and its appeal to the categories as conditions for the possibility of synthetic unity.

Index

Lightning Source UK Ltd.
Milton Keynes UK
20 March 2010

151672UK00001BA/17/P